a collector's guide

CONTEMPORARY
ARTIST
DOLLS

Published by

HOBBY HOUSE PRESS, INC.
Cumberland, Maryland 21502

susanna oroyan
and
carol-lynn rössel waugh

Additional copies of this book may be purchased at $19.95
from
HOBBY HOUSE PRESS, INC.
900 Frederick Street
Cumberland, Maryland 21502
or from your favorite bookstore or dealer
Please add $1.75 postage

ISBN: 0-87588-271-4

our thanks

To our artist friends who took precious time away from their art to gather materials and to write long and serious explanations to our "daunting" and "provocative" questions.

To our families, friends and colleagues for patience, support and understanding.

To Ariel Vert-Légume and Pompilia de la Terre who gave us the inspiration and the flights of fancy.

and

To Kaypro 4/a:wordstar and IBM PC/a:wordperfect who made it all possible.

contents

AN INTRODUCTION TO THE ART...... 5

SEEING OURSELVES —
The Interpretive Figure 35

Elizabeth Brandon 36
Christine Adams.................................... 41
Helen Kish 45
Sonja Bryer 49
Kezi 52
Nancy Villaseñor 57
Edna Daly.. 60
Robert Raikes 63
Rebecca Iverson 68
Patricia Ryan Brooks 71
Kenneth von Essen 76
Susan Wakeen 79
Cathleen O'Rork 83
Ruth Ann Eckersley 88
Mary Ann Oldenburg 91
Debby Anderson 95
Margaret Hickson.................................. 98

MOMENTS IN TIME —
The Portrait Figure 102

Charlotte Zeepvat................................. 103
Marilyn Stauber 107
Cecilia Rothman 112
Gillian Charlson 117
Don Anderson 121
Paul Crees 124
Ann Parker.. 129
Sheila Wallace 134
June Gale 139
Margaret Glover 144
Michael Langton 147

FLIGHTS OF FANCY —
The Character Figure.................... 152

Edna Shaw 153
Ellen Turner.. 158
William Arthur Wiley 163
Julia Hills 167
Tuck Dolls 172
Robert Keene McKinley 176
Jean Heighton 181
Lisa Lictenfels 185
Beverly Port 190
Blythe Collins-Kretschmer 195
Nerissa 199
Susanna Oroyan 204
Van Craig 209

BEGINNINGS —
The Prototype 214

A COLLECTOR'S GUIDE............. 227
LEARNING MORE.................... 244
SOURCES AND SUPPLIES 245
DIRECTORY OF ARTISTS............ 246
ABOUT THE AUTHORS 247

an introduction
to the art

Up through the moldering sandwich crusts, dried up paint brushes, dismembered doll parts and general creative litter on our worktables surface a number of letters and notes, and essay fragments written on the backs of old envelopes. All these bits relate to the art and science of doll art.

In the odd, late hours, we ponder and add a bit more to our notes, and finally come to the conclusion that the time has come to speak to you of dolls and their makers. Although there is a lot of photographic and biographical information on the subject (a good deal of it written by us), there really has not been much discussion of doll art in the abstract or the general conditions of the business.

Therefore, in hopes of broadening the base of understanding between artist and collector, we take keyboards under fingers and speak to you of ART.

(Oh Oh! Heavy stuff coming?)

No, indeed, we are going to keep the discussion just as light and easy as possible because as Carol-Lynn says, "Dolls should be fun, just as art should. I'm an art historian by training. I have two degrees in the subject and know more than most people forget about effete aesthetic intricacies. I always wondered, when I was studying art, why so many scholars were so stodgy, why they didn't seem to enjoy what they were doing. Because art should bring pleasure to the viewer, and pleasure, for me is equated with fun. Ergo, art dolls, too, should be fun."

We are going to keep it simple because what we have to say is absolutely crucial to understanding the artist designed original doll and all the things involved in the making, collecting and appreciating of it.

Taste for doll artist dolls is usually an acquired one. Many doll collectors are unfamiliar with the term as are artists, museums and gallery owners. You have to be initiated, as it were, into the rites of collecting original dolls, but, once the introduction is made, you will probably be hooked for life because as their collectors agree, there is nothing that compares to a doll created by an artist.

What we really aim for, in our heart of hearts, is to give you a general appreciation of artist dolls...be you collector, artist or just a curious reader passing the time.

To appreciate, let us remember, does not mean to like something. It means something more like understanding it and allowing it to exist on its own terms. We do not expect each reader to like every doll shown here. It would be most unusual if he or she did as each one of us has individual tastes, likes and dislikes. We show here a selection of artist work which deserves to be appreciated. Each portfolio is worthy of any collector's wish list or any museum's attention. You decide which fit your likes, but, in the end, we would like you to be able to look at a work and know why it should be appreciated, why it is good or not good by design standards even if you do not like it yourself.

Let us begin by defining some boundaries.

"Humans," said artist Jean Ray Laury in the introduction to her book, *Dollmaking: A Creative Approach*, "have a natural inclination to make images. Dolls are manifestations of this propensity expressed in three-dimensional form. Within its scope, doll making has many different possibilities. First, there is a group which includes dolls that are the spontaneous products of traditional folk art. Second, there are dolls produced as toys, playthings for children. And third, there are dolls which, through personal and aesthetic statements, make an effort to communicate."

She goes on to say about handmade dolls, "the single most delightful thing about these dolls is that each one is completely unique. In the hands of the doll maker, the various materials come to life, and no two dolls will ever be the same."

In the doll art world we have representation of all three types. Folk dolls, which we might define as those dolls made at home by mothers for children or human-like creations with the specific cultural meaning like the Kachina or the harvest festival "corn-dollies" of England and their American derivations, the cornhusk dolls of Appalachia, do not figure as large as they could, however. In the doll art world most have come to doll making through a love of dolls as playthings (number two on the Laury list) or they have come to dolls as part of their exploration of design and sculpture (number three). The same is true for those who collect artist dolls. Most of

those collectors and artists who have the same basic interests usually seem to find each other, too.

The unpretentious *Nosalie* by artist-author Carol-Lynn Rössel Waugh was made specifically to be a child's companion. She is huggable, lovable and washable. *Waugh Collection and photograph.*

It boils down to three very distinct types of doll making. One product is a toy and is strictly judged by the attributes of playability...can it be loved? Can it be the vehicle for acting out games and fantasies? Can it be slept on or can its "mother" wash its hair? Another, the sculptural type, we usually refer to as a "figure." Figures are dolls in that they are small representations of human beings, but after that the field is wide open to interpretation of what that figure can be. Then, sort of in the middle is the doll figure that <u>looks</u> as if it could be played with, but is not really meant to be given daily handling.

Artists who make the first type often work in the design development departments of doll companies or sell their work primarily to parents and grandparents, rather than a collector market. The figures and the "not for really playing with" dolls, often constructed with more fragile materials, are made by individual artists as well as companies who produce dolls directly for the collector's shelves. All of these doll types, either made by an artist independently or by a company team designer, are essentially "dressed sculpture." They may reflect any one of a number of human characteristics or conditions. They are, if successfully done, a personal or esthetic, or educational statement by the artist. These statements may be humorous, serious, caricature or expressive of a certain relationship. They may be very real figures or totally ideal. They help us to see ourselves as humans. (We do like ourselves or we would not create more images to look at or to show us what we can be!) They help us to see our history and they help us to take a

Definitely a non-washable, "look at only" figure, Susie Oroyan's *Dumbdolly* is made of felt and wears a silk dress. *Oroyan Collection. Photograph by W. Donald Smith.*

ABOVE: Making "no bones about it," Oregon craftsman Kim Allen created this "doggie doll" of stoneware. *Oroyan Collection. Photograph by W. Donald Smith.*

BELOW: What is it? Is it a play doll? Is it truly sculptural? It certainly is "different!" The velvet bodied *Scarlett Ribbons* with her inked in face and extraordinary hairstyle can only be classified as pure whimsy. Figure by Susanna Oroyan. *Photograph by W. Donald Smith.*

break from the sometimes grim everyday realities by giving us a little of the fantasy world.

Getting down to the nitty-gritty, a doll should have a humanoid face which is shown by painting, sculpting or other applications such as needlesculpture or embroidery. A doll really cannot be totally an animal form. It can have animal attributes--say, a mermaid's tail, or butterfly wings, but it really should not have an animal face. The particular manifestation of art we are talking about is an outgrowth of man's making images of himself whether for religious statements, fashion messengers or children's playthings. Dressed cats and bear heads on doll-type of bodies really belong to the field of representational sculpture in general and to the art and craft of toymaking in particular...if you want to be strict about it. Carol-Lynn, as expected, would prefer not to be strict about it! She says, "Bears are more human than people and bear dolls are definitely dolls." A doll artist has imagination and if that imagination says, "Let's create a neat dog person," then that doggie person is just as valid a statement of art. Realistically, though, the "all doggie" artist will find a hard time breaking into the both the art world and the doll world as most of the organizations imply or expressly state that they are specifically concerned with representations of the human figure.

Next, a doll is more than a static piece of sculpture. How much more brings one to the shadier areas of definition. It seems that one can accept molded clothes when a doll is jointed, but, on the other hand, molded clothes on a non-movable figure make it a figurine. Does a doll have to be jointed? Does it have to have mobility? Some say yes and some say no. It depends on who you are talking to. Those who come from the doll/toy persuasian will say yes, a doll should be movable. And yet, many play dolls were not movable. Corncob dolls are not: handkerchief dolls are not: "pillow flat" dolls are not. It does seem, however, that movement must at least be implied in a doll artist piece. That is, for instance, with a wire armatured piece one could move it into a different position, if desired (though the artist would probably have a fit!). Or that in the position and arrangement of the clothing, there is an <u>illusion</u> of movement.

Can we make a conclusion at this point? Let's try!

What is a doll artist doll? It is a doll that was designed and made by a doll artist...a small replica of the human form whose object may be pure art or plaything. It seems it must be humanoid, may be made to represent the human condition or personality, may or may not move, may or may not represent the historical or folk cultural aspects of the world...can be a toy, can be at least part animal....a very wide ranging area for creative endeavor, indeed!

And matters are made even more complex when you get into the "academics" of contemporary doll artists and what they do. There are different types of doll artist dolls. Some are one-of-a-kind, some are limited editions and some are done as prototypes (which are the originals of "store bought" dolls), and then reproduced by people other than the artist who designed them--either commercial firms or reproduction craftsmen in a cottage industry. All of them get their integrity from the fact that they are original works of art, sculpted by the artist himself, and are derived from no one else's work. By this we mean they are not "adaptations," re-sculpted from a casting or mold of a doll done by another person, either living or dead, or derived from patterns or sculpture by others. Every stitch, every bit of clay of that doll has to be the design of the artist who makes it for it to be an original doll.

This is a lot of hard work and, to do it well, an artist must be adept at many facets of art: design, sculpture, needlework, pattern drafting, painting, mold-making (at times), ceramic techniques, wig making and other skills such as just a good sense of proportion. A doll artist is a jack-of-all-trades and usually, a master of them all, too, or his work does not work.

Many people never take the time to realize that the dolls they buy in the store were designed and made by artists, as well as were the antique dolls that are now so highly prized. Unfortunately, most of the names of these early doll designers have been lost. Grace Storey Putnam, who designed the Bye-Lo Baby is a case in point. An American artist, she sculpted the baby from life (although some say the model was actually a dead child). Her designs, universally popular, were reproduced in Germany for a world market. The original sculpture of the Bye-Lo baby was the prototype for the doll and was the "original artist doll." The myriads of *Bye-Los* extant are all replicas, reproductions of her designs.

On the other hand, the work of the German artist, Käthe Kruse, raises paradoxes in the definition of artist designs and leads to a clouding of the issue. Perhaps we can shed a bit of light on the differences. Käthe Kruse designed a line of charming fabric and felt children with molded faces. The part of her creation that was original, as we understand it, was the concept of the child, the painting of the face and the design of the body. The heads and faces were pulled from a mold made from a commercially and commonly available plaster sculpture...a head that any craftsmen could have purchased in a ceramic supply shop. In any definition of doll artist work today, these would not be allowed, as the most important part of an original is the basic sculpture.

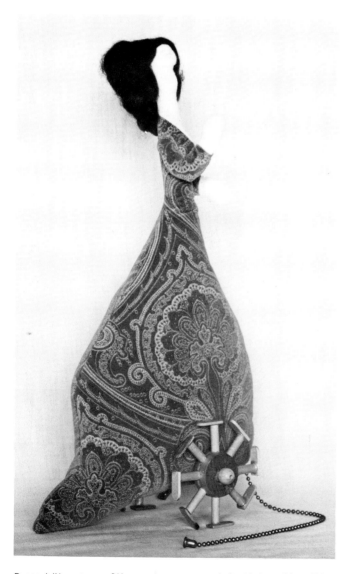

Does a doll have to move? How much movement and what kind must it have? Most would probably classify "Autoperipetitikos" as a pull toy rather than a true doll. Mobility in this figure constructed by Susanna Oroyan is effected by tinker toy wheels with wooden little feet for spokes. *Oroyan Collection. Photograph by W. Donald Smith.*

Sasha Morgenthaler's internationally famed creation, *Sasha. Oroyan Collection. Photograph by W. Donald Smith.*

The designs of the late Sasha Morgenthaler, a Swiss artist, have been made with great integrity in Great Britain for the world market. The "keeper of the flame" of Mrs. Morgenthaler's designs, Sara Doggart, was very careful to keep her new Sasha dolls faithful to Sasha's intentions. If it does not "feel" right, if it does not seem like something of which Sasha, herself, would have approved, a design was not done. Contemporary Sasha dolls are a fine example of a translation of an artist's work into a play doll -- which is what both their makers, Sasha and Mrs. Doggart wanted them to be.

Gorham-Textron in 1984 began translating the work of a contemporary doll artist, Kezi, into porcelain-headed dolls of a very high quality. Often, the translation of an artist's prototype into a commercial product is unsatisfactory because the artist may not have designed her model with the limitations of commercial manufacturing in mind. Then the doll head has to be re-cast and re-sculpted by others and the product ends up a pallid ghost of the original crisp and vital design.

None of these horrors happened to Kezi's work. The Japanese craftsmen who translated her originals into reproductions excellently reproduced her ideas, much to the artist's relief and pleasure. They have enabled people who cannot afford Kezi's limited, very expensive original dolls, to purchase her work.

Grace designed by Kezi for Gorham-Textron, 1984. *Waugh Collection and photograph.*

Doll artist originals are expensive. They have to be. First of all, they are works of art. They take countless hours to develop and to construct...more time than a doll artist ever wants to admit. If they are one-of-a-kind dolls, then these hundreds of hours go into one-- count it -- one doll. Even if the doll costs $800. or $900., (and some very nice pieces can be had for a great deal less), the doll artist would not be making the minimum wage.

Now, let us take a run at it from the art standpoint. Lots of artists, themselves, have a hard time describing the difference between what they do as craft and what they do that is art. This was made very apparent by the arguments and rebuttles to Carol-Lynn's article about those differences in a 1981 issue of Doll Reader®. Naturally, collectors listening to all that get even more confused.

Why is there such a fuss between art and craft, or artist and craftsman? Why, indeed, when the definitions seem fairly inter-changeable on the basis of the first dictionary listings?

In the first place, in semantics, one describes a definition as a *set* of denotations or meanings necessary to distinguish one word from another in the same class, e.g. what points differentiate "chair" from "bench" or "stool?" So, if we look at the set of denotations for "artist" as compared to "craftsman," we find that an artist is one who, in addition to using a skill, uses his imagination to make objects which have beauty or aesthetic value --value for themselves alone and not for any particular function that they may serve. The object that the artist makes <u>does not have</u> to be useful or educational, although it might be intended or interpreted to be so. For instance, one artist may wish to portray an American child of a certain historical period (as Mirren Barrie does with her colonial children series) and another may wish to portray a universal notion of "youth" as part of the general human condition. By contrast, a craftsman is no more than one who is skilled at technical construction -- handwork, toolwork or uses of materials -- and usually this is a set of highly precise procedures which he uses to make many repetitions of an object invented by someone else. The object a craftsman makes <u>does not</u> require him to use his imagination creatively nor does the product of his skill need to be anything more than functional. It does not have to be interesting or different so long as it is made well and works. The craftsman uses patterns and molds of designs made by others (artists); whereas, the artist uses his imagination to make his own designs and such skill as he can pick up to bring the idea into visible form. More importantly, an artist is often the inventor of the technical processes of craft because he is often forced to find a new way to work with raw materials in order to bring his idea into being. Although many artists are skilled craftsman, and many others strive to be, they are judged by imagination, interpretation and expression of form. Good art can be crude, but good craft cannot.

Alexander Phimister Proctor, American, 1862-1950 "Indian Maiden and Fawn," 1926. University of Oregon Museum of Art. Gift of Narcissa J., Washburne estate. *Photograph reproduced by permission of the University of Oregon Museum of Art.*

Coincidentally, a news feature appeared in the Eugene, Oregon, paper which serves to illustrate these differences. The story told that a bronze sculpture on the University of Oregon campus had been damaged by vandals and, as it was rather a favorite landmark, the University retained a person to repair it. The sculpture had been done in wax or clay by an artist nearly 60 years ago. The original sculpture was then cast in bronze by foundry metal craftsman, thereby creating the first and only "edition" and also destroying the original in the process. During the restoration of the damaged piece, the craftsman hired by the University certainly used his imagination, but he was not using it to create new expression. He was imaginatively drawing on his skill and knowledge of techniques in metalwork to restore and, in some places, reconstruct another's work. Furthermore, as the earlier bronze work was flawed, the modern restorer had to employ more skill than those foundry men who did the original casting work. Both the original foundry craftsmen and the restorer knew more about making the metal pieces than did the artist himself, who was primarily concerned with bringing a new shape into existence and who trusted others to make his work in the final medium. This is very like the situation which exists in the reproduction of antique dolls today. We know very little about the original artists who created the sculptures and the craftsmen who made the editions, though competent, were primarily engaged on mass production for a low cost general market. Craftsmen of today, however, reproduce antique dolls for a far more limited and discerning market and can take time to demonstrate better skill at painting and working with ceramics. In most cases, our reproduction doll makers can truthfully claim that they are making technically better dolls than the antiques they copy.

The annoying confusion between the terms "artist" and "craftsman" is, we think, a fairly recent phenomenon. Up to the time of, roughly, Rembrandt, there was no particular differentiation -- all creative endeavors from architecture to portraiture came under the heading of craft. Michelangelo would have called himself a craftsman and Cellini certainly did. The technical aspect was also reflected in the heavy percentage of study and work time devoted to its pursuit in the great art studios of the Middle Ages and Renaissance. Only in the last two centuries has there been a division of art and craft and that division has primarily separated sculptors and painters from everyone else. The confusion was not helped any by the so-called "crafts Renaissance" of the late 1960s. At that time people who were essentially artists producing limited amounts of their own imaginative work and selling it on the streets let themselves be called craftsmen. Adding to the confusion is the fact that many of these people were working in media not traditionally associated with the fine arts. Definitions and standards, however, are changing, and, as we know, many artist dolls are being added to permanent museum collections and sold in established galleries.

All these definitions of dolls, art, crafts and so forth have circled us closer to a definition of the contemporary art doll. We know that a doll must be human-like, at least in the facial expression, if no where else. We now that it must be the product of an artist's imagination. We know that it can be called dressed sculpture. We do not necessarily know what makes a good one.

What makes a good doll is *design*. The requisite parts might be there. The artist's idea might be there. The idea might be new and different expression, but if the whole thing is not executed with good use of design, it will be a failure.

Volumes have been written about design. It is, basically, harmonious combinations of such elements as line, form, texture, color, balance, proportion and scale. The emphasis really is on harmony. All those elements must work together, no one dominating, to form one whole expressive piece. We could also say that anything in a figure that jars the senses, seems out of place or that is incomplete is poor design.

If hands are out of scale to the type of body being portrayed, then there is no harmony and design fails. If colors do not work together for good effect (that does not mean that they all have to be the same hues), the harmony is not there and the design fails. If one is trying to make a beautiful lady and the waist is too thick, then it is out of proportion. If large scale prints or textures are used on a small

realistic person figure, then it is out of scale, out of harmony and fails. Design elements can be bent...and often are bent to make a point for the total figure, but when they are bent, they still must be balanced. For instance, if one is doing a character with a big, warty nose, then it might be desirable from a design standpoint to make big, hunky feet.

Hobbit. Note exaggeration of hands, head and feet. *Oroyan Collection and photograph.*

In the figure shown, the head, hands and feet are all out of scale for the height of the figure, but that bending is allowed because all of those elements balance. If only the hands were large, it would be a design balance failure and out of scale. One of the biggest failures of doll makers working wire armatures is the neglect to consider the width of the hip and the placement of the legs as they come down from the hip socket. This is a proportion problem and if not corrected, destroys the whole line of the figure. (In this particular figure, the legs are purposely triangulated downward to draw the eye to the unusual feet.)

In the figure of "Betsy Ross" there are several things that jar. The top is just a bit too big for the bottom of the body. The hair, though fine human hair, is still too big for the whole figure. The style is also not historically accurate. The print of the dress and the lace

Betsy Ross, the first sculpted work made by author Susanna Oroyan, exemplifies several problems that can occur in an otherwise ordinary seeming original. Just for starters, the head is too large for the body, the trims and patterns used in the costume are disproportionate and the hair is simply awful! Look again and see what other anomalies you can find. *Photograph by W. Donald Smith.*

Gauguin Lady, a two dimensional cloth figure made by artist Susanna Oroyan. Arguments vary as to whether this type of construction classifies as having sufficiently "re-shaped the material" to be called "sculpted." What do you think? *Oroyan photograph.*

that trims it is too large in scale. Furthermore, if you were to look underneath, you would see that the trim of the underwear did not at all work well with the trim of the dress.

The problem with understanding design is that quite often taste gets in the way. Perhaps an artist has made a doll and put a big curly wig on a head that should not have such a hairdo. It is poor design, but it might be to someone's taste. The big problem arises when poor design happens to be the artist's taste!...usually artists who have had art training are fully aware of design because every project they had in art classes was graded and critiqued on design. When one has to defend one's design, one learns quickly. Those who come to doll making without this experience usually learn it quickly or know it naturally, but unfortunately, some do not.

A good artist or a good critic can look at a piece and be able to tell right away what things combine to make good design. As a collector, one should learn to be a good critic. And it goes without saying that all artists must be their own toughest critics.

THE MEDIA

As we have seen, the bottom line in the definition of an artist's doll is "sculpture." What is sculpture? It is any process using the hands or the hands and tools that takes away from, adds to, or changes a hunk of raw material so that it resembles a three-dimensional form. In the case of a doll, the form is one that resembles a human being. The doll art world, however, puts a few more restrictions on the definition of sculpture than does the fine

arts world. The art world might accept an assembly of materials or a collage as sculpture, but the doll world feels that sculpture must re-form the raw material. Doll art does not accept "natural" processes such as the drying of an apple as sculpture, nor does a surface change such as painting a purchased clothespin amount to significant art work or sculpture. It might be well argued that a two-dimensional "pillow" type doll is a designed and sculpted piece because the fabrics have been shaped; however, at this time such forms have not gained much recognition within the field, possibly because artists enjoy the challenge of complex sculpture more.

The doll artist is not limited to any one medium for his sculpture. He or she uses what he "feels in tune with" and may combine two or more materials to build the form he wants.

The traditional materials for doll art are those that have been long associated with the better known art forms: wood, wax, clay (porcelain, china), papier-mâché, composition and fabric. Doll artists, however, are always curious and willing to experiment and innovate and, as a result, in recent years, we have seen very nice work from synthetic clays, improved papier-mâchés, stronger waxes, and that very contemporary product of our "age of plastic," polymer resin.

Clay

Clay can be synthetic or natural (as it comes from the earth), or a combination of the two. Doll artists use all three. Here we will discuss natural, water-based clay and its derivatives.

Stoneware, terra cotta and porcelain are all "natural" clays; although, porcelain often has elements added to it. This type of clay can be left as is to dry gradually under close supervision, then polished and fired in a kiln. If a mold is not made of the piece, it produces a one-of-a-kind doll.

Other clays use natural clays, sometimes, as a base, but add petroleum and/or some other elements to prevent drying. One clay of this sort, very good for modeling, is a favorite of professional sculptors and is called plastilina or plasticene. It is usually greenish-gray in color, tends to be greasy and comes in different hardnesses. Medium hardness seems best for making dolls. This clay seldom dries out, cannot be fired and sculptures made with it must be reproduced in another medium.

Clay to which a liquid, usually water, which dissolves the clay, and sometimes chemicals, has been added, is called "slip." Almost any natural clay can become slip, which is often the consistency of a thick milk shake and has to be thoroughly stirred before using. You can make your own slip; however, since it is available at ceramic shops, to do so is not worth the trouble.

Goddess by Julia Hills. One-of-a-kind, directly sculpted porcelain clay. *Photograph courtesy of the artist.*

The two most popular "slip" clays used by doll makers are porcelain and "ceramic" slip. Although they look similar, they have different properties.

"My Friend Bear," 9in (22.9cm) tall Teddy Bear doll prototype by Carol-Lynn Rössel Waugh. Some dolls have their own dollies to play with...shouldn't a doll have a Teddy Bear to play with? Children do! Ceramic clay. Jointed limbs. © 1985. Signed on left foot. *Waugh photograph.*

"Ceramic" slip is grayish in liquid form. It fires to a chalky, porous white and is rather fragile. It should be "stained," or painted with china paints or glazed with ceramic glazes. Some doll makers begin with ceramic clay and graduate to a more sophisticated stuff. The most practical use for it is in making a "master sculpture" from a mold. An artist can pour his work in ceramic slip and fire it. He then has a permanent master, in almost the same size as his original, from which he can make numerous successive molds.

Most doll artists work in porcelain. It is extremely fine-grained. It can be used in several states of plasticity and it affords a wide range of artistic possibilities. It is, however, very delicate and frustrating to work with. It is also hazardous to the health and many people have been affected by breathing in porcelain dust or have contracted skin problems from direct contact with it. Breathing masks and plastic gloves should be used when polishing or cleaning porcelain and it should never be ingested.

In an unfired state, porcelain is maddeningly fragile. When fired, it becomes so strong that many doll makers have to resort to whacking away at their "seconds" with mallets to destroy them.

After firing, porcelain clay shrinks from 17 to 20 percent. Details on the clay become refined and intensified. Successive molds can be made of a porcelain item and increasingly smaller dolls can be produced, thereby. This is how old-time doll companies obtained so many sizes of the same doll head.

Fired (in a kiln), unglazed natural clay is called "bisque." Glazing (coating the clay with a substance which, when fired, has a glass-like appearance) is not necessary with porcelain as its fine particles preclude leakage. Other clays, like stoneware and ceramic slip, must be glazed or they will leak. Some dolls are glazed all over and have a "teacuppy" appearance like the old "china dolls." Others are glazed selectively. Some clays are chalky if not glazed --ceramic clay is. Porcelain bisque is, if properly polished, sort of velvety in appearance.

Natural clay dolls are often china-painted. An art in itself, and a difficult process, it involves grinding and mixing pigments on a glass palette with oil vehicles and then firing in a kiln. Often successive reapplications and refirings are necessary to obtain colors and blends desired. Since they are lead-based, china paints should never be put in the mouth.

Wood

Wood as a medium for sculpting figures has been in use for equally as long as clays as is witnessed by such figures as the "Sheikh-el-Beled," a portrait in wood of an ancient Egyptian courtier. Undoubtedly, some of the finest figure sculpture that has ever been done are the beautifully carved people made for the gorgeous creche scenes of the 17th and 18th centuries. When wooden "babies" or dollies for children began to find their way into the market stalls of Europe, the material was wood. More elegant versions of the early wooden dolls formed traveling fashion reports throughout Europe and across the Atlantic to the American Colonies. Most wooden dolls made up through the 20th century were carved and then painted over to achieve a realistic flesh color. Our contemporary artists, however, have generally chosen to let wood grains become an integral part of the sculpture, often working with the grains present to achieve special effects in skin tone and texture. It is interesting to note that while carved wooden dolls are almost a given in the American folk tradition, until the early 1970s, only NIADA artists Helen Bullard and Fred Thompson had taken wood seriously as a medium for dolls. It is also curious that of the four artists working in wood covered in Carol-Lynn Rössel Waugh's book, *Petite Portraits,* each carving their first doll between 1975 and 1977, two of the four admitted to getting the inspiration from a *McCall's Magazine* craft project. One wonders how many artists were started off in wood by that one article.

Not much is required to describe the basic principles of wood carving. In her book, *Babes in Wood*, NIADA artist Pat Brooks describes the process as follows: "Start with a piece of wood large enough for the object you want to make and then with knives, or chisels, or whatever, cut away everything that does not look like what you want it to be." This approach is similar to the ancient

A typical 17th century creche figure. Even though the hands are slightly too large for the rest of the body, they have been sculpted with extraordinary sensitivity to modeling of flesh. Given the differences of style between the head and hands, it is quite likely the piece is the work of more than one artist. *Photograph by W. Donald Smith.*

This little black girl created by Sharon Howard, ODACA, is sculpted of the synthetic clay Fimo. *Oroyan Collection. Photograph by W. Donald Smith.*

Chinese feeling that there is a spirit in the wood which you must free by cutting away.

There is, of course, a bit more to wood sculpture than that. The artist has to become familiar with the workability of several types of woods, has to be an expert at selecting and caring for the proper tools, and has to spend long hours polishing and finishing in addition to the basic carving.

Synthetic Clays

Synthetic clays are relatively new -- products of our contemporary "plastic" age, they are petroleum based, plastic derivatives which can be fired or cured in the low temperature of the home oven.

Many doll artists who do work cast from molds have taken to the use of synthetic clays for their original sculptures as the cured synthetic clay is extremely durable and stands up well to the rigors of being buried in plaster. For the artist who makes one-of-a-kind figures, the synthetic clays are an excellent choice of medium -- especially for those whose sculpture is not amenable to the mold making process. On the other hand, some artists have felt that the longevity of the synthetic products are in some question simply because they have not been around long enough to see what will happen over a long period of time. At this point, synthetic clays have been in use for well over ten years and so far no significant changes in finished work as regards to deterioration or loss of finish has been

reported. So far, nothing has been observed to indicate that they will not be a durable product. It is quite likely that as these products are plastic types, they will last as long as or even longer than the natural forms...damage or deterioration to any doll form is more likely to result from mis-handling than from the material itself. Most artists are fully aware of the potential risk points during construction and take great pains to avoid them.

There are difficulties for the artist who begins to work in synthetic clays, but most involve perfecting necessary technique and learning the skills and processes necessary to achieve satisfactory work...no more than one would have to do with any other medium.

The major types of synthetic clays in use today are Sculpey, Super Sculpey (known generically as "polyform"), Fimo, and Cernit. Sculpey is very similar to the more commonly known plasticine modeling clays; although, perhaps not quite as resilient to work with. Super Sculpey is a harder version of the regular Sculpey and while very easy to sculpt, it cures to a very hard, cement-like finish which is extremely difficult to polish. It also requires a great deal of patience to manage a well-painted surface. Both Sculpey and Super Sculpey are not compatible with lacquer based paints and must be either primed with gesso or painted with oils or acrylics.

Fimo and Cernit are rather similar synthetic clays which, when cured have a lovely, translucent quality that resembles wax or porcelain. These two are relatively expensive and preferred for use

Head of the synthetic clay, Sculpey, being modeled. Artist is Susanna Oroyan. *Oroyan photograph.*

by those working in miniature scale.

Figures of synthetic clays may be sculpted whole and jointed or assembled as in the standard china doll body or they may be modeled over a wire armature skeleton.

Charlotte by Gillian Charlson shows the realistic portrayal of flesh allowed by the medium of wax. *Photograph courtesy of Gillian Charlson.*

Wax

The medium made famous by Madame Tussaud has been around for many years for the making of figures. Works in wax are treasured because of their wonderfully life-like flesh tones.

Wax is favored by artists because it can be used in a number of different ways. It can be sculpted or carved to make an original first sculpture. It can be poured into a mold to create an edition. It allows re-modeling of spot areas for changes or corrections easily and it allows the insertion of rooted hair. It can also be used to coat composition or works in other media to tone down bright colors and to produce a flesh-like surface.

The wax artist has the mixed blessing of having his work admired for its life-like qualities and at the same time the frustration of the public's lack of trust in the medium's durability. Modern waxes, however, are extremely hard with most requiring higher temperatures to melt than would ever be encountered under normal home or ordinary weather conditions. One would have to burn the house down or create a solar exposure to melt a modern wax piece. Very little worry, truly. If you like the piece, buy it and take good care of it.

Composition

Composition is a catchall term without good definition. It is used to define a variety of combinations of substances which form a number of different compounds which may be used for doll making. Most compositions are developed and kept secret by individual doll artists.

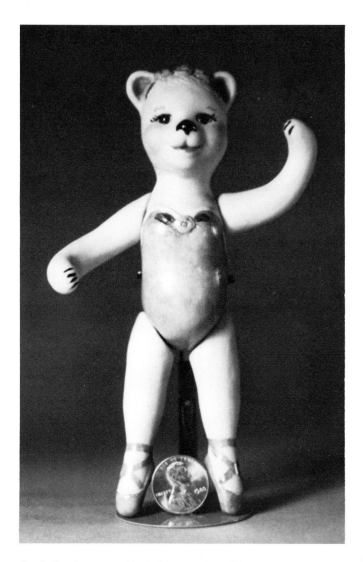

Bearisnikova latex composition by Carol-Lynn Rössel Waugh. *Waugh photograph.*

The traditional composition used for many years is formed from fine, sifted sawdust, glues, clay and/or plaster mixed together in varying parts. This is the type of composition that was used in the United States between the First and Second World Wars. Generally pushed into molds, trimmed and painted, the material was cheap, lightweight, relatively durable. The one failing was a tendency for paint to chip and peel.

Few doll artist dolls are made of this sawdust composition these days. Most makers have experimented and developed more successful formulas.

A more commercial type of composition is a mixture of water, clay, liquid latex (a rubber like material) and silicon. It can be mixed at home or bought already prepared in gallon or five-gallon jugs. This latex composition is a "slip" which is water based and pours. It works in plaster molds, setting up very much like porcelain slip. It is poured into molds, allowed to set up, and then decanted. Castings are trimmed and allowed to air dry. Then they are sanded, painted with latex paints and finished.

Latex is hard on molds, but altogether it is surprising that more artists have not adapted its use as it is safe, durable and produces a lightweight object.

Rings on Her Fingers and Bells on Her Toes, a fabric doll by Susanna Oroyan takes the traditional flag fabric doll "a few steps beyond." The figure has been made three-dimensional by "jointing" seams at the knees, elbows, wrists and hips and by the articulation of the fingers and toes. *Photograph by W. Donald Smith.*

Artist Ann Parker finishing her portrait figures which are made of cast resin. *Photograph courtesy of Ann Parker.*

Resin

Resin, another product of the age of plastics, is very new to the doll world and at this time it is difficult to say if it will catch on. Artists who use it like it because it is lightweight and can be poured into a mold. The hesitation in use seems to be coming from the fact that there have been reports that artists who have worked with resins over a number of years have developed health problems.

Cloth

The fabric doll is one of the oldest forms and certainly the one most traditionally associated with the warm feeling of childhood playmate dolls. Many, many doll artists have started out with fabric as a medium and most will admit to a lasting pleasure in working with it. Of course, all doll artists do have to be proficient with fabric in general to design and costume their figures, but to actually sculpt with fabric takes a special skill. In sculpting fabric to form a doll one either cuts and sews shapes such that the contours, when filled with stuffing, take on a three dimensional sculptured effect or one "needlesculpts."

Needlesculpture is almost impossible to define and is usually only learned by trial and error or by observation and imitation. Ordinarily, the artist works with a nylon stocking or piece of stretchy fabric with stuffing behind it. A threaded needle is put in and pulled out, picking up and poking the fabric and stuffing into shapes that finally resemble a face. Nylon stocking needlesculpture when well done has an uncanny resemblance to real human faces...with all the sags, bags, wrinkles and creases.

CLASSIFICATIONS OF WORK

Within the field of original doll art there are a number of production modes that an artist may choose from to make a doll. All except reproduction are equally valid statements as original work. Choice of one or the other method depends on the individual artist's preference, work capabilities and/or media.

The one-of-a-kind

A one-of-a-kind figure sometimes called a "one of" means that a doll is made as a separate and unique entity and that there are no molds made from the original sculpture...usually because the original sculpture material can be finished without having to make a mold. This is often the case with wood, fabric, Polyform, and, in some cases, ceramic materials. Sometimes the artist will make one-of-a-kind pieces because he simply does not have the desire nor the facilities to make more than one. (Producing even five of

The limited edition

Artists who work in forms and materials that can be pulled or poured from a mold often do "editions." Essentially, the finished dolls in an edition are castings from molds made from one original piece of sculpture. The original sculpture is used in this case to make a plaster or rubber mold. A liquid (porcelain slip, resin, wax) or a pliable material (felt) is put into the mold, allowed to set up and removed as many times as the artist desires. The additional time and expense involved in making a good mold or set of molds makes it only sensible to produce more than one item. Artists making editions of their work will produce anywhere from 5 to 50 or more pieces which are in essence reproductions of their own work. Most limit their editions to no more than 20 pieces so that the comparative rarity of the work is not diminished and, also, so that they can get on to new ideas without the odious obligations of hundreds of repetitions. One always has to feel a bit sorry for the beginning artist who advertises a work in an edition of several hundred or more. Even with good studio help, it will not be long before he is thoroughly sick of the same thing and, of course, the discerning collector will not be especially eager to have a piece he thinks will be in every other household in the country.

The members of the artist produced edition will always have some minute individual differences. The artist will, consciously or unconsciously, change the depth of color, the line of an eyebrow or the like. Quite often, an artist will also purposely vary the costume design or "message" in the figures...for instance, one of an edition of children may be shown as a "sleepy head" in nightclothes with eyes painted to look droopy while another may be shown in wide-eyed surprise opening a birthday gift. As the question of originality hinges on the artist's design and sculpture, these changes do not detract from the value of the doll as long as the creating artist does them and no one else.

When the limit set for an edition is reached, the molds are destroyed to guarantee the number. Because of the shrinkage of porcelain slip during firing, copies made by taking a mold from a member of an edition will always be smaller in size and easy to identify then as copies. Identical copies of the original can only be made if one has the original sculpture. Editions in other materials such as wax or resin could be copied, but, as they are usually painted and/or covered with finishes when sold, it would be virtually impossible to achieve an exact replica.

A very realistic needlesculpture by artist Lisa Lichtenfels. *Photograph by Lisa Lichtenfels.*

something can be extremely tedious when you want to get on to something new and exciting!)

The one-of-a-kind is the most rare type of figure. It is THE ONLY ONE that will ever be available of that sculpture. If you have a one-of-a-kind, you can be sure that you will not find any unexpected twins popping up on a fellow collector's coffee table or in every store window. Occasionally, an artist will refer to his work in fabric or wood as an edition, but this means that he has separately and by hand sculpted a number of figures which appear to be the same thing. The actual "hands-on" process of sculpture and assembly required for each figure of this type still makes them one-of-a-kind -- even though they may look identical. The key thing that distinguishes the one-of-a-kind is that each sculpture is done from beginning to end without the "short cut" of reproducing a head or body part from a mold. A very rare exception would be in the case where an artist must make a mold to make the final one and then destroys the mold in order to guarantee that it is the only one. In fabric, only those types pressed with a metal mold can be qualified as "editions."

Artists who do one-of-a-kind work usually have a very difficult time letting one go. Ideally, the "best of all possible worlds" would be to be able to make three-of-a-kind: one for the artist, one for permanent display in a museum and one for a collector.

"Variations." The artist's original prototype (center) can be the basis for the artist's own production of a limited edition (left) as well as a manufacturer's production of a commercial edition (right).

A collector should always be aware of what the artist is doing with his or her original sculptures. For example, it would be possible for artist X to create an original sculpture of a doll we can call *Baby Billy* in polyform. This polyform original can be used to make a mold. The artist may then produce an edition of 20 *Billies* in porcelain from those molds. The artist can make another set of molds from the same original sculpture and produce an edition or authorize someone else to produce an edition of 1000 *Billies* in vinyl...and on top of all that, the artist could go back and finish up the original polyform *Billy* as a doll. Each type of production is equally valid and there is no rule against it. The first *Billy* in polyform finished up by the artist personally will always be the most rare and most desirable. The 20 porcelain *Billies* painted and dressed by the artist

RIGHT: *Prince William*; porcelain portrait doll by June Gale. *Photograph courtesy of June Gale.*

BELOW: *Marie*, a porcelain toddler by Nerissa. *Photograph courtesy of Nerissa.*

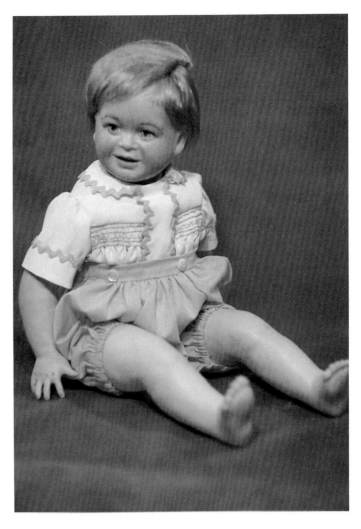

Jack Hill, unclothed, all-porcelain figure by Edna Nell Shaw. *Photograph courtesy of Edna Nell Shaw.*

LEFT: *My Friend Bear,* 9in (22.9cm) tall Teddy Bear doll prototype by Carol-Lynn Rössel Waugh. Ceramic clay. Jointed limbs. © 1985. Holds small gray bear made by April Whitcomb. *Waugh photograph.*

ABOVE: *Edward* and *Emma* by Gillian Charlson. Wax. 26in (66cm). *Photograph courtesy of Gillian Charlson.*

LEFT: *Dutch Doll* by Margaret Hickson. Papier-mâché. Chair decoration hand-painted by the artist. *Photograph by Betty Lorrimar.*

One of Van Craig's papier-mâché ladies. *Photograph by M. J. Magri.*

ABOVE: Lisa Lichtenfels' *Ruby*, a New York street woman. Nylon stocking needlesculpture. © 1983. *Photograph courtesy of Lisa Lichtenfels.*

RIGHT: *Chasing Butterflies,* polyform one-of-a-kind by Susanna Oroyan. 9in (22.9cm) tall. *Oroyan photograph.*

LEFT: *Sarah Goings.* Cloth on wire armature by Ellen Turner. *Photograph by Ann Hawthorne.*

ABOVE: The *Diva*, 26in (66cm), is a porcelain figure designed and made by Helen Kish. This piece is all-porcelain with jointed arms and legs. She is posed in such a way as to look like she may be singing and is not really meant to be moved about. As with all of Helen's dolls, her features are painted. In this case the hair (very short) is molded. The elegant gown and cap is of beaded silk charmeuse. So far only the one figure has been made. If the artist decides to do an edition in the future, no more than three will be made totally. She is incised on the back of the head, "Diva, copyright 1984, Helen Kish #1." *Photograph courtesy of Helen Kish.*

LEFT: *Carol Di Donna* by Robert McKinley. Latex composition head, sculpey hands, cloth body. *Photograph by Robert McKinley.*

Katie designed by Nancy Villaseñor, produced in vinyl by Jesco. Approximately 10in (25.4cm) tall, fully-jointed. *Waugh photograph.*

ABOVE: Kezi's *Contrary Mary*, porcelain, swivel head, 13½in (34.3cm). © 1979 Kezi. Part of Kezi's "Arabella Series." *Photograph courtesy of Kezi.*

LEFT: *Jeanne, Patty* and *Cynthia* by Susan Wakeen. 15½in (39.4cm) tall all-porcelain dolls with glass eyes, fully-jointed. 1984. *Photograph courtesy of Susan Wakeen.*

ABOVE LEFT: *Beatrix Potter*, cast resin portrait figure by Ann Parker. *Photograph courtesy of Ann Parker.*

ABOVE: *Humpty Dumpty.* Porcelain limited edition by Blythe Collins-Kretschmer. *Photograph courtesy of Blythe Collins-Kretschmer.*

LEFT: *Puss in Boots* by Beverly Port. Porcelain. *Photograph courtesy of Beverly Port.*

RIGHT: *Bride* and *Groom Rabbits,* 21in (53.3cm), fully-jointed carved wood figures by Bob Raikes with removable clothing made by Carol Raikes. © 1985. *Waugh photograph.*

BELOW LEFT: *Marley's Ghost* by Charlotte Zeepvat, *Photograph courtesy of Charlotte Zeepvat.*

BELOW RIGHT: *Sherlock Holmes* by Jean Heighton. Porcelain. *Photograph courtesy of Jean Heighton.*

LEFT: *Queen Elizabeth I.* Wax portrait figure by Sheila Wallace. *Photograph courtesy of Sheila Wallace.*

BELOW LEFT: Small *Lady Beth* by Marilyn Stauber. 5½in (14cm), No. 1 of an edition of 10. Porcelain. Costumed in 1873 blue silk walking dress. *Photograph by Marilyn Stauber.*

BELOW RIGHT: *Oberon* by Julia Hills. *Photograph courtesy of Julia Hills.*

would be next most valuable. The 1000 vinyl *Billies*, initially cheaper, would take quite awhile longer to appreciate in value, whether they were made up by the artist entirely or whether they were produced by others... primarily because there would be so many of them and because vinyl is not considered as "classy" a material as porcelain.

In speaking of one-of-a-kind and edition work so far, we have assumed that all the work was done by one individual artist; however, there are a number of variations possible and they are all differentiated by the degree in which the artist directly controls and/or participates in the actual design and production.

Artist ORIGINALS, either one-of-a-kind or editions, are those dolls which are designed and constructed by the one creating artist. That artist does all the work, sculpture, makes all the parts, designs and drafts the patterns, and usually makes the majority of all accessories like clothes, wigs and props.

Artist-PRODUCED dolls, usually limited editions which do not exceed 15 or 20 pieces, are those in which all the work is done by one artist. He or she sculpts the figure, designs the clothes and paints the faces. In artist-produced work, others (artisans/craftsmen) may help in making molds, wigs, clothing and accessories. The important part is that the artist personally and directly does all the design work and supervises all stages of the production from the beginning to the completion of the piece.

Artist-DESIGNED dolls, limited or unlimited editions, are those that are produced by others (home craftsmen or manufacturers), in any medium, from the artist's original sculpture and design. The artist usually designs and executes a prototype which is sold to a commercial manufacturer and, in doing so, may forfeit all control over the execution of the finished product. Because these designs must be adapted to the requirements of mass production and economic feasibility, when the artist forfeits control, what remains in the finished work is often no more than a "flavor" of the style of the artist. Fortunately, more and more manufacturers are coming to value the importance of allowing the artist to work with them in quality control and, more and more, artists are learning to design specifically for the requirements of mass production. Farther along, we include a section detailing the day-to-day experiences of an artist as she creates a prototype for commercial production.

And then there is the sticky question of reproduction! It should be clearly understood that A REPRODUCTION IS IN NO WAY ORIGINAL ART. The work is entirely copy work done by craftsmen or artisans.

Reproductions may be work made by a manufacturer from a prototype made and purchased from an artist. Reproductions may be made from molds that the artist has sold for craftsmen to use. Reproductions can be made from the artist's personal molds or original sculpture by permission of the artist. Reproductions of any kind, done where the artist is not in control should be clearly marked: "Reproduction by _____" and this marking should be visible on hang tags as well as marked on the body of the doll. In cases where original work is certified and registered with the National Institute of American Doll Artists, the reproduction should be of a different medium or size and should be sufficiently different in appearance so as to be readily distinguishable as not the original piece or a member of the original edition.

A very good example is seen in the recent reproduction of NIADA artist Dewees Cochran's work. Dewees, famous for her "Grow-up" series, made her original editions in a latex composition material. Dewees is now retired and no longer able to produce her own work, but with the realization that collectors who have just discovered "artist originals" might like to have a replica of her work, arrangements were made for reproductions to be made from her molds. These reproductions, made in porcelain, are clearly marked as the work of someone else, and are of a different size and medium than the original Cochran dolls. Sadly, on the other hand, there are people who acquire an artist original piece and figure it is all right "to make just a few for fun" but sooner or later, these "funsies" turn up on a dealer's table as an original work by the artist. If the dealer and the collector are not really well up on that particular artist's work, both can be fooled. Again, reproductions are never original art

pieces. To produce them and to allow them to be purchased as such is essentially fraud.

Before leaving the subject of reproductions, we feel we ought to say something about the delicate question of "tweekling." Very often when a hobbyist gets into making porcelain dolls, he is tempted to short-cut into originals by casting a head from a mold made of an antique doll. He then takes this reproduction head and "tweeks" it here and there to change the features or the expression...a closed mouth may become a grin, a dimple may be added, and so forth. This is a "fun" thing to do in one's own studio for one's own collection, but, again, these dolls get out into the public and the unaware are taken in. Some inexperienced doll makers think that this constitutes original work. It does not and never will. The worst of it is that often doll makers who know better try to pass off tweekled work as original. Knowledgeable artists, collectors and reproductionists can spot these dolls right off. How often have we stood next to an expert who recognized a "Jumeau QT 476" or the like under a doll that was presented as an original. How embarrassing for its fabricator! Any kind of "tweekled" work is fraud. The wise doll maker would be sure to do his or her own sculpture or stick to good reproduction work. There is no middle ground.

THE STATE OF THE ART

In the doll world, the doll artist has just taken his first steps past the toddler stage and is poised to break for a dead run.

The artist-made-doll has existed since the beginning of doll collecting. Most notable among the early originals were those of Dorothy Heizer, Muriel Bruyere and Gertrude Florian who worked in the 1930s, 40s and 50s. Fortunately, for doll art, their output was outstanding and set a high standard for the field.

During the 50s, a few more artists began to make dolls doing their own sculptures and producing them in doll form. At the end of the decade, a handful of these artists, feeling rather like lost children in the doll collecting world, formed the organization called the National Institute of American Doll Artists. Magge Head Kane and Helen Bullard, the early driving forces behind the organization, worked against great odds to establish recognition for original doll art, and doll artists everywhere owe them thanks for they made it possible for us to sell, speak about and display our work at national shows and conferences.

Through the 1960s, even with a national artist group, things progressed slowly; artists were still scarce. In the early 70s, however, a sudden explosion of interest in doll artistry occurred. Perhaps, it had its roots in the crafts revival which revered originality and creativity and rejected the mass-market and the so-called "plastic" society.

Much of the crafts movement was based in California and on the West Coast, and many early doll makers seem to have stemmed from the American West, also. But, as doll making seems to have universal appeal, doll artists began experimenting all over the country, and concurrently a need arose for organs of communication between them for supplies, sources and support.

By 1975, two more doll maker's organizations were in operation, ODACA (The Original Doll Artist Council of America) and IDMA (The International Dollmaker's Association). Doll makers began to have conventions, shows, seminars, classes and impressive displays of their production.

Simultaneously, prices for the increasingly scarce antique dolls took a tenfold leap. Discerning collectors began to see that the collectible of the future was the original doll. From 1978 to 1985, commercial companies began using talents of independent artists to put out "name artist" editions. The original doll, by 1985, had "come of age" in the collector's world.

Unfortunately, the art world takes a different view. Doll art falls through the cracks in its power structure. Much of mainstream art society has never heard the term "doll artist," and, when introduced to it, often dismisses it, perhaps because of unfamiliarity. One never studies about doll artists in history classes or in studio classes and the art form combines so many media, so many diverse techniques that it is extremely hard to classify. Then, too, there is the "toy

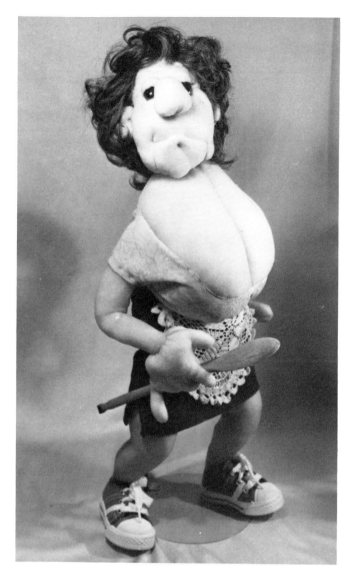

Don't Mess with Mama, needlesculpture by Susanna Oroyan. Some dolls are not made to be pretty or lovable! *Oroyan photograph.*

to make a supremely beautiful play object for a child. He may create a sculptural form that recreates the ambience and feeling of old toys in fragile materials that can only be "played with" mentally, or with great care by adult hands. Or he might want to make a social statement, be it gentle or rankling, a commentary on the state of mankind, and bring it to his audience in doll form. Sometimes these statements are not so sweet and the doll artist runs the risk of alienating the doll collector, or, at least, not attracting him. But, if the intention of the designer is to alert the public to the existence of his subject matter, which might be, for example, child abuse or drunkenness, or crime, and not to make sales, a three-dimensional piece in doll-form can be a powerful statement. It might, however, scare buyers away forever, especially those who are uncomfortable with anything but sweet-faced children with vacuous eyes in Sunday School dresses and Mary Janes. Traditionally "safe" subjects like this are usually the realm of the neophyte and the reproductionist.

A doll artist's acceptance by the art world has a lot to do with how closely his work approximates what is being shown by other artists in other forms. Most galleries are looking for "new" expressions, "avant garde" work. They want pieces that will cause controversy, create sales and publicity. They stick with what has gone well for them and what they understand. Doll artist work, which runs the gamut of artistic experiences and intentions, is alien, and, at the same time, too "tame," too familiar to consider. After all, everybody knows what a doll is; what can possibly be new about dolls or toys? And besides, how is a gallery owner to decently display these things?

At this writing, the doll artist still has an uphill climb for recognition in both the doll collecting and the artistic world. The job description "doll artist" still receives almost universal lack of comprehension from the general public...which is why Carol-Lynn's business card reads "writer/artist." She may never change that designation. For a doll artist is almost a Renaissance man or woman. He must know about and combine many more artistic techniques and media than any other form of practicing artist, and they all have to blend harmoniously, seamlessly, for his work to succeed. Of all the designations, that of doll artist may be one of the most difficult to practice and to explain. The term "artist," plain and simple, suffices. "Renaissance Woman" on a business card may be ostentatious!

THE ARTIST

"Doll artistry" defies neat classification. The products of doll artists are diverse in intent, material and construction. They may or may not be moved, may be covered (with paint or fabric), may be limited to the expression of the human form, and may employ several technical skills and media. To call doll artists "multi-media sculptors" comes close. They add, subtract from, bend or manipulate raw materials to reflect their visions. This, the creative aspect of his work, tends to be the most important to the doll artist.

How does one become a doll artist? Since we are handy, we will rely on ourselves as source material. As we have approached the field from diverse starting points and come out with different products, media and philosophies, we are a pretty good cross-section of the movement.

Practically none of us start out to be doll artists. Looking back on it, though, it seems that everything we have done has led to this goal. Basically, all of us started out with a love of dolls, or of art, or both.

Carol-Lynn:

There are a few constants in my life and three of them have been, in order: a love of dolls, a love of books and a love of art. Almost every page of my childhood album contains a photograph of me with a doll. Somebody once told me when I was eight that I was "the dolliest girl in town," a dreadful expression which stuck in my brain for obvious reasons.

I had lots of dolls when I was growing up, and, amazingly, I've kept most of them in playing condition. Right up front, I'd better mention that I consider dolls, even artist dolls to be playthings --even when they are art. Grownups "play" with their dolls (and their Teddy Bears -- see my book *Teddy Bear Artists: The Romance*

syndrome." Dolls are toys, playthings, vaguely functional objects. How can they, too, be considered fine art? Are they not more in the realm of crafts?

The problem is that in Western Art traditions, the doll has never been considered an art object, as opposed to, for example, Japan, where doll making is a revered art form and doll artists are honored by the government as "living national treasures."

Art galleries, museums and historians have always had problems with new art expressions and with art forms that combine media such that they are not readily classifiable. They have convenient places in which they display objects, and if one comes through their doors that mixes definitions, they face a dilemma.

Dolls have always been stuck in historical displays. Museums usually acquire them reluctantly because they are considered of minor importance, when, actually, they have major importance because they reflect and interpret society at the time they are made and also help formulate the way in which children, the most important members of that society for the future, will act towards their children and other people.

Dolls have always been a historical record, a mirror of the populations, whether made as toys or as art objects. And it is our position that there is no reason for exclusivity in dealing with dolls; they can be both aesthetically beautiful and playthings. On the other hand, they do not have to be either of these.

When a doll is made by an artist, as a means of aesthetic expression, he may have any number of goals in mind. He may want

Carol-Lynn Rössel, Christmas morning, circa 1950, Tottenville, Staten Island, New York. One doll in arm, one on the floor, a box of bride paper dolls are there, too. My gifts always centered on dolls. Notice the easel, with my name on it, yet! *Photograph by Carl Rössel.*

Second Bear (left) and *First Bear* (right), life-long companions of Carol-Lynn Rössel Waugh. "Second Bear" wears the first bear outfit I ever designed, at the age of six, of red polished cotton. It has a pocket, one real button and a snap that still works. This was the beginning of my career as a doll and bear couturiere -- 1953. *Waugh photograph.*

of Making and Collecting Bears for a harangue on that subject) in lots of ways. If they don't, they shouldn't have them around because otherwise they are nothing but big dust magnets.

I play with mine. I stash their boxes, sit them on the bed and see what other clothes I might have on hand that might fit them. Bears I always find a new sweater for (I believe bears are furry dolls) and a honey pot. The other day, Kezi's doll, *Grace*, arrived in her lovely official box. I chucked the box, checked out the doll and played with her for a half an hour on the bed before handing her over to the three bears she shares the deacon's bench in the bedroom with. Every once in awhile I pick her up, wind up her music box and have fun.

As I said above, dolls should be fun. Always have. So, I carried my love of them with me as I grew up. Dolls taught me things. I sewed my first dress for a *Ginny* doll and had to learn to read dressmaking patterns and the intricacies of my grandmother's treadle sewing machine to do it. I have now, at age 39, been sewing dolls' clothes for 33 years, most of the time designing my own, just because my *Ginny* dolls and my unclothed Teddy named *Second Bear* needed wardrobes.

I had a squadron of *Ginnys* -- still do -- and prefer them. There's something, to my way of thinking, magical and just right about a doll sized from 6in (15.2cm) to 9in (22.9cm) in height. This is why, by and large, I made dolls of this scale when I started to design originals. They are fun to sew for and to play with.

In the third grade I made dolls from crepe paper and cloth, I still have a couple of these virgin doll making experiments. In sixth grade I designed marionettes, made, as I remember, from newspaper rolls, painted and dressed. These are long-gone.

In college, after abandoning French, I studied art history and acquired B.A. and M.A. degrees in it. My specialties were American art and architecture, but I was fascinated by William Blake, William Morris and the 19th Century Arts and Crafts Movement which were all English.

I got married and had a daughter (the daughter came in between the B.A. and the M.A. So did the son, but he was ten years later), moved to Maine and began teaching sewing, the skill my *Ginny* dolls taught me because nobody in Central Maine has a burning need for art historians.

When Jenny-Lynn was three, I designed my first doll for her. *Nosalie* was a rag doll with a predominant round proboscis, a big smile and fringe hair, 24in (61cm) tall. She was a Christmas gift for Jenny-Lynn's first Christmas in Maine. When the doll was done, I wrote a children's book about the doll making experience to go with it with a pattern in the back. It was my first never-published manuscript, deservedly so. But it established a pattern.

I began to create dolls and simultaneously write about them. I joined the crafts circuit and designed over two dozen fabric dolls which I purveyed over a three-year period. I began to study about dolls and make contact with other doll makers.

Just before I met Susie at that 1974 IDMA Conference, I discovered clay and experimented with sculpting originals and reproducing them in low-fire ceramic clay. Nobody, to my knowledge, was making original porcelain dolls in Central Maine in 1974. Until I went to Reno that summer, I hadn't a clue to their existence.

Susie:

It seems pretty obvious that there are three ways that a person can get hooked into this doll making business. One is, like Carol-Lynn, a person grows up playing with, loving and living with dolls. Another route in is though pure art, where one is connected to pencils, paints and so forth before he even learns to read. These are the guys that are good from the first try. They know design and they have the eye. The third, or probably middle route, is mine. If there is one constant in my life outside of loving books, it is making things. I am a compulsive "putter-togetherer," builder, project person and general "putterer arounder." If I see one I think I should make one...whatever it is. I have incredible lists of things "to do."

Artist-author Susanna Oroyan and her *Old Ted*...when they were both much younger. *Ted*, minus one eye and sole survivor of the toy box, now enjoys a much deserved retirement. *Photograph by L. B. Scruggs.*

This muu-muu clad rag doll adapted from a pattern by Edith Flack Ackley was the first "successful" doll made by Susanna Oroyan. *Oroyan photograph.*

Making things was very big at my house. My dad always was building and re-finishing and adding to: my mother and both grandmothers did all the sewing and needle arts between them...everything from quilts to nuts. My brother was given, to his immense joy, a truck load of balsa blocks and spent most of his youth building the Seven Cities of Cibola in the basement when he wasn't drawing castles upstairs. Altogether a very can do, will do environment.

Sure, I had dolls. But the truth is that I took them all apart to see how they worked and, mostly, never got them back again (which probably explains why there are no pictures of me as a child with a doll). Poor things never survived me.

My youthful doll making never satisfied me. I took the dolls apart, intended to dress them in wonderfully fantastic costumes, but lacking the skill, couldn't even get close to what I saw in mind's eye. Frustrated, I gave up. But, under the bed, a small box of gleaned fabric scraps began a multiplication of species which is still going on to this day.

My first real concentrated experience with making a doll happened in my fourth grade year. I discovered Edith Flack Ackley's book, *Dolls to Make for Fun and Profit*, in the school library. I had it checked out so much the fall of that year, my parents tracked down a copy and put it in my Christmas stocking. I still have the book. I sometimes suspect that half the attraction was that word "profit" in the title (I have since learned better!) and the other half was the wonderful sketches that made it all look so easy.

The experience was over soon. Again, my small and inexperienced hands could not reproduce the patterns and sketches...not even for fun, let alone profit!

Meanwhile I played dress-ups, drew or tried to draw paper dolls, and generally became known for the little messes of "crafty" projects I left around behind me.

School and related activities pretty much put doll making attempts in the shade until after I was married and a mother. For my son's first Christmas, I got out the Ackley book and tried again. Much to my surprise, I came pretty close in reproducing a clown doll in cloth. Then I made a few more for nieces and baby gifts...and then I made a few more for myself. School intervened again while I

completed degrees in English and linguistics. But, by this time I was experimenting with all kinds of dolls (except sculpted) during vacations and, sometimes, when I should have been studying.

Now, I still wasn't thinking of myself as a doll maker. Dolls, at this time, were just one of several things I was making. I was into weaving, collage, creative clothing, decoupage, jewelry making -- you name it. Somehow, there was an attraction to learning more about art for why else would I have spent the majority of one college summer session reading my way through the library's art sections.

I suppose, in the end, two things decided my course in dolls. One, was a love of character. I think what I have always wanted to do in dolls is somehow to bring my favorite people in books, and off the streets, to life in three-dimensional form. The other, more down to earth reason, was that I discovered the world of doll making and collecting just after finishing up school at a time when I had time to make dolls, was making dolls as a result of the influence of Jean Ray Laury's 1971 book, and the introduction to "capital A" doll art by colleague Anne Luree Leonard in Sacramento, California.

I made a few, I advertised, I met Carol-Lynn through the ad and you know the rest of the story.

The Technical Artist

How artists "get there" is one thing, but what they are is quite another and rather helpful to understanding the whole phenomenon of doll art.

One cannot help but pick up a large, bright entwined thread of similarites running through the artists' lives. If we were to make a list of artist characteristics, we arrive at the following:

Most artists are very serious about their work. By work, we mean the process of working with new ideas and the actual sculpting and constructing of each new doll idea. They know each creation intimately because they spend long hours bringing it into being. Most are very aware of things that they will be wanting to change, correct, or improve and experiment with on the next piece. Most artists love to figure out how to use materials or to put things together to get their ideas in finished form.

Make no mistake -- a doll artist is a craftsman, too. A doll artist is a mechanic and an engineer. He has to be. The business of building dolls is essentially the business of assembling a vast amount of unrelated materials into a unified and workable object...a communicating figure. In all cases, a doll artist is just as serious about what goes on under the surface as he is about the finished top. Obviously, those who make complex jointed figures become very adept at the actual "physics" of motion and connection. This task becomes even more difficult when trying to achieve human

movement -- in itself an amazing phenomenon -- and do it while trying to achieve a surface that looks smooth and rounded as the human body does.

Would it be easier to do a bendable wire armatured figure? No. Take away the joint processes and you still have problems involved in building a skeleton and covering it with materials like fabric and stuffing which in no way resemble human flesh and muscle. If anything, those of us who do wire armature work would probably say that clay sculpture was easier because there is only one raw material to work with and it is fairly easy to make look human.

A doll artist has to become a fairly decent chemist...at the very least a student of the properties of materials. He has to know how to make and mix paints. He has to know how to achieve proper consistencies in mixing a number of exotic materials including solvents, lacquers, resins and rubber. He has to become an expert in applying tools to wood and he has to know how the various types of grains will behave. He has to learn to be aware of the increments and effects of high temperatures on such things as wax and ceramic clay. And you have to realize that it is one thing to know what these things will do, but it is quite a good deal more to adapt and to innovate with them.

The business side of doll art may not be so important, but it cannot be ignored. A doll artist has to be his own tax expert, accountant, promoter, agent, advertising executive, graphics department, photographer and shipping clerk all at the same time. Even those artists with studio help have to know these things well enough themselves to insure work gets done efficiently by others. Many do this all very well as a matter of course. To others, it is a pain in the neck because it takes away from creating time. (Fully one-third of the time it takes to produce a doll and to present it to the public is taken up by these kinds of non-doll making activities.)

The Creative Artist

The points that distinguished art from craft were imagination and the use of imagination, or, in a word, creativity. The creative process, while it may seem somewhat "magical" to those who do not often engage in it, is really a combination of two very related things: A strong urge to make something from nothing and the ability to visualize what that something will be.

The urge, itself, is both selfish and generous. The artist has a desire to capture some bit of reality around him or something he has conjured up in his imagination -- a beautiful child, a mythical creature, whatever, and he wants to be able to see and hold it in his hands. He wants to re-create that image in his head and have the satisfaction of knowing he made one for himself. It is sharing in that the artists wants others to see and enjoy and appreciate that same joy he has had in the creation and completion of his vision.

The actual process of creating is possible because of the personality and mental make-up of the artist. It does not have to be something one is born with...it is possible to learn.

Basic to all artists is the receptiveness to stimulus and the ability to compound one, two or more stimuli. If we were to try to explain what goes on in the artist's head when he is coming up with an idea, it might go something like this:

Two or more things come together in his mind as a result of seeing something in the outside environment or as the result of making mental images -- "mind play."

A lightbulb flashes! Fission or fusion, the idea is born!

A near comparison to the actual split second flash might be to the ignition of a firework sparkler. First, there is a sputtering of light and that is when the color, form and line of the idea appears -- along with, in the case of the doll artist, the image of persona. Perhaps, it might be a flash of a word along with the visualization of a concept like "pretty lady, blue dress with stars, seated on a moon." But it is a neurological fact that the brain abhors a vacuum or an incomplete picture so the time that it would take a sparkler to go from first ignition to full display, is just about as fast as it would take the artist's brain to fill in a complete picture image -- a full visualization.

Now, this first image is not anything like a complete picture. It is fuzzy, ill-defined and definitely uncrisp. It is an impression. A good receptive artist will have a lot of flashes like this -- if in a receptive mood, several a day. Occasionally, it gets "messy" and an effort has to be made to shut off the creative "noise" in order to get work done. From the point of the artist saying "aha, I have an idea" to beginning work might be rapid or slow, depending on the individual. At this point, however, the work actually becomes problem solving. The artist has to think how he can use his experience and knowledge of materials and skills to make the idea real. Some artists will organize themselves immediately into a problem solving work mode. They will outline, research, sketch and even work out full sized patterns...do real work. They will photograph, draw the image, and they will go looking for materials and learn new methods if they have to. Some actually write out instructions for themselves to follow.

About half the artists who read that last paragraph nodded their heads and said to themselves, "Of course, naturally, what other way could there be?" This reminds us of the time when one of the artists who had been engaging in that dangerous pastime, reading, discovered that some people actually do not dream in color. For those who dream in color, it is impossible to conceive of dreaming any other way. For those who work with a pencil in designing, it is impossible to imagine any other way.

But other artists -- probably a good half -- will "go with it" a bit. They will hold the idea in their head and mentally play with the design for awhile. And if you were able to see inside their heads at the time, you might see images being put together or tried and rejected in much the same way as a person puts together a jig-saw puzzle. The mental conversation goes like this: "I need such and such a body to get this effect. How can I get from here to there?" In the mind's eye, using their experience as well as known procedures, they will cast around for solutions. Many design options are taken up, played with, thought through, rejected or kept in the scheme of creation. Some rejections actually become bases for other new ideas.

All this is very much like the mental process described by the great engineer, Nicola Tesla, who said he built the machine in his head, started it up, and ran it for a week or so -- all in his head -- to see if there were any bugs in the design. During this period the artist might seem to be laying around staring into space, but the majority of the design work is being done, and, in many cases, no words are involved. For a lot of us, this is the part that is most fun. The artist would not be able to tell you rules, or methods, or reasons for what he did because all he did mentally was move shapes and colors until "it looked right." "Right" means that it looked like what he had

imagined it ought to in that first flash. The "mental" designer usually does not draw much...maybe a couple rough sketches which no one but the artist would recognize as meaningful. This artist starts to work by snapping his feet off the worktable and plunging right into action. He does not need to draw a paper pattern. He already drew one in his head.

Either way, when the mental work is done and physical preparation of sketches is complete, the figure is still a long way from being a real, tangible object. It is still subject to change, but changes in construction are usually the result of miscalculation of process, inability to find the visualized material, or lack of technical expertise, and very occasionally, because the artist sees something that looks like it might even be a better solution as he is working. Very frustrating sometimes, but sometimes, being thwarted will actually make the artist work harder to solve the problem and the result might be even better than the original intention.

The creative process may take a long time -- as many as several months -- or a much shorter time depending on the particular artist. Some artists have mastered one medium and create all their work using the same technical procedures. Some artists choose modes of expression like portrait or historical recreation where the image is, more or less, preset. In these cases the problems to be solved involve catching the desired image in the sculpture or everyday problems such as finding the right materials.

Parenthetically, we should take a minute to say something about time and the artist. Almost any doll artist you talk to will tell you "there is never enough time." There are always more things waiting in their heads than there will ever be time in a life to do. This is because every time one is working on the path to one design solution, all the options considered in between can also lead to new ideas (one of the reasons why doll artists often conceive of ideas in sets of or series of dolls). It also takes longer to do good work...lots longer. A good artist works to satisfy himself. Few artists make their living from doll work because they do not wish to be bound to the daily pressures of producing to keep the bills paid. Many work at other jobs and many have families to care for -- the doll making often has to take a back seat to these other needs.

The artist at leisure? For the life of us, we cannot think of a thing that the waking artist does that is not in some way or other connected with doll making. Watching television, reading, doing things with friends all are possible sources for ideas and solutions. Those things that most people consider leisure time activities... things like potting, painting, are for a doll artist fun but also add up to increasing skills and experience which will, sooner or later, be applied somewhere in the doll making process.

The Professional Artist

The difference between amateur and professional is usually defined by the presence or absence of payment for work done. An amateur or hobbyist works when he feels like it for his own personal satisfaction. Although he might sell a piece, he is not in it for the money. A professional is one who is engaged in providing goods or services for a profit. Take for instance, Aunt Minnie who makes very nice and very original soft sculpture dolls for the grandkids and, maybe, sells a few extra at the church bazaar or local crafts show...Aunt Minnie is a hobbyist or amateur. On the other hand, take the case of Cousin Jane who makes dolls for the fun of it, too. Because Cousin Jane sets out to make a number of dolls for the purpose of selling them (even though she may give one or two away) and because she invests time and money in studying various skills, printing business cards, order forms and photo brochures, renting sales tables, and traveling to shows, she is considered to be a professional.

The difference between amateur and professional is also defined by the element of ability implied in the term professional. A professional person has more specialized skill or knowledge than the hobbyist, in theory. In the traditional professions, this skill and knowledge is usually gained from academic study and recognized in professional licensing as in the case of doctors, attorneys, architects, certified accountants and the like. In the doll world, however, we know of some extremely skilled amateurs and we know of no governmental or professional licensing requirements (business licenses may be required in certain areas, but they do not relate to "professionalism" per se). Recognition of specialized knowledge and skills in the doll world comes by reputation and/or by invitation to join a professionally oriented doll artist organization.

Professional also strongly implies the adherence to good business and work practices. A professional, or one who calls himself a professional, should be one who can be counted on to provide well-crafted pieces, to be honest and on-time in business relations, and to conduct himself in a generally ethical manner.

In doll art a person is pretty much a professional if he says he is, if he sells his work and if he behaves in a "professional" way. You know a professional by experience and "feel." Fancy letters after a name and gilt-edged certificates do not a professional (or a good doll) make.

The Organized Artist

When you read an advertisement or artist brochure, you may encounter the words, "member NIADA, ODACA, or IDMA," or the like which signifies membership in an organization for doll artists. As there is often some confusion about what each organization entails, a general outline might be helpful. Basically, they are all groups independently organized by the common interest of their members in making dolls and promoting doll art. Each group varies to a certain extent as far as structure, activities and membership requirements, but membership in one or another group does not necessarily mean that work being produced is any more valuable, expensive, or of different quality.

The official logo of the National Institute of American Doll Artists.

The eldest of these doll artist organizations is the National Institute of American Doll Artists (NIADA). NIADA is a smaller, very professionally oriented group dedicated to aesthetic and technical excellence. Of the current active membership, nearly one half have designed for or are actively engaged in designing professionally for toy manufacturers or are engaged in operation of doll making studios. Other members concentrate on the production of specialized small editions or one-of-a-kind work which is frequently seen in gallery and museum exhibits. Membership is extended to those who demonstrably achieve and maintain the highest quality in their work. In general, a NIADA artist is one who it is felt has shown full creative use of a chosen medium. Any artist may apply for membership. Letters of recommendation from member artists are not required. A doll maker wishing to apply for membership first submits his work for an anonymous preliminary slide review by the NIADA Standards Committee. The Standards Committee consists of nine nationally known artists with extensive background in art and design. Those selected after review are invited to submit a portfolio for further, more rigorous examination. If the Standards Committee agree that merit is definitely shown, the artist is invited to bring samples of his work to show first-hand. After the Standards Committee review process, applicants felt to meet NIADA standards are referred to a vote by the general membership.

NIADA artists may issue certificates for the dolls they make; although, not all NIADA artist work may be certified. In cases where the individual artist has not participated in the production of the figure (as in commercial or licensed manufacture), no certificate is issued. It is the doll itself -- its painting, sculpture and design -- that must be the hand product of the artist to carry certification. Certification records are kept within the organization so that a collector can always have the ability to verify work.

The official logo of the Original Doll Artists Council of America.

In response to the explosion of interest in doll making in the early 1970s the Original Doll Artist Council of America (ODACA) was organized in 1976 with a core group of six artists and has, within a very short span of time, come to comprise nearly 100 active and energetic artists whose goals are to promote original doll artists and their work, to maintain a high quality of doll making, and to educate collectors about the field of original dolls. To become a member one should be a professional artist (making dolls to sell) and show demonstrable ability as well as an indicated desire to work actively towards maximum potential. Many operate studios and cottage industry businesses as well as teach courses in sculpture and technical processes. Artists are invited to join ODACA on the basis of achievement in their own work and a willingness to participate in organizational, educational and promotional activities. Applications can be obtained from the Membership Chairman and must be endorsed by two active members. Applications and artist work is reviewed by the membership committee and, if deemed to meet qualifications of originality and technical skill, are submitted for vote by the general membership. At this time the organization does not issue certification; although, several of the individual members do issue certificates as a matter of their own business procedure. These are usually

The official logo of the International Doll Makers Association.

statements to the effect that the doll is an original, either one-of-a-kind or member of an edition, and that is guaranteed to have been made and designed by the artist or under the artist's supervision.

The International Dollmaker's Association (IDMA) is an organization which includes both makers of original dolls and those who make reproductions of antique dolls as well as those who reproduce commercial molds and patterns. Anyone may apply for membership and the organization serves the excellent purpose of joining all those with similar interests in doll making. Beginners with talent and ambition are given assistance and encouragement. Professionals constantly strive to improve their work and compete with each other in the annual exhibits and the Silver Award Category. IDMA has members in several countries and holds annual conferences in the United States each year. Their annual conferences include workshops, exhibits and competitions for their members.

The official logo of the British Doll Artists.

A few years ago, in Great Britain, artists formed the British Doll Artist Association (BDA). The basic requirement is, again, that the work must be totally original and that the artist must be producing work for sale. BDA has been actively engaged in setting up a number of fine exhibits of their members' work throughout the British Isles. Annual meetings of BDA provide workshops as well as competitions for their members.

In general, all of the doll artist organizations are formed for the purpose of promoting good work and awakening the public's interest in doll art. Dolls produced by their members must be judged each one on its own merits...all doll artists will have the occasional "potboiler," and, of course, each collector will have his or her own individual preferences as far as media and type. It should be noted, however, that many first-rate artists have not opted to be members of organizations and this does not in any way detract from the value or collectibility of their work.

Both NIADA and ODACA have non-artist members classifications for collectors and those who are interested in doll art and its promotion. Both groups have been a great help to their organizations in putting on shows, exhibits and educational lecture-demonstrations.

The Artist on the Road

One of the great joys for many doll artists is "going away"...that is, going to a doll show or conference where he or she gets to share dolls, to learn about what is happening in the doll making field, and to share experiences with fellow artists. There are, of course, all kinds of nasty problems to face in actually going...things like getting work done to show or sell, (this need is probably responsible for more artist finished work than all the artist's best intentions!)...and packing, which can be a truly nerve-wracking experience frought with all kinds of worries about committing one's "babies" to the hazards of transport. Then there is also the fact that one simply just does not "feel right" about covering up dolls or taking down settings. And there are things to consider like making the investment in time and travel expense at the risk of maybe only selling a few or just breaking even. If you see a doll artist at a conference or show, you can be sure all these things were considered greatly before he made the decision to go.

Once arrived at a doll show or conference, the artist has a great time. Normally, quiet, introspective artists "get high" on the discussion of their work, having their work appreciated by others, seeing what new and wonderful things their colleagues have come up with as well as learning about new materials and sources of supply.

Unfortunately, there are few opportunities geared for doll artists and collectors of doll art specifically...certainly not as many or not nearly as close enough for all who might want to go. Commercially organized shows are really sales experiences and if only one day affairs, they allow very little chance for artists to get a good chance to visit. Doll club get-togethers such as mini-regionals, regionals and national conferences do offer a bit more chance, but again, the emphasis is on general collecting interests and doll artists and collectors can only search each other out in odd minutes.

The doll artist groups themselves usually try to meet once a year. At the time of this writing, all three major groups in the United States and The British Doll Artists hold some sort of an annual meeting. The Original Doll Artist Council of America has had its annual meeting in conjunction with the United Federation of Doll Clubs (UFDC) annual national convention. As most are usually involved with the overall convention activities such as sales and exhibit rooms, at this point it has not been possible for them to hold workshops or special lectures outside of the UFDC scheduled programs; although, a luncheon is held. Competition is limited to entering the appropriate UFDC categories for doll art.

For the last three years, the National Institute of American Doll Artists has held a conference in April and is intending to continue meeting this way every year in various major cities around the United States. In addition to the general business meeting, the NIADA conference includes three days of special workshops (including sculpture), programs, lecture demonstrations, and featured guest speakers from the art world in addition to a salon exhibit. The NIADA conference is open to any who wish to attend. Dates and specifics are advertised and announced in the major doll collector publications each year.

As the number of artists working with the toy industry or building their own businesses in manufacturing dolls grows, the annual Toy Fair held each winter in New York, New York, is coming to be included in the traveling plans of more artists. There artists and/or their agents can meet with toy and doll buyers, present their work, and, we hope, increase the numbers of well-designed dolls available in the mass market place.

In conclusion, each doll artist is a highly individual -- ourselves included -- so there will be some differences of opinion and practice amongst us all. Not every artist will have had the same experiences as we have, nor will every case discussed here apply to every artist and collector.

What started out to be some brief answers have turned out to be somewhat of an extended treatise on the whole state of the art, but one, we hope will fill in the gaps about doll art in the abstract as well as in practice.

....Meanwhile, the list of things waiting to be done grows longer, and the stack of things to be finished grows higher. New ideas are impatiently waiting their turn to be "hatched"...the sandwich crusts have turned to dust, and the paint brushes still need cleaning....

Artist friends at the Original Doll Artist Invitational.

Margory Novak, founder of the California Original Doll Artist Seminar and Show, with her creations *Father Christmas* and *Little Mischief.* Oroyan photograph.

ABOVE: Elizabeth Brandon and *Jael.* Photograph by Dorothy Aspinwall.

ABOVE: Janice Riggs with her petite *Fashion Lady.* Oroyan photograph.

Cecilia Rothman with *John Muir, Theodore Roosevelt* and *Princess Lovelia.* Photograph by Dorothy Aspinwall.

seeing ourselves —
the interpretive figure

Essentially, all doll artists are illustrators of the human condition. Some, like those who make portrait and character figures, have narrowed their focus and specialized their type of interpretation. Others, like those in the section immediately following, are wide-ranging generalists who seek to help us define ourselves by illustrating humanity in terms of everyday thought, action and emotion.

These artists illustrate every stage and condition of life from the innocence of childhood through the joys and frustrations of parenthood to the quiet reflection of old age. They also show us how the human form can be abstracted to make a child's play object...in doll form. They also show us pursuing cultural and aesthetic interests and in personal relationships. They illustrate our ethnic, festival and holiday past times and they show us as we define ourselves in terms of such abstract concepts as love, beauty, and even death.

They are very much concerned with finding and illustrating the shared patterns and truths which make us human beings. They help us to realize what a unique phenomenon humanity is. They celebrate life.

elizabeth brandon

Picture this: In the wee small hours of the night, under the light of a single naked bulb, a doll artist sits hunched over an unfamiliar and menacing typing machine. She is plumbing the depths of her vocabulary, scraping and raking through all her stylistic knowledge in the struggle to find just the right words and rhetorical framework to tell the world about Elizabeth Brandon.

Why would she do this when making dolls would be so much more fun?

(The accusing stare of an overhead shelf full of bodiless doll heads gives rise to shivers of guilt along the back of the artist.)

The midnight writer chews another hangnail, drains yet another cup of coffee and tries again.

Remember the "Who, what, why," she thinks.

Why is this all so frustrating?

Because Elizabeth Brandon is an artist who prefers, nay, insists that her work be appreciated, or not appreciated, as it stands by itself and she is most insistent that she not become a "personality" associated with her work...and, just to underline that feeling, she has only supplied the writer with four (count'-em four) useful quotes!

The "writer rat" struggles to cope with this maze and decides that maybe some attempt to define the role of the writer/critic and journalist might help.

Okay, then here goes...

The function of the art critic is to provide a means for the reader to see what it is that the artist's work communicates and in what ways this communication is exceptional or outstanding. The critic's function is also to present one, or more, or maybe several points from which to view the work. These points may deal with the technical execution, elements of design or thematic treatments. It follows that the critic has an obligation to be very familiar with the processes of construction and must be able to recognize ways in which form, line and texture are approached. He must also be able to see and define messages present in the work. Most importantly, the critic's function is to be able to communicate what he or she sees and feels in such a way that the reader is able to understand and appreciate a body of work which may only be shown in part.

So far, so good.

Now a journalist, on the other hand, reports. For example, a journalist writing about Elizabeth Brandon would say that she was born in Colorado, has lived most of her life in Kansas, is a life-long musician with conservatory training in violin and piano, is married to Berkley Brandon who crafts the accessories for her pieces, is the mother of two grown sons, and is one who, after experimenting with many media, started making porcelain dolls in 1969. These items of information place the subject in a geographical location, a rough time-frame and describe general interest and family structure. They do not, however, bring the reader to any understanding of Elizabeth as an artist or the work she produces.

The forward roll of the would-be critic comes to a screaming halt!

What to do?

A ha!

The thing to do is to take a good hard look at the work and try to see what it is that Brandon builds.

And that is just what your reporter/critic did.

She looked, and she thought, and she made several satisfactory (to her) deductions and she wrote them all up in four or five tidy paragraphs...all neatly tied in with those four elegant quotes.

But she made the big mistake of telling Elizabeth what she had concluded and.....

Back came an equally elegant argument for at least three or four alternative conclusions from the artist herself! And since the artist has a silly streak a mile wide, this "rebuttal" was accompanied by some delicate verses describing the artist's life and woes.

At this point, your writer is about to follow Elizabeth's desire and head the chapter with her name, eliminate the prose and just let the pictures tell the story!

(And, maybe, give said artist a heavy threat about the possibility of printing her poem to boot!)

Wait a minute...Let's go back to the why of Elizabeth's desire to disassociate herself from her work.

This attitude does not mean that Elizabeth does not care what a person thinks about her work. Significantly, it means that as totally involved as she may become with each piece as a technical challenge and an emotional struggle, she is able to make the gift of appreciation to the viewer without forcing him or her to agree with her statement.

As Elizabeth feels the eternal things are invisible, the challenge to her as doll maker becomes, therefore, to see how closely she can translate some eternal reality into a material object. On first look at her work, one could say that they are "just people." So they are --ordinary housewives, children, potters and the like, but each one carries at least one theme and, perhaps, more than one theme in its personality type. The message or statement that will be taken from each piece will be and should be in Elizabeth's thinking, just what

Jael, 9in (22.9cm), is a seated baby wearing pink smocked dress and bonnet. *Copyright Brandon Porcelain Originals. Photograph by Betty Hodges.*

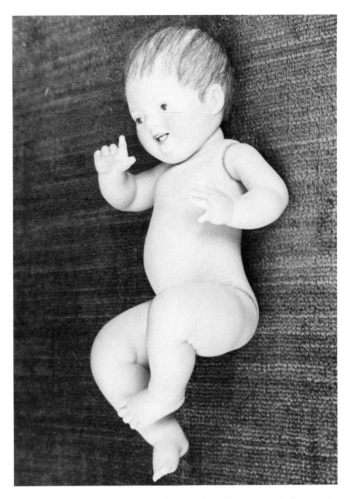

Katie, 5in (12.7cm), is an open-mouth, brown haired, brown-eyed all-porcelain baby. Note how successfully Elizabeth Brandon has modeled the contours of flesh...and has been able to preserve those details in reducing the form to a small scale. *Photograph by Betty Hodges.*

the viewer can put into and bring out himself. She realizes that her own definition of an eternal reality may not be the same as someone else's.

Her goal or work is aimed toward working out her own definitions and expressions. She does not say, "This is a representation of X and you must like it or not like it on that basis." She says rather, "I have tried to express something within myself and, whether or not I feel that I have expressed that idea to my satisfaction, the piece is available to you so that you can see if it mirrors a part of your internal feelings."

What Elizabeth was trying to point out to me in her rebuttals was the fact that while my deductions were perfectly valid for me, I really should not let them affect the interpretation of another. More precisely, she did not want me to tell you how to see the work.

Therefore, dear reader, please turn to the photographs to see for yourself and decide for yourself what Elizabeth's work says to you.

The little "writer rat" did not give up the Brandon maze without yet another run.

Cagily, on the pretext of needing help, she conned a few more useful notes out of the artist at the other end of the Yellow Brick Road (Kansas, remember) because she wondered why Elizabeth --with a super musical education and ability -- would choose the struggle with expression in a medium as demanding as porcelain and with a form as demanding as the human figure.

Elizabeth answered that "in the material configuration of the human form, its unlimited expressiveness and universal application, I have my best chance at mirroring the internal truths which have become so important to me."

She chooses the medium of porcelain for a lot of the same reasons other doll makers have: its smoothness, ability to hold intricate detail, strength and durability.

There are, of course, drawbacks to porcelain. It can look stiff and cold, the very materials, if not handled properly, are messy and dangerous. And, unless one models directly (which results in very heavy pieces), there is a long delay between idea and execution because of the many steps involved.

Many interesting immediate materials such as wood, cloth and wax are subject to decay, she notes, as is the case with the bodies we, ourselves, live in. But with porcelain, here is a material that has the possibility of lasting for ages after we are gone.

"And there is another reason I like porcelain," Elizabeth says, "the fire." I am not an outdoor person -- I never tiptoe through the tulips, and I cry when there are no sidewalks, but the first time I saw a big gas kiln in action, roaring its way up to cone 9, actual fire belching out of the tall brick chimney outside, I felt a call and an affinity.

"I feel a definite thrill to be part of producing a metamorphasis, clay to porcelain, through the basic element of fire, even at the remove of electricity. I used to go about saying absurd things about wanting to tame the capricious nature of porcelain, but, through the years, have finally learned that there is always going to be a degree of chance involved because of the fire. I have come to respect and enjoy the challenge of that chance-factor, to look forward to seeing what the fire might do to my weeks of work.

"But perhaps, the greatest advantage of porcelain as a medium is its range of possibility. Like the piano, the veriest amateur can produce something lovely; yet at the same time, the instrument is sufficient to intrigue a Horowitz for his entire lifetime. There is no end of personal development possible using the medium."

Jann, 10in (25.4cm), is an all-porcelain younger sister of *Jody* with the same composition. *Photograph by Betty Hodges.*

Hakamon by Elizabeth Brandon is the personification of a real clown. Head, multi-jointed body and outsized hands on this 15in (38.1cm) figure are porcelain while the jointed arms and legs are of wood. *Photograph by Betty Hodges.*

Close-up of *Hakamon's* porcelain shoes with their untied laces and piece of cloth stocking showing through the worn sole. *Photograph by Betty Hodges.*

As Elizabeth's work is basically that of a sculptor, not of a toy maker or an illustrator, accessories do not often take center stage in the presentation of a piece. As a sculptor involved with the human form, most of her figures are only lightly clothed and only as much as is necessary to define the character type. Most of her figures are highly expressive of particular actions or emotions demonstrated by the contours of face and body and as such they are only given those accessories which are necessary as a rationale for this motion...such as a chair for a reading grandmother, or a bench wheel for a potter.

After an examination of Elizabeth Brandon's work, it is not surprising to find that although she works ten hours a day, six days a week, her annual output may be only one new creation and, perhaps, as many as ten (in a good year) pieces of the various editions that are open. Her work is never static. Each new doll is more difficult than the one that went before it. She, herself, says, "Most of us have to dedicate ourselves to perpetual study in order to develop enough technique to realize our ideas in whatever media we have chosen.

"For me, armed with self-study, none of this has never been easy and is not now easy.

"All my doll making comes with great difficulty and never meets my expectation, but in each case bestows a gift of just a little more insight, a little better understanding of our human form, and a great and deepening respect for all those artists who have spent their lives in trying to explain the intangible in material form."

Obviously, it is a fortunate collector who realizes the opportunity to own and enjoy one of Elizabeth's rare and unique pieces for each one is a part of herself...risks, dangers, challenges, emotions and all!

(The writer/artist/critic -- whatever, stretches, yawns, throws the cats out, and crawls wearily off to bed.....the pen is mightier than the reticent artist!)

LEFT: Close-up of *Alexandre Beaumont* showing depth of her painted eyes. This depth is achieved by judicious applications of paint and by as many as ten firings. *Photograph by Betty Hodges.*

BELOW LEFT: *Alexandre Beaumont-Devant le Bal*, 20in (50.8cm), has a porcelain head, arms and legs on a cotton body. She is dressed in a pink peignoir and is about to powder her nose and put on her jewelry in preparation for the ball. Her furniture is custom made for her. The chair has hand carving on its back and the dressing table, with its operable drawers, holds her powder box. *Photograph by Betty Hodges.*

BELOW: *Alexandre Beaumont's* graceful hands with their clearly defined fingernails are as fragile in appearance as the real flower they are holding. *Photograph by Betty Hodges.*

Detail of Mother's hand holding baby from Elizabeth Brandon's *Trouble at Breakfast* vignette — a three figure all-porcelain group of expectant mother holding crying baby and gazing down at a small son who has just spilled his milk. The mother in this 1977 group is 13in (33cm). *Photograph by Betty Hodges.*

Mexicali Rose, 14½in (36.9cm), by Elizabeth Brandon, one of a series of dolls based on songs with the name *Rose* in their titles. *Photograph by Betty Hodges.*

christine adams

Cloth ranks among the simplest and most difficult doll making media to master. Many doll makers begin with fabric. It is easy to measure, sew and craft. "Rag" dolls have a special tactile, homespun appeal. They yield and seem to respond to embraces. The warmth of the textiles used in their construction is an emotional allure that, for many doll collectors, outshines that of the finest porcelain.

Few doll makers are able to fashion sculpted art dolls from this material, however. Christine Adams is one who has succeeded, creating a line of charming toddlers and babies with molded calico faces. But the going has been rough.

"If I were to start making dolls again, I wouldn't work in cloth," she says. "It is an incredibly difficult and unpredictable medium, and after seven years of production, I still cannot overcome certain problems. I would choose felt or wax as my medium."

Fortunately for collectors, she has persevered and has developed techniques which turn her clay sculptures of children's faces into molded fabric-headed dolls that remind one of the work of the woman who most inspired her: Käthe Kruse. But Adams' dolls are contemporary English children and stand on their own as artistic statements.

Christine describes the effect she strives for.

"I think a doll has to have a soulful, pensive look to satisfy me. On the whole, I prefer the face to be under-stated rather than very precise -- almost an impression rather than a statement...They don't have to be terribly realistic, but to have a feeling of reality in the mood they express and, of course, they must be professionally finished."

Adams' dolls are all of the above. Her chubby British children pout and challenge the viewer to explain himself, and then to take them home. They find homes with collectors on both sides of the Atlantic. "I think my dolls appeal to different sorts of people," the artist says. "Children like them, too. I imagine they can identify with them."

Her unusual doll making techniques make her work particularly collectible, and they were derived through experimentation, with a little help from some knowledgeable friends.

She describes her process.

"I start by modeling the face I have conceived. This can take many hours, until I'm really satisfied. I always model in clay. When it is finished and dry, I rub the surface smooth and then make a mold over it in plaster of paris. This mold is removed and cleaned and when ready, silicone rubber is poured in to make the patrix.

"When this is set, it is removed and over it is poured resin, forming the final mold or matrix.

"The calico which forms the head is pre-stitched to form the basic shape of the head; then it is stretched over the patrix, soaked with a resin glue and inserted in the matrix. Clamps are fixed over both parts of the mold and tightened to produce great pressure.

"Forty-eight hours is usually sufficient to allow the glue to set, and when the cloth is removed from the mold, it has the contours of the face permanently fixed. Once out of the mold, the glued face cures. It is during this process that the distortion can occur.

"The head is than stitched up the back, stuffed and the ears attached. It is then ready for painting.

"Five or six coats are necessary to give a good finish, and each coat must dry thoroughly before the next is applied. When the features have been painted on the face, it is varnished, and finally the wig is attached.

"The body is made of calico which is stitched and stuffed firmly. Discs are inserted at the hip to enable the doll to sit or stand.

"After the head has been stitched to the body, the doll is dressed and the hair styled; then it is ready for the customer."

Working out of her kitchen and dining room, Ms. Adams considers doll making a full-time job and depends upon it for her livelihood. Her many orders have necessitated jobbing out the clothing and wigs, which will be made to her specifications.

Currently she makes between 100 and 200 dolls a year. Before 1983, production was about 45 a year. Numbers are small because, she says, "I have a very high failure rate (again because of the unpredictable nature of cloth). If it weren't for this I could make more dolls."

Dolls entail approximately 20 hours' work and most procedures are done by the artist.

"The part of the process I enjoy most is the painting of the faces and the final dressing," she says. "The part I like least is the stuffing of the body, which is tedious and difficult, especially the insertion of the disc joints. I haven't found anyone good enough to take over this part of the production."

She works at a model until she tires of it, and then goes on to fresh ideas, although she does keep some early molds she is still interested in the fills orders on them. About four new models are designed each year, each one adding something new.

"I have made hundreds of modifications over the years, to make the results not easier, but better. There seem to be NO shortcuts in my medium."

Adams' great care in executing her work is evident. Many incorrectly believe the dolls to be portraits. "A child in the high street, a picture in a book, or a face on T.V. might inspire me to make a certain doll. But when I'm in the process of modeling a new face, it's usually a composite of several children. I rarely model from life," she says.

But she tries to capture life and emotion in her sculpture, and in the doll as a whole. "Many aspects contribute to the 'feel' and 'mood' of a doll -- like the stance, the clothes, the angle of the head and hairstyle...I want people to feel that they have a real little person in one of my dolls, with all the faults and charms of a child. I don't want my dolls to be beautiful and unapproachable."

Her medium renders her work approachable to both children and adults and she terms her dolls "play dolls," bearing in mind that collectors "play" with their dolls, too.

The art doll occupies a rare position, incorporating the qualities of plaything and art object. Often collectors find this combination perplexing, and do not know how to categorize their possessions or their creators. Ms. Adams has strong opinions on this dilemma.

"I think a doll artist may be looked down upon by the art world, and yet doll making incorporates sculpture, painting, dress design and technical skill of a very high standard.

"The trouble is that the collector who wants an artist's doll isn't always 'au fait' with what is aesthetically good, and doesn't necessarily want a work of art. I think the doll artist could be more accepted as more people go in for doll making."

Christine comes to doll making from an extensive artistic background, having studied three years at Bath Academy of Art, emerging with qualifications as an art teacher. Her dolls have won awards and have been exhibited with the works of fellow members of the British Doll Artists Association.

They are sold only by mail order, directly to customers, or wholesaled to shops. She refers to them as "series," which are alphabetically chronological. A complete listing (as of 1984) follows:

Series "A." First child doll. 1976-81. About 200 sold.

Series "B." Sleeping baby. 1976-the present. Still available.

Series "C." Older child. 1976-77. Only about a dozen sold. Molding problems were daunting.

Series "D." Child doll. 1980. Only five sold.

Series "E." Character baby. 1982. Only five made.

Series "F." Awake baby. Based on "Zara," Princess Anne's daughter. Still available. Eight sold to date.

Series "G." Replaced Series "A." 1982-84. Soon to be replaced. About 40 sold.

Series "H." Older child. 1982-84. Soon to be replaced. Molding problems. About 25 sold.

Series "I." *Flora.* (Girl only. All other dolls available as boy or girl). This doll is based on Mabel Lucie Atwell's drawings. Very popular. 1982-present. Still available. About 50 sold.

Series "J." Child doll. Not very popular. Phased out soon. 1982-84.

Series "K." Child. 1984.

Series "L." Chubby child. 1984.

Series "M." *Christopher Robin.* 1984. Exclusive to The Toy Shoppe, Midlothian, Virginia.

"Another three models in the pipeline -- all children."

Adams' dolls all carry a tie-on round label, and are signed on the back of the body as follows:

CAdams
Series 'G' No. 14

Adams' dolls are still evolving. Their creator would like to experiment with felt doll making. "This is a medium that I would like to adopt eventually, mainly because felt lends itself so beautifully to the idea of the understated 'impressionistic' approach. (You cannot be too precise and fiddly with felt.)"

The doll making challenges inherent in cloth doll making are the failure rate high. But Christine Adams has overcome the odds and produced art dolls worthy of the shelves of the fussiest collector, or the embrace of a child.

Rosemary by Christine Adams, 16in (40.6cm) tall. Molded cloth head; fair hair; gray eyes; disc-jointed cloth body; floral cotton dress; leather shoes. Series "A," No. 17. 1977. One of 200 made. *Photograph courtesy of Christine Adams.*

Christine Adams' tag which hangs from each of her dolls. *Courtesy of Christine Adams.*

RIGHT: No Name Toddler by Christine Adams, 16in (40.6cm) tall. Molded cloth head; disc-jointed cloth body; fair hair; blue eyes; woolen jumper; cotton shorts; leather shoes. Series "G." No. 44. Edition of 50. 1982-84. *Photograph courtesy of Christine Adams.*

BELOW: No Name (boy or girl) Toddler Doll by Christine Adams, 16in (40.5cm) tall. Molded cloth head; disc-jointed cloth body; fair mohair wig; blue eyes; smocked cotton dress. Series "L" prototype. 1984 (new model). *Photograph courtesy of Christine Adams.*

BELOW RIGHT: Close-up of No Name (boy or girl) Doll by Christine Adams. *Photograph courtesy of Christine Adams.*

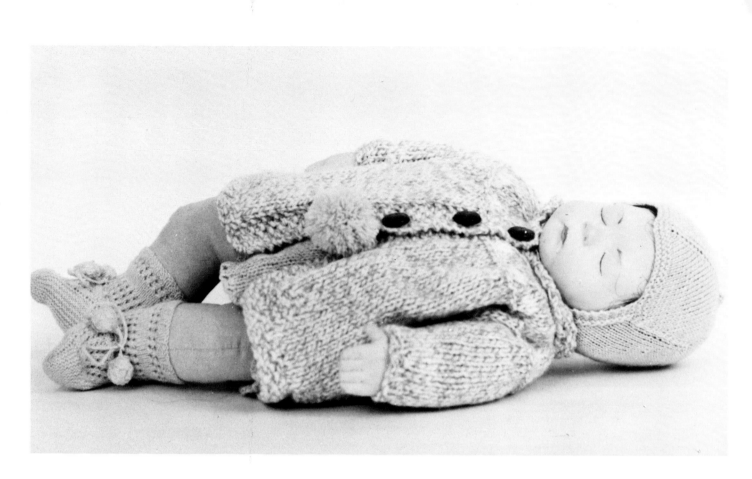

Christopher Robin by Christine Adams, 14in (35.6cm) tall. Molded cloth head; detail of cloth disc-jointed body; head and arms hand-stitched to the body; fair mohair wig; blue eyes. *Photograph courtesy of Christine Adams.*

ABOVE: Sleeping Baby by Christine Adams, 16in (40.6cm) long. Molded cloth head; dark hair, soft floppy body weighted with sand; knitted outfit. Series "B." Prototype. 1977. One of 20 made. *Photograph courtesy of Christine Adams.*

BELOW: *Zara* or *Neil* by Christine Adams, 18in (45.7cm) long. Molded cloth head; soft floppy body; fair hair; blue eyes; cotton and lace robe; knitted bonnet. Series "F" prototype. 1983-84. One of 15 made. *Photograph courtesy of Christine Adams.*

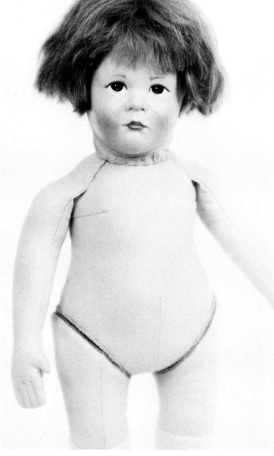

helen kish

Helen is a sculptor with a feel for what it takes to design dolls for mass production. Not just any artist can, you know. Helen is able to create dolls...sculpted dolls... children who are just the epitome of the ideal darlings that all collectors associate with their childhood dreams of the perfect doll.

Helen's sculpting hand has the ability to bring out that wonderfully detailed modeling which can capture the rounded softness of a child's body with fat little knees and chubby dimpled cheeks with happy smiles. But more than that, all finished and in settings, her children always look like real children. Just look at *Little Brother* and his *Little Mother*...how many times have you seen just the identical pose and expression in children you know. These kids could be playing on the sidewalk in front of anyone's house. Helen knows her children. Make no mistake. Notice also that this particular vignette is complete. There is a stroller and a toy bear for the baby (another of Helen's designs in dotted felt and snappy bow)...poor Ted, typically, he has been tossed out of little brother's stroller. Here are children one is tempted to pick up and hug, but what a surprise to find they are of porcelain and not flesh.

Helen does not limit her expression to children's forms only. Like all artists, she has her dream visions. One of Helen's loveliest visions is portrayed in her *Diva*, a beautiful tall, expressive singer costumed in exotic silk charmeuse with a beaded bodice. The inspiration for this figure was a beautiful opera singer Helen had seen. She says the singer's elegance and grace along with her exquisite voice simply haunted her. She found it a particular challenge to sculpt a figure that looked as if it were singing.

Diva is a one-of-a-kind and she says that she is not sure if she will do any more, but if so, she would not make more than three...and this is a good part due to her desire to preserve the feeling or the "high" of the first creation. When many, many dolls are repeated, some element of the first excitement begins to fade away and, as the numbers multiply, it often seems to the artist that the original charm and spontaneity fades. *Diva* is posed and jointed although her limbs are not meant to be moved. Underneath her shimmering, all beaded cap, *Diva* has very short molded hair.

Readers may remark that almost every single artist has portrayed figures that represent theatrical themes. Why is this? Because the theater is colorful, graceful, full of interesting combinations of color and texture and expressive character. Practically no doll artist has been able to resist taking up the challenge of trying to re-create the motion of the dance in hard and resistive media of their expression. Perhaps it is because clay and wax and such artists' materials are so totally and diametrically opposite to the fluid grace of the human body.

Helen, like many an artist, finds she has a special love of the ballet and an irresistible desire to bring to preserve its beauty in doll form. One of her earlier works was a small porcelain wire-armatured dancer shown doing her barre work.

She admits she is one of those who can watch the ice skating championships and get a lump in her throat from the sheer beauty and grace of human movement...she also says one of the influences just might be the fact that she has a brother who has been a dancer and is now a ballet choreographer. Not too surprisingly, Helen has done a poor, sad Petrouchka, ballet's famous crumpled clown, in mauves and blue-grays.

In the commercial world, Helen's work first came to the attention of an agent for the Dakin Company at the Harrisburg 1983 meeting of NIADA. He didn't say anything to her at the time so a later call to ask if she was interested in designing for commercial production came as a surprise. Naturally, the idea was a challenge. It was also a whole new world for both Helen, as an artist, and for the Dakin company, itself. Dakin had never produced dolls before.

A call from Dakin's Chairman of the Board to Helen got things under way. The general outline for a series of collector dolls limited, valuable, made in the United States and geared for the adult collector was proposed. When Helen admitted to being a bit unsure, Dakin replied that perhaps they could learn together. This comment has formed the basis of a successful working relationship.

When Dakin approached Helen about designing dolls to produce in vinyl, she says, she faced a number of problems. First was, of course, the fact that Dakin had not done a line of dolls before and so there was nothing for Helen to go by with reference to quality, design preference, color or anything. (Dakin, as you know, is noted particularly for its line of stuffed animal toys.)

The Dakin management, however, convinced Helen that they were going to go all out to produce a first class product and, as she noted in the winter of 1985, her experience has been extremely satisfactory.

Helen sent her portfolio of work to Dakin and they picked out the various types of work that she had done that they felt fit the idea they had in mind. They indicated a general size range and types that they liked -- a baby and a little girl, but otherwise gave the artist carte blanche to follow her own hand and eye.

Helen went to work to produce the prototypes in porcelain. She sculpted the little girl *Meggie* and the baby *Annie Laurie*, and

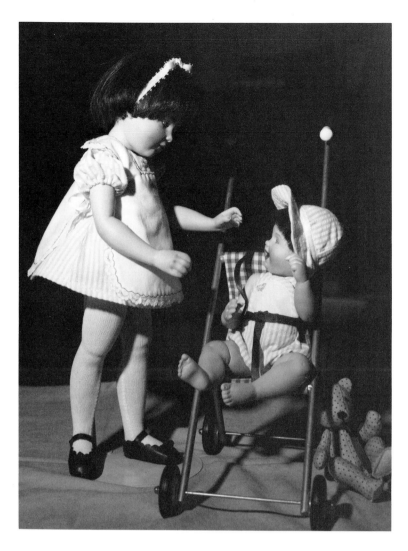

PREVIOUS PAGE: *Kathie*, designed by Helen Kish and produced in an edition limited to 15, is a 17in (43.2cm) porcelain child. She has a dark brown human hair wig and brown painted eyes on a stationary head. Her body is constructed of porcelain arms and legs on a torso of amara suede and the legs are jointed at the hip and knee. In the edition of 15 *Kathies*, there were three different costumes. The one shown is a pale mauve rayon faille coat dress with matching fur-trimmed beret or bonnet. The others were a black Gunne Sax print dress in waltz length and an ecru batiste dress trimmed with blue ribbons. A NIADA certified cloth label is sewn into the clothing. These dolls were made from 1982 to 1984 when the edition was completed. *Photograph courtesy of Helen Kish.*

Little Mother and *Baby Brother* are 14in (35.6cm) and 6in (15.2cm) respectively and made in porcelain by Helen Kish. Both dolls have human hair wigs of dark brown, painted blue eyes and jointed bodies. *Little Mother* wears a simple dress of green seersucker stripe topped with a white panel pinafore. *Baby Brother* is wearing a sunsuit of the same material as his sister's dress with a white bib and sun hat. Both the boy's bib and the girl's pinafore are decorated with hand-painted ducks. *Baby Brother's* 3in (7.6cm) polka dot Teddy Bear was also designed by Helen. Each doll is incised on the back of the head with their names, copyright symbol, dates, artist's name and the number in the edition. Each set also has a paper tag with the number of the edition and the artist's signature. The prototypes of these dolls were completed in May 1984 and the first sets were offered for sale in August of that same year. The idea for this set, says Helen, was to present a contemporary pair of children much like any you might see in a shopping mall, complete with the very modern umbrella stroller. *Photograph courtesy of Helen Kish.*

finished them in porcelain with painting and costuming just as she saw they should be.

Meggie is shown as the porcelain prototype which Dakin designers and engineers adapted for production in vinyl. Notice Helen has posed *Meggie* on a perfectly scaled stuffed pony. Doesn't she look just like the serious little girl learning to school her pony in a grown up fashion?

Carefully boxed up, Helen sent her doll prototypes off to the mysteries of production, most likely with great apprehension at what they might "do" to her work in translating it from porcelain perfection to vinyl edition.

The first samples were not quite what Helen had envisioned. But, at Dakin, they were true to their word about working and learning. Helen found that the company was willing to listen and made all the important changes. Before long the finished baby, *Annie Laurie*, arrived all complete in vinyl and Helen was very much pleased with it.

Meggie, still in production at this time, will be a series of three little girls in different costumes. *Annie Laurie* will be the baby of the Dakin series...all doll lines ought to have a baby, naturally. And what a scrumptious darling she is, all dolled up in the most delicate embroidered batiste bonnet and gown.

The completed artist series for collectors from Dakin will include some of Faith Wick's delightful characters...a clown with masks, *Alice*, the *White Rabbit*, and the *Mad Hatter*, as well as some fashion and costume ladies. All will have made their debut at the 1985 Winter Toy Fair.

Helen, meantime, is working away on her sixth prototype and looks forward to working further in the area of commercial collector dolls as well as exploring her own visions and impressions of the human form and personality.

made exclusively for the Toy Shoppe
by helen kish originals

Little Mother & Baby Brother

member of DBADA

ABOVE: *Petrouchka* is a 24in (61cm) porcelain and cloth doll designed by Helen Kish, NIADA, and made in an edition limited to five pieces. The hair, hat and collar are all part of the porcelain head. The eyes and features are painted as well as the hat and collar. The hands and legs are porcelain and the body is made of amara suede (jointed at the knees and hips). The arms have a wire armature for posability. The smock under *Petrouchka's* collar is made of lavender silk with an applique edge and his trousers are purple silk. This doll is marked (incised) on the back of the head: "Petrouchka ©1982 helen kish" and the number of his edition. On his smock the NIADA cloth tag is sewn in on the underside. *Petrouchka* is an outgrowth of Helen's love of the ballet. *Photograph courtesy of Helen Kish.*

RIGHT: The *Diva*, 26in (66cm), is a porcelain figure designed and made by Helen Kish. This piece is all-porcelain with jointed arms and legs. She is posed in such a way as to look like she may be singing and is not really meant to be moved about. As with all of Helen's dolls, her features are painted. In this case the hair (very short) is molded. The elegant gown and cap is of beaded silk charmeuse. So far only the one figure has been made. If the artist decides to do an edition in the future, no more than three will be made totally. She is incised on the back of the head: "Diva, copyright 1984, Helen Kish #1." *Photograph courtesy of Helen Kish.*

ABOVE: *Annie Laurie*, another prototype for production in vinyl, has a cloth body with porcelain head, arms and legs. She is the first doll Helen designed with sleep eyes (at the request of the commissioning company, R. Dakin). Helen reports that this doll is without a doubt her five-year-old daughter's personal favorite. *Photograph courtesy of Helen Kish.*

RIGHT: This photograph shows the porcelain prototype, *Meggie*, designed and made by Helen Kish for production as a vinyl doll by the R. Dakin Company of San Francisco, California. *Meggie*, who made her debut with the Dakin Company's Spring 1985 line, is available in vinyl in three costume versions. *Meggie* in pink leotard and lace net tutu as a brunette, *Meggie* in a blue party dress with reddish hair and *Meggie* in her riding costume similar to the prototype shown here. These dolls were designed as all-porcelain prototypes with movable heads, arms and legs and painted in the artist's usual way for adaptation to production in vinyl as part of Dakin's "Elegante" line. Designed: 1984. *Photograph courtesy of Helen Kish.*

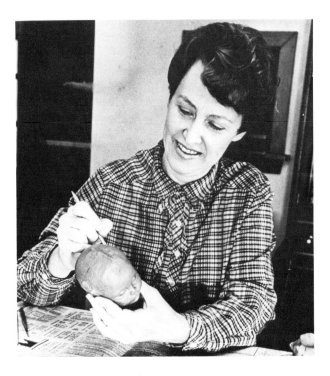

sonja bryer

Sonja Bryer is a perfectionist. Her husband, Paul, has told her, "You're too much of a perfectionist for this imperfect world."

The second force in her life is a need for challenge. "Everything has to be a challenge," she says, "If it's not, move on to something new." The Ohio native has found an outlet for both these needs in porcelain doll making.

Her formal art training began with four years of art and of sewing in high school, followed by two years of fashion illustration at the Dayton Art Institute, as well as seminars in many areas of art all over the country.

For a decade and a half, she taught ceramics, and was drawn towards porcelain work because of the difficulties involved in the medium.

"It's stronger after it's fired than ceramics," she says, "but the firing is more fragile because the temperature is so high to cure porcelain. The kiln goes to 2300 degrees. The piece may melt in the kiln, or it can boil if it is fired too fast. Blisters form all over the surface of the piece."

Sonja, who formerly flitted from one project to another, as she mastered it, found in porcelain's unpredictability, ample challenge, and has remained with it for a decade.

Doll making began with porcelain reproductions in 1976. "I wasn't happy with doing that very long since it wasn't creative enough," she says. "I started sculpting in 1977 but did not make a doll to sell until 1979."

Sonja's dolls are realistic, usually children, and she is insistent on verisimilitude. "I like to make my dolls look like real people most of the time. Sculpting the human from birth to adult, since the body is always changing, is a real challenge. I feel that the anatomy and proportions are the most important things," she says, "and I'm not happy until I feel they are right." She studied doll sculpture with doll artists Janet Masteller and Mary Ann Oldenburg, and collects pictures from which to study anatomy.

Her children and miniatures have won many ribbons, among them the Best of Show in Originals for her portrait doll of her daughter, Cindy, in 1980. A member of the Original Doll Artist Council of America and the Guild of Ohio Dollmakers, her dolls are in demand because of the high caliber of her work, which comes from a need to push the medium to its limits.

"I am always experimenting for a better way," she says. "My first dolls had a swivel bisque head on a shoulder plate and bisque arms and legs. The bodies were cloth with a wire armature inside. Last year (1983) I made an all-bisque baby with jointed arms and legs, plus a lady doll 7in (17.8cm) tall made very differently. Her head sits on top of her neck and swivels. Then the arms are in three pieces, jointed at the shoulders, elbows and wrists. She has a leather body, which her bisque legs and bust are attached to."

Doll making is a full-time occupation and Sonja works five to six hours at it a day, five days a week. When preparing for shows, she starts eight weeks before the date, and works eight to ten hours a day, six or seven days a week. One doll requires at least 25 hours to complete.

They are brought to life in her basement studio which is organized into seven work stations, one for each doll making operation: mold making and pouring, cleaning greenware, kiln firing, china painting, assembling, sewing and shipping. "It looks like a factory," she says, "and most of the time I'm so busy, I must admit it is usually messy. I have to clean up my mess each time I need to work in that area."

She describes her doll making process.

"To start, if I have a certain age child in mind, I search through my collection of pictures of children. Since my dolls, up to now, have been made with a bisque head, shoulders, arms and legs, I would start out checking the size doll I wanted, especially if they were miniature 1in (2.5cm) = 1ft (30.5cm) scale I had to be very precise. I had to be very sure I sculpted it big enough to allow for shrinkage.

"Sculpting the head would come first; then I would lay the head down on paper and draw around it, sketching the proportions of the age I have chosen to give me a chart to go by for the rest of the body and limbs.

"After I sculpt them of plastelina or Super Sculpey, I make a mold of plaster. When the mold dries, I pour in the porcelain. The porcelain must dry also and then the mold seams are cleaned off and the piece is polished till it is smooth. This, after it is fired, becomes my new model to make my good mold for the limited editions. The firing makes the porcelain shrink about 20%.

"If everything comes out of the firing the right size, I can proceed. If not, back to the drawing board, and this has happened to me several times."

Painting, for Sonja, as much as sculpture, makes or breaks a doll. "I have seen some really terrific work ruined because it wasn't painted nicely," she says.

She describes her painting methods.

"Painting is with china paint mixed with a slow drying medium so I can blend color into the flesh while it is wet. For the features I add lavender oil to thin the china paint just enough so the tiny brush

Sophie and *Jennifer* by Sonja Bryer in room setting of 1880. Clothes also are styled from 1880 fashions. *Sophie* is 7in (17.8cm) tall. Her head, bust, arms and legs are made of porcelain. Her head swivels on her neck and arms are jointed in three places. Limited edition of 75. 1983. *Photograph courtesy of Sonja Bryer.*

will flow easily. If too much lavender oil is added, the color will fire out in the kiln."

Bryer dolls all wear original clothing from Sonja's patterns. She is proud of the way the garments fit her miniature dolls, in particular. "They are put together like real clothes," she says, even though they are on 1/12th scale. "Some are even lined, since the seams would pull out if they were not. All the stitching is done on a sewing machine since this makes the seams stronger."

Never an easy medium, porcelain presents many obstacles for Sonja to overcome. "Things that bother me the most are fumes from the china paint and the porcelain clay dust. We have put in an exhaust fan, but in the winter it makes it awful drafty, which creates other problems and illness. Of the whole doll making process I think I enjoy the sculpting and the clothes making the most. Mold making is the process I dislike the most."

Sonja's production in 1984 was approximately 125 dolls. "Of the 125," she says, "about 80 of them were new creations." A complete listing of Bryer dolls, through 1983, follows.

Eddie and His Teddy, 17in (43.2cm) tall. 1979.
Portrait of Cindy, 15in (38.1cm) tall. 1980.
Little Dumplin, 13in (33cm) tall. 1980.
Annie with Her Kitty, 17in (43.2cm) tall. 1981.
Mammy and Sara. 1in = 1ft (2.5cm = 30.5cm) scale. 1981.
Santa, Billy, Beth and *Elf*. All miniatures 1in = 1ft (2.5cm = 30.5cm) scale. 1982.
Sophie, Elizabeth, Scarlett and *Rose*, all ladies. 7in (17.8cm) tall. 1983.
Jennifer and *Jamie*, jointed bisque twin babies. 1in = 1ft (2.5cm = 30.5cm) scale. 1983.
Pattie Cake, made for souvenir doll for the Guild of Ohio Dollmakers Convention, April 1984. Worked on for two years. 12in (30.5cm) tall.

All dolls are signed and dated when they are made. A tag comes with them telling the name, number and date sold of the doll. Limited editions are registered in a special file.

Bryer dolls are available by mail order and at shows. "I try to keep dolls made up so I don't have to take orders," Sonja says. "People are happier if they can choose the one they want rather than take what you send. Plus it makes my schedule easier to organize. I have to set aside eight weeks before each show to prepare for it. If I schedule more than five shows a year, it is hard to find time for sculpting and filling orders, plus any other things that have to be done."

Clearly, porcelain doll making is the proper medium for Sonja Bryer. She enjoys tackling its difficulties, and has not been tempted to switch to any other art form, contrary to her former method of operations. Her explanation is simple. "I make dolls because it's the most challenging and rewarding art I have ever done."

ABOVE: *Portrait of Cindy* by Sonja Bryer, 15in (38.1cm) tall. 1980. Head, arms and legs are porcelain. She has a cloth body with a wire armature inside. This doll is sculpted from pictures of Sonja's daughter, Cindy. *Photograph courtesy of Sonja Bryer.*

BELOW: *Pattie Cake* by Sonja Bryer. Made for souvenir for the Guild of Ohio Dollmakers' convention, April 1984. The doll was a two-year-project. 12in (30.5cm) tall with curls sculpted all around her head and an open-closed mouth. *Photograph courtesy of Sonja Bryer.*

Elizabeth by Sonja Bryer, 7in (17.8cm) tall. 1983. Her head, bust, arms and legs are made of porcelain. Her head swivels on her neck and arms are jointed in three places. Leather body. *Photograph courtesy of Sonja Bryer.*

Scarlett by Sonja Bryer. 7in (17.8cm) tall. Her head, bust, arms and legs are made of porcelain. Her head swivels on her neck and her arms are jointed in three places. Limited edition of 75. 1983. *Photograph courtesy of Sonja Bryer.*

kezi

"For me, the doll is a universal yet highly subjective art form that has some mysterious, symbolic connection to the human psyche."

Kezi's definition, many collectors would agree, aptly describes her work. There is a sensitive, almost mystic quality to the faces of many of her dolls. But they lack saccharine nostalgia; Kezi's work is deliberately contemporary.

"Probably the minimum requirement of any practicing artist is that works created accurately reflect the times in which the artist lived," she states. "This is not to say doll artists can't create period dolls such as Queen Annes if they choose, but they should make personal, contemporary statements and not try to go back and do something that has already been done better than they can hope to do it because it sprang naturally from its own time. Artists should rejoice in their own times, incorporating the emotions and perceptions of their own personal worlds into their work so that it connects in a natural, refreshing way with artistic predecessors."

Dolls are a recent development in Kezi's repertoire.

"After an early career in radio and television that took me from Illinois to Alaska to California," she says, "I moved to Oregon in 1957 and began doing what I had always wanted to do--artwork on a full-time, independent and self-supporting basis.

"I consider myself fortunate to be a self-taught artist for I approached art on my own terms with no preconceived ideas of what I could or couldn't do. Economic survival forced me to teach myself the things I had to know and rewarded me with incredible 'highs' of discovery that, for me, would not have been the same in a structured academic setting. I am still in the process or learning. It has become a way of life for me. My greatest joy is sensing something new and wonderful in my style or attitude."

The "new" tangent of doll making came after a long illness, in which she recalled a doll she met at summer camp at the age of eight. *Clarinda's* face crept back into her mind and reappeared in a vivid dream in which she "led me into a room filled with dolls in various stages of development. I intuitively knew this was the artistic course I would set out upon as soon as I could."

She spent five years studying porcelain, and learned from a master mold maker how to craft molds that would yield the finest detail possible, then settled down to create dolls for the most difficult of all audiences -- herself.

She talks about her doll making philosophy.

"Above all else, an artist has to be true to his or her own inner voice. I don't make dolls, or any other artistic statement, with any specific audience in mind. I make my art to please myself, to fulfill a need, to satisfy a longing. I think if an artist, even a very good one, falls into the trap of trying to please others, his or her work reflects a loss of freshness and vitality and takes on a rather boring plastic look. Often this kind of vapidness is indicative of over-anxious, eager-to-please novices who cast about endlessly for a successful 'look' instead of applying elbow grease to practical theory and gradually developing their own style."

Kezi's style is unmistakable. Her sensitivity of facial expression, combined with a simplicity of design, a shunning of froufrou and superfluity in clothing construction leave the viewer with a fresh, clean, reflective experience.

Kezi originals, however, are seldom seen. Sold my mail-order only, and never wholesaled, they are treated as art objects by their purchasers and rarely exhibited. "They are primarily in private collections in the United States, South America, Australia and Europe," she explains. "While some of my collectors occasionally take their Kezi dolls to their local doll shows, many have written to say they consider their dolls too valuable as artwork to put them at risk. This, of course, is most gratifying for an artist to hear."

Kezi works constantly at doll making, is a perfectionist and holds her chosen form of artistic expression in high regard. She explains her rationale.

"Why does an artist turn to creating dolls? Why not? I don't think a doll artist is basically any different from any other type of artist. Any specific difference is to be found in the individual artist's perception, sophistication and integrity. If mastery of technique and execution is equal, a doll artist of great sensitivity and originality rises above a fine artist of faulty perception or unsure integrity. I think a doll artist's place in the art world is exactly where he or she is willing to work and fight for it to be. An artist's stature, regardless of medium or subject matter, is based on enduring quality of performance lit with ongoing expansion of insight and expression."

When creating a doll, she molds a personality, working in concert with that still-unborn persona until it comes to life. This may be why her dolls have such uncanny presence.

"My working method for my porcelain dolls begins with sketchpad in hand. I first commit my ideas to paper, working general impressions of size and attitude into concrete details. In this way I discover exactly what it is I expect from this new character -- and more importantly -- what it is willing to actually give me. If all goes smoothly and we agree, my next step is the clay model.

"I do not build my doll as I would build a figurine. I build it in

Sunday's Child (close-up) by Kezi, 13½in (34.3cm) tall. One-of-a-kind. Mohair wig, light blue painted eyes, cloth hips, intaglio painted shoes. Wears short frock, bonnet and petticoat; carries purse. © 1979 by Kezi. Copyright notice on back of head and torso. Part of Kezi's "Arabella" series, her first completed porcelain dolls. *Photograph courtesy of Kezi.*

sections. For an all-porcelain doll, I build the torso, neck to crotch, on a wire armature anchored to a working platform. I leave enough room between the platform work surface and the bottom edge of the clay torso for legs. I work with an adjustable stand so that I can view my work from all angles and heights.

"Since my all-porcelain dolls, when fired, are seldom taller than 14in (35.6cm), I build the limbs and head over tightly wound and taped paper armatures. These parts are modeled for close fit to the torso. If I'm aiming for good mold release, it's here that I eliminate any prominent undercuts and awkward angles that might cause mold-making problems. Before making the first set of molds, I study the assembled model, trying to determine exactly how much 'relaxation' high firing will effect upon the various porcelain pieces, and if it will be acceptable. I always incorporate allowances for these firing changes into my clay models.

"I'm often asked how I create such radiant lifelike 'skins' on my dolls. Though I sometimes use a premixed flesh-colored porcelain slip as a base, I prefer a superior white slip to which I add oxides to obtain individual flesh colors. After adjusting and blending, I always strain my slip several times to ensure smoothness and clarity. I spend hours bringing dry greenware as close to flawlessness as possible. Basically, what you put into the kiln dictates what you're going to take out. Firing does not reduce or 'melt' flaws; it magnifies them. All of my porcelains are slow-fired. I have too much respect for the medium to subscribe to the 'pop 'em in the oven and turn up the heat' cookie baking attitude. Porcelain greenware is not cookie dough. The difference between a properly matured piece of porcelain bisque and a piece from a fast-fire practitioner is clearly visible to the naked eye.

"I polish my fired bisque until it feels like silk beneath my fingertips. Then it is rinsed in clear water and set up to dry. Just prior to china painting, I swab each piece down with denatured alcohol to remove any trace of dust or lint."

Kezi's work really comes to life in the china painting process.

"The painting of a porcelain doll's face requires sensitive handling of one's materials....I apply my semi-gloss paints in thin washes much as a watercolorist would. Lips, for example, may have as many as three washes plus final accents, each fired after application. This technique results in a supersoft 'glow' when finished. Nor do I care for the often vacuous stare of glass eyes. I think a doll's individuality, character, if you will, is best conveyed when its eyes are painted by the artist. I also think this increases the doll's value as artwork. I paint my dolls' eyes in several sequences of light to dark, fired after each application. I rarely paint in highlights but instead let the fired gloss of the eyes capture highlights from any surrounding light source. The results are natural and expressive. The final painting is an application of warm blushes over the forehead, ears, palms of hands, wristlines, fingernails, knees and soles of feet."

Because of these high standards, demand for Kezi's work far outran her capacity to fill orders, and, in August 1983, she signed an exclusive contract with Gorham-Textron to produce her dolls in series, each for a limited time span. This milestone in her career was undertaken after much consideration.

"From the artist's point of view, I concluded the SECOND most important ingredient in the successful transition of one's work to the commercial arena is a realistic comprehension of the logistics of commercial production. The most important ingredient is, of course, the integrity of the contracting company. I consider myself fortunate to have a company of such impeccable reputation present my designs to the mass market. Besides, let's not forget that the priceless antique dolls of today were almost without exception factory-produced consumer goods in THEIR day."

Vision and introspection are what Kezi's work is all about. "The connection between doll and human is a deep and emotional one," she states. "Deeper still, I think, is the connection between an artist's doll and its creator. Yet, I do not think of my dolls as people. They are expressions of some facet of my inner self."

It is fortunate for doll collectors that Kezi has been able to express the ineffable, mysterious qualities of the human psyche in a thoroughly concrete and appealing manner.

Celine by Kezi, 18in (45.7cm) tall. Doll No. 5 of "American Gold Series." Edition of 16 dolls. Porcelain swivel head, shoulder plate, half-arms, three-quarter legs. Lined cotton print cloth torso. Open crown with pate. Chestnut brown synthetic removable wig. Deep blue painted eyes. Wears cotton dress, batiste combinations, suede belt, beaded suede sandals. Kezi Artist's edition wrist tag. © 1983 Kezi. *Photograph courtesy of Kezi.*

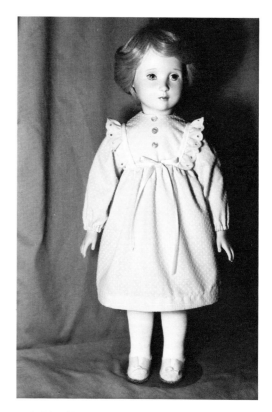

Faith — a musical doll, 18in (45.7cm) tall. One-of-a-kind, the original prototype for Gorham's "Golden Gifts Series." Porcelain dome head and hands. Upright cloth body with musical movement in upper torso. Blonde synthetic removable wig. Light blue painted eyes. Wears cotton dress, matching bloomers, cotton stockings, felt shoes. © 1982 Kezi. Copyright notice on back of head. *Photograph courtesy of Kezi.*

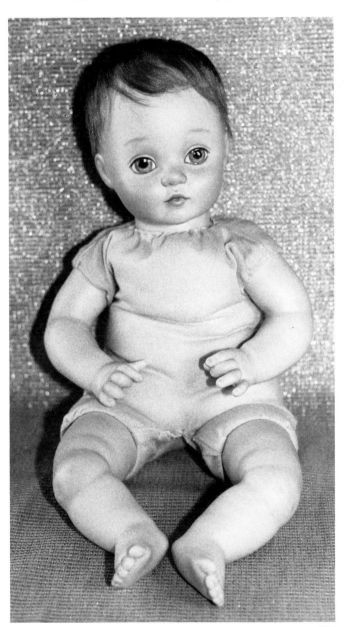

Little Mary by Kezi, 14in (35.6cm) tall. One-of-a-kind. Porcelain head and limbs. Soft-stuffed floppy body. Golden red mohair wig. Blue painted eyes. Unclothed. © 1982 Kezi. Copyright notice on back of neck. *Photograph courtesy of Kezi.*

Contrary Mary by Kezi, 13½in (34.3cm) tall. Porcelain swivel head, jointed shoulders, elbows. One-of-a-kind doll with mohair wig, brown painted eyes, cloth hips, intaglio hand-painted shoes. Dressed in dotted swiss frock, vest, petticoat and hat; holds flower basket. © 1979 Kezi. Copyright notice on back of head and torso. Part of Kezi's "Arabella" series. *Photograph courtesy of Kezi.*

LEFT: *Ryan* by Kezi, 20in (50.8cm) tall. Doll No. 4 of Kezi's "American Gold Series." Edition of 15. Porcelain swivel head, shoulder plate, half-arms, three-quarter legs. Striped cotton denim torso. Open crown with pate. Reddish-brown synthetic removable wig. Hazel painted eyes. Wears cotton plaid shirt, cotton short pants, suede sandals. Artist's original edition wrist tag. © 1982 Kezi. Winner of Blue ribbon and Best of Division, 1982 OCA professional porcelain competition. *Photograph courtesy of Kezi.*

BELOW LEFT: *Felicity* (left) and *Prudence* (right). Dolls by Kezi for Gorham-Textron. © 1984. 18in (45.7cm) tall with porcelain dome heads and hands, upright cloth bodies with musical movements in upper torsos, synthetic wigs, painted eyes. Wear cotton frocks with matching bloomers, cotton stockings, felt shoes. Hallmarked, dated, limited to a production of two years, gift boxed with a certificate of authenticity. Part of the "Golden Gifts"™ Series. *Felicity* plays "Always," has brown braids and brown eyes. *Prudence* plays "Love Me Tender," has blonde wig and brown eyes. *Photograph courtesy of Gorham-Textron.*

BELOW: *Kikki*, a musical boy clown by Kezi, 18in (45.7cm) tall. Edition of 10. Porcelain dome head and hands. Specially designed loose-jointed body for easy placement on shelf, and so forth. Musical movement in upper torso. Bright auburn forelock. Light blue painted eyes. Clown suit, neck ruff, felt cap with flower trim, felt slippers. © 1981 Kezi. Copyright notice on back of head. *Photograph courtesy of Kezi.*

nancy villaseñor
JESCO

Many doll makers, artists and designers secretly dream of their ideas reaching the mass-market, of children playing with their brain children. But this dream has come true for a relatively small percentage of them. At the 1985 American International Toy Fair, New York, Carol-Lynn noticed an encouraging new trend. Many commercial firms were openly and proudly showing the work of doll artists and designers.

During Toy Fair, Carol-Lynn met with doll designer Nancy Villaseñor, to conduct the following interview. They had met the previous fall at a show in Toldeo, Ohio, where the writer fell in love with Nancy's doll, *Katie*. Nancy is President of Jesco, a young, growing doll company in Monrovia, California. Her role as a doll maker differs substantially from everyone else in this book. She does not claim to be a doll artist, but a designer. Through her ideas and influence, dolls are born. Carol-Lynn Rössel Waugh (*)

*How did you get started in the doll business? Nancy Villaseñor (+)

I was working in the toy department in Sears and started interviewing with Fisher Price. I had probably four interviews. I really wanted that job more than anything in the world. I thought, from a consumer standpoint, they made the finest toys in the world.

They decided not to hire me because I was planning to be married. They felt they would be investing too much money. Of course, now, those things are illegal to say. But they were very upfront about it. One of the gentlemen who worked for them, who was involved in the interview said, "I'd like you to meet my brother. He's a sales rep for the area." And that's Jim. So, Jim hired me to work as a sales rep. He was selling Effanbee dolls at the time.

Shortly after that, we decided to go into the European import toy business, which was really how we began Jesco. At one time we imported 20 or 30 different product lines out of Europe. No matter how much I got involved in it, my true love was always dolls. I was involved with a company called Corolle -- a beautiful doll line. I think they're probably my favorite dolls of all time. We marketed those products from Europe for five years. Now they've set up their own U.S. company, so that got us out of that, but my love was in dolls. After 30 years in the toy products business, Jim has seen a lot of dolls come and go. He'd always had a tremendous love for *Kewpie*. We began an association with Joseph Kallus, who was the founder of Cameo Doll Company.

He was a very old gentleman, and, over many, many months he flattered me by deciding, over a lot of big toy companies, that he wanted me to take over and buy Cameo from him. Big companies

wanted to buy the rights and, as he used to say, "I'm 89 years old. What do I need the money for?"

We began by bringing out *Kewpie*, but, then, in the whole property we bought, there were molds for many, many dolls. I had an idea that it would be really neat to tie in what was old in the doll business -- which I love -- with what was new in the doll business.

When we made the shift from more of an importer to a manufacturer, we decided to produce dolls from the old molds. That process is very slow, because the molds were very old. We had to treat them very delicately and we had to make sure that they stayed in very good shape. We could never service the mass market with that approach.

Once we started doing that, we decided to build a doll company that was really for children. Yes, *Kewpie* was being gobbled up by the collectors, but dolls touch children, and it doesn't matter if you're 50, you've still got the child part of you, so that's the orientation that we developed when we started our own company as far as manufacturing goes.

I love the idea of making dolls for children. *Katie* -- for example -- she's really for a child.

I have been criticized a lot by the doll collectors, the *bona fide* doll collectors, the true blue doll collectors who are really down and dirty about it. I've made some very unpopular statements about that industry and I'm sure they'll all come back to haunt me someday, but, nevertheless, I want to make dolls for children. I think that's what this company is about. I would never be comfortable exploiting the collector market. I just can't do it.

That doesn't go to say that you can't do something more special, and something less special, and something that may have a particular characteristic that might be more appealing to collectors, but a doll is good for some very intrinsic things, that touch people. I can't say that I'm going to make this doll and it's going to have a certain value ten years from now, because that's not what it is about. It has a value because it was important for a child.

*I grew up with *Ginny* dolls. They always were my favorites. They're a little girl, about the same size as *Katie*. It's the same type of philosophy. *Ginny* dolls now are very collectible because people my age grew up with them and they were their favorite dolls.

+I think when you say the word "collectible," I always say you have to qualify that. Yes, I want to make a doll a little girl will remember when she grows up. She'll remember that it was special to her. That's the reason for collecting. It's not for the value of it.

*I feel there are too many sophisticated dolls for little girls.

*When did you design her?

+I began her in October of '83.

*How long did it take you to sculpt her?

+I didn't do the actual sculpture because there are a lot of technicalities involved. First of all, I'm not an artist. I say that right out front. I know how to get things done and I see it in my head, but I don't do it myself. I had a sculptor in New York whom I showed literally zillions of pictures of Katie to. I must have driven him crazy. I showed him close-ups of her cheeks, close-ups of her eyes when they wrinkled, how her arms were posed when she was not standing.

Dolls are not meant to stand straight up and down. I pointed out to the sculptor the way I wanted her head to turn, not just straight around, but sort of on an axis -- on a tilt, to bring out the expression on her face. I flew back and forth to New York literally every step of the way to look at the sculpting.

There are a lot of intricacies in sculpting a doll that will eventually be made into a mold for a doll. For vinyl. First of all there's the shrinkage factor.

First they make a sculpture and then they make a master mold. The master mold is the mold from which they cast all the other molds.

When that master is made, say, 50 years from now, somebody wanted to remake *Katie*, a new mold could be made.

*Is it made of metal?

+Yes. From that master mold the doll shrinks down seven percent. You have to build it up to get it down. But there's something else, too. When you have a moving eye on a doll, when it shrinks seven percent, you have to build that into the sculpting, but when it shrinks, the eye opening enlarges in relationship to the head. There are people in New York who have been involved in the doll industry for years who are expert at doing this.

You have to know what you're doing or you'll never get the eyes to go in.

*Do the eyes go in from the front or from the back? I know the stationary eyes go in from the front.

+Yes, we have a tool that we use. That's why I say a doll is much more beautiful than the sum of its parts. If you see arms and legs and heads and heads without the hair, it's not beautiful. They make fun of me in my office, because when I'm working on new products, I have dolls all over the place, but never, ever do I have a doll without a head on it.

We have a factory in Monrovia, which is a suburb of Los Angeles. If you go out on assembly line, you'll see dolls without heads, but never in my office. I just don't want to look at them. I'm rather fanatical about it. That does take the romance away.

*There must be all sorts of things that people who work in porcelain have no idea about, concerning working in vinyl. I heard that when you design a doll, the mold opening the doll is pulled from is the smallest part in the body.

+Right. Because they strip the mold. Vinyl, plastisol, has a memory to it. It's poured in liquid form into the mold. The caps are put on. You may have 12 arms so they're done simultaneously. There's a compressor that shoots the material into each arm, for example. It's premeasured. The cap is put on. It goes into the oven, along with the other parts.

Vinyl dolls have such nice soft feel to them -- or *can* have a soft feel to them; not all of them do because they rotate around a 360° axis. In other words, they rotate this way, this way and this way all at the same time. There are no seams inside the doll.

In any case, they have a very small opening to strip the vinyl out of. If it's distorted in any way -- say, the worker has a tool, and he grabs the doll part and he pinches it too tightly, in that real critical cooling-off period. That defect will stay in the material. Sometimes when they strip a whole bunch of heads, they will put them in a box. If they're still warm, they may tilt the head on its side, causing a dent in it. If you heat up that dented head to its original temperature, the memory from the mold will make it pop back into shape. Plastisol is a wonderful material because you can get tremendous softness and still have a play doll. Vinyl is a wonderful play material because it lasts forever.

You can create a soft look because there are no seams in it. You don't have parting lines like in porcelain. And I think that does lessen the softness.

I want to work with soft-bodied dolls and I will be doing that.

Katie by Jesco, 9¾in (24.9cm) tall. 1983. All-vinyl doll, fully-jointed. Brown hair, green eyes, white dress, shoes and tights. Comes with a cameo locket. Other colors available. *Waugh photograph.*

Katie by Jesco with blonde hair in original packaging, designed by Nancy Villaseñor. 1983. *Photograph courtesy of Nancy Villaseñor.*

Katie by Jesco, designed by Nancy Villaseñor. 1983. The nice thing about *Katie* is her wholesome, childish quality and her play value. This photograph illustrates some of her clothing and accessories, an ensemble called the "Katie Kollars Kollection," designed for the 1985 market. *Photograph courtesy of Nancy Villaseñor.*

The doll will have a vinyl face, soft body, vinyl arms and legs. I think that's going to be an exciting new material to work with because it will have a different softness.

*What made you decide to make *Katie* the size she is?

+I wanted to make a small doll that little kids could handle. I wanted her to be at a price that's affordable. She was going to be about 7in (17.8cm). It appeared to me very early on that if I did her small, I couldn't capture the dimension of looking like a real child. If I did it much larger, merchandising-wise, it would get lost, among a lot of other products that were available.

I wanted her to be just big enough so I could capture all the poseability of her.

Also, I started thinking that some of the things I wanted to do with *Katie*, to make her have a lot of play value, couldn't be done so small because a child couldn't do them. It wouldn't work right. So, that's how I came up with her size.

I think it works just fine. People ask me what size she is and I don't know. I don't know the number of inches. I know dolls are sold as a 10in (25.4cm) doll or a 12in (30.5cm) doll. I think she's a little over 9in (22.9cm), and she's almost 10in (25.4cm). She's some size. She's the right size.

*You did a Storybook doll, and it was bigger. Was that your first one?

+That was the first one. I think my motivation was a little different. I guess everybody looks back on his first thing and wishes he could do it over again. And I imagine ten years from now, looking back, if I've done a doll I love as much as *Katie*, I'll look back and say "How could I have done *Katie*?" I don't think so, but everybody goes through that creative process.

I knew Storybook dolls were a popular category in the toy industry. But I also did something else with them that has made them fairly successful. A lot of companies who do Storybook characters or international characters sort of make the consumer feel like they have to buy all of them to be successful at collecting. I wanted dolls that could be bought alone and that would still be a fun doll to have. I didn't want them to *have* to be the Storybook characters. I didn't want them to have to be anything. I wanted them to be just pretty little dolls.

Sometimes you have to do things that will sell. It costs a lot of money to develop *a* new doll, *a* new doll face. From the sculpting to the master mold making for the wax models to the molds, it's very expensive. So, before you make one doll, you have to be sure where you can sell it.

*Where does the wax model come in? Is that after the first sculpting? You make a mold and then a wax model from it, and then it's refined?

*Yes, that's where you can get a lot of the detail on it. I don't know that I know a lot about it. I know that I have good people doing things that need to be done to make the doll good. I trust those people.

*How many people are involved in making the dolls?

+The molding is done on the East Coast, because vinyl molding just isn't an industry that's developed in California. And I certainly don't want to move to the East Coast, so I have to kind of live with that.

*So that's done over here and shipped to California?

+Yes. We buy parts from all sorts of suppliers: eyes from one company, the hair is rooted by another company, a lot of things like that. But, as far as our factory's concerned, we have ten people in the office, we have as many as 35 to 40 people in the factory in the height of our season. I think it's down to maybe 25 the rest of the year.

*They're assembling the parts and dressing dolls?

+Putting trinkets on them packaging, stocking the shelves, putting the shoes on, socks on. A lot of things go into every doll. It may seem funny, but if you get ready to run the assembly line one day, and you're missing the red shoes, you don't make that doll. And it happens sometimes.

*Did the same person who sculpted *Katie* sculpt the Storybook doll?

+It was a different person, but I had a different thing in my head. The Storybook doll never turned out the way I wanted it to look, but I was too timid to rant and rave and say "No, this is NOT what I want."

I was very timid about creating my first doll, so it isn't what was in my head. *Katie* IS what was in my head.

*When were the Storybook dolls started?

+In 82.

*And then *Katie* came out in 83?

+I started her in 83, but she came out in 84. It's a year to develop a doll -- for me, it is. Maybe other people could do it quicker, but I've decided that's my style. It's a year.

A lot of things I've done come out of something that was real special to me personally. *Katie* was designed from a very special child. She's somebody I have a real connection with -- not my own daugher, although I have a different connection with my own children -- she's a niece.

But, since the very beginning of her life I've felt very bonded to her. She's a very unusual character and a lot of what I do really relates to this connection.

A lot of the outfits I do, I draw out, and the seamstress and I work on them. A lot of my ideas come from seeing her in a particular environment. I mean, she runs around in a running suit all the time, so I had to have a running suit in the line this year.

Katie is the youngest grandchild in our family and she's pretty special to everybody. She has a unique personality to say the least. I wanted to do something for my mother -- her grandmother -- for Christmas. So I bought some European fabric. And I wanted some long curls, some wigs, to make her real fancy, just the way I saw her sometimes. People saw it, and said, "Gosh, this is just great. Why don't you do that in your line?" And it's one of the best-selling things we have. It came from some place very, very special. It came from my whole family. I have two sisters. We all have kids. We're all very close. It came from this connection I had doing that doll for my mother.

*What gives you the most satisfaction about your dolls?

+I suppose, probably, that kids enjoy them, and that I can run a business based on a product that does do that.

Fairy Godmother and *Cinderella* by Jesco. 1982. *Godmother* has dark hair and eyes, pale blue dress, magic wand. *Cinderella* has blonde hair, pale blue dress and shoes. *Photograph courtesy of Nancy Villansenor.*

edna daly

Edna Daly became a doll maker by serendipity.

She trained to be a social worker, receiving her degree from Bear Sheva University in Israel. With ten years' experience under her belt, the mother of three fully intended to continue her career when she moved with her family to America in 1981. But a chance encounter changed her life.

Her husband is to blame. It was he who took the children to the park that afternoon and met the husband of doll artist Avigail Brahms. But it was the beauty of Mrs. Brahms' dolls that enchanted her, when Edna accepted an invitation to see them.

The two women made an agreement: "I helped Avigail with the sewing (for her dolls) and she taught me her technique of doll making," says Mrs. Daly.

The dolls brought together all the loose ends in Edna's life, which to this point skirted the edges of doll making, perhaps unconsciously. She had had little practical experience with dolls. As a child on a farm in Israel, she had very few toys and only one used rag doll. However, for as long as she can remember, she has enjoyed working with her hands at crafts. She took courses in sculpting, needlepoint, crocheting, painting and even doll making. One of her dreams was to "play" with antique clothing, in particular, beads. In Europe she spent many pleasant hours combing the flea markets and antique shops.

By the time Edna met Mrs. Brahms, she was ready to learn. She absorbed her lessons quickly and after almost a year of apprenticeship, began to work on her own.

"When I worked with Avigail Brahms, I enjoyed it very much and was excited when sewing the clothing for her dolls. I fell in love with them and felt that I must learn how to sculpt. At the beginning, I did not have any proportion, but in time, with a lot of work, ups and downs, I succeeded", she says.

Her style was not, however, that of her teacher. Whereas Mrs. Brahms' dolls are Victorian, Mrs. Daly prefers the era of the 1920s and 1930s, the slightly worldly-wise, decadent decade of Art Deco and Erté. Her dolls are sumptuous and attenuated, elegant and refined. They exude a "knowing" air and a restrained sadness.

Each doll is individually sculpted. The arms, legs and shoulder plates are formed of a "special hard-fired material that has the properties to simulate the natural skin pigmentation," in the words of the artist.

She describes her sculpting procedure. "I always start with choosing a pair of matching eyes, in the early morning. Then I begin to work on the raw material for a minimum of two hours, continuing to sculpt the doll's head. The sculpting is from my imagination only; I do not look at any pictures. The head sculpting takes me at least two days. Most of the work with the doll head is directed at the expression of the eyes."

The torso, thighs and upper arms are stuffed fabric over a wire armature. Sculpted limbs are attached to these. "When I am sculpting the hands and legs, I already know the position in which they will stand," Edna notes.

"The most enjoyable and surprising part for me, when making the dolls, is the face painting. Although I know more or less what kind of a character I have sculpted, it always astonishes me when I finish the painting and put on the hair," she confides. Hair is mohair, of often surprising colors: bright red, floozie orange, striking yellow, complementing the other worldly characters of the dolls, their makeup and costumes.

The ladies stand 22in (55.9cm) to 24in (61cm) high; the children are approximately 12in (30.5cm) tall. They are completely hand done. Great care is taken in costuming, incorporating difficult-to-find antique materials in the construction. Lace overlays, feathers, marabou, hand-sewn silk or nylon stockings, intricate beading work, specially made hats of antique felt all take time and consideration. The clothes are sewn onto the body; leather shoes are glued on because "I consider the doll as a piece of art and I do not want anyone to change it," Edna says.

Edna describes her work area: "A small room with many windows, packed with cabinets and drawers half open: antique dresses and hats hanging on the walls; lots of tissue paper, material, threads on the floor; a sewing machine and a messy work table. But each time, when I begin to sculpt again, I clean the room for I do not want the dust to affect the material."

She spends an average of eight hours a day there, doll making, working sometimes until the very late hours of the night, producing about four dolls a month. "I have a full-time job as a mother to three children and another full-time job as a doll maker," she states. "I love making dolls."

Each doll is unique. No molds are made; nothing is repeated. One detects, however, a "family resemblance" among her creations, a flair that unmistakably marks a Daly doll.

They are signed at the back of the neck, and with a tag sewn to the back of the belt. Because of her limited output, Edna's dolls are very collectible, and are available only through art galleries, doll shops or from her studio, which is light-years from the social worker's office she occupied a short while ago.

LEFT: Lady doll 22in (55.9cm) tall. One-of-a-kind doll of wax-like oven-fired material made by Edna Daly, © 1983. Wig of blonde curly mohair. Blown blue crystal glass eyes. Body is made of cotton and fabric on wire armature. Cream silk gown beaded with white beads. Purple felt hat with flower and feather. Gold leather shoes. Signature and date on the back, at neck. *Photograph courtesy of Edna Daly.*

BELOW LEFT: One-of-a-kind girl doll, © 1983 by Edna Daly. Head and limbs of wax-like oven-fired material. Body of cotton and fabric on a wire armature. Black mohair hair. Brown blown crystal glass eyes. Cream net lace dress. Pink felt hat. Holds pink flowers. Pink leather shoes. Signature and date on the back at the neck. A tag attached to the belt in the back. *Photograph courtesy of Edna Daly.*

BELOW MIDDLE: One-of-a-kind lady doll 22½in (57.2cm) tall, © 1983 by Edna Daly. Head and limbs made of wax-like oven-fired material. Body of cotton and fabric on a wire armature. Blonde straight mohair wig. Blown blue crystal glass eyes. Black silk gown beaded in gold, green and blue. Green felt hat. Green feather fan. Black leather shoes with gold stripes. Signature and date on the back at the neck. A tag is attached to the belt in the back. *Photograph courtesy of Edna Daly.*

BELOW RIGHT: One-of-a-kind girl doll 10in (25.4cm) tall, © 1983 by Edna Daly. Head and limbs made of wax-like oven-fired material. Body made of cotton and fabric on wire armature. Blue blown crystal glass eyes. Light brown mohair wig. Wears pink crepe chiffon dress and dark orange felt hat with flowers. Signature and date on the back of the neck. A tag is attached to the belt at the back. *Photograph courtesy of Edna Daly.*

LEFT: One-of-a-kind child doll 10in (25.4cm) tall, © 1983 by Edna Daly. Head and limbs made of wax-like oven-fired material. Body made of cotton and fabric on a wire armature. Brown mohair hair. Brown blown glass eyes. Holds fruit basket. Wears dark blue silk velvet rompers with lace collar and cuffs. Bare feet. Light blue felt hat decorated with fruit. Signature and date on the back of the neck. A tag attached to the belt in the back. *Photograph courtesy of Edna Daly.*

RIGHT: One-of-a-kind lady doll 22in (55.9cm) tall, © 1983 by Edna Daly. Head and limbs made of wax-like oven-fired material. Body of cotton and fabric on a wire armature. Blonde curly mohair wig. Blue blown crystal glass eyes. Gown of red silk chiffon, beaded with dark red beads. Beaded hat. Black and orange feather. Handmade leather shoes. Signature and date on the back of the neck. A tag attached to the belt in the back. *Photograph courtesy of Edna Daly.*

BELOW LEFT: One-of-a-kind bride doll 23in (58.4cm) tall, © 1983 by Edna Daly. Head and limbs made from wax-like oven-fired material. Body of cotton and fabric on a wire armature. Brown blown crystal glass eyes. Brown mohair hair. Holds white bouquet. Gown of cream beaded silk. Lace veil. Wax flowers on crown. White bridal bouquet. Signature and date on the back at the neck. A tag attached to the belt in the back. *Photograph courtesy of Edna Daly.*

BELOW RIGHT: Two one-of-a-kind lady dolls each 22in (55.9cm) tall, © 1983 by Edna Daly. Heads and limbs made from wax-like oven-fired material. Bodies of cotton and fabric on a wire armature. Left doll has blonde mohair wig, blue glass eyes and wears a red chiffon beaded dress. Completing her costume is a boa and a black felt hat with a long red feather. Right doll has a black mohair wig, brown glass eyes and wears a black net gown with sequins on a gold slip. She has a gold beaded hat. Signature and date on the back at the neck. A tag attached to the belt in the back. *Photograph courtesy of Edna Daly.*

robert raikes

Bob Raikes is a modern Gepetto, carving new life into wooden boughs.

His charming, often largish dolls, they go to 26in (66cm) tall, reach out and seem to speak to the viewer. Purchasers seem to be captivated by the animism of these little "people," and occasionally act in peculiar ways.

"I have received several letters," Raikes relates, "written as if the dolls wrote the letters. One couple bought one of our baby dolls, which wore a hand-made christening gown for their newborn premature granddaughter. Later they told us the baby wore the doll's gown when she was christened."

What is it that makes people act toward Raikes Originals as if they were animate? Perhaps it is their construction. Their bodies, which are often fully-jointed, allow naturalistic, child-like, dolly-like posing, and are extremely appealing to collectors who want their dolls to, also, be "play-toys."

This aspect of Bob's work has been noted by a major manufacturer, and commercial versions may soon be available -- none too soon, for these dolls have an immediate appeal to both children and adults.

Their maker has been sculpting for many years. He views doll making as an all-encompassing art form, and an aesthetic challenge.

"As a sculptor I always enjoyed working with the human form," he says. "Doll making gives the opportunity to artistically express the human form using a variety of materials and colors. For the artist it affords limitless creative opportunities. In my opinion doll artistry is one of the highest art forms, yet unrecognized. I would like doll artists to be recognized as true sculptors. I would like my field to be open to not just the doll world. Some doll artists can stand up to the best sculptors in the country. The doll artist has not been properly recognized in the art world."

Self-taught, the sculptor has been working in wood since 1970, creating dolls from miniature scale to 36in (91.4cm) tall. Because of the nature of his medium, each is an original. Some body types are repeated -- faces, never.

"I feel comfortable working in a subtractive art form," Bob says of his medium. "I'm interested in experimenting with subject matter".

Early bodies were soft, sawdust-stuffed, with wooden hands and head (a limited number of cloth-bodied dolls are still made). Later ones are fully-jointed, with what Bob calls "sophisticated joints," and posable. Either type has a delightful "dolly" quality to it

that makes the viewer want to pick it up and play, especially in the case of the children, or the animal dolls.

The latter are pure visions of fantasy. Bob seems tuned in on alternate realities, and his rabbit dolls, especially, are fully-realized individuals with definite personas. Dressed with skill, insight and tenderness, usually by his wife, Carol, they seem like characters from a half-forgotten nursery story, familiar, and yet almost beyond the bounds of memory. The *Faerie Rabbit*, dressed in flower petals, and the wedding couple, ready for nuptuals in the meadow, are two examples. Fully-jointed, posable, with removable, excellently-constructed clothing, they accost the viewer. Their eyes speak in a barely intelligible language, which can be interpreted only if the viewer is of a certain mental set. This writer speaks the above from experience.

Not long ago, two Raikes rabbits lay in a box for a while in the bedroom, waiting for their photographs to be taken. Nineteen inches (48.5cm) tall, they completely filled the carton, and, as I passed one day, I could have sworn small noises came from its depths. I opened the lid and peered in. The lady rabbit, clad in eyelet lace, wonderful underclothes, ribbons, veil and garter, with flower garlands in paw, peered back.

"That's better," she seemed to say. Rabbits don't speak too loudly, so I wasn't sure. "It's awfully stuffy in here, you know." I reached down, lifted her out, and sat her on the desk. "Just for a while," I told her. You're in danger around here. Not from the bears, but from peanut butter and jelly. You have to go back before school is out." I lifted her companion, sat him beside her and found a plastic carrot in my prop box. It would have to do, I thought. I had been lured into Bob Raikes' fantasy world, as have many others.

It is his preferred place, methinks, too.

"My favorite dolls are those dealing with fantasy and the elegant ladies. "It gives me a chance to separate myself from the ordinary. It gives me a chance to daydream in an art form."

His fairies, usually 12in (30.5cm) tall, are another example of creative daydreaming. They are in line with the qualities he looks for in a doll.

"It has to evoke emotion or a sense of wonder from those viewing the dolls. I have to feel the work has challenged my creativity," he explains.

Bob's dolls are really a family project and are the source of income for the household. Everyone is involved in their construction and sale, and household activity revolves around their creation. Twelve to sixteen hours a day are spent at doll work. Dolls take from a minimum of two days for small ones to two or three weeks for some more sophisticated ones.

Bob describes his workplace.

"There is a carving shop, a material storage room, and assembly sewing room. This sometimes overflows into the dining room, which we try to avoid at all costs to keep an orderly house for the family. This is not always easy to do."

A doll-making studio can be a hectic environment in which to raise a family, as Raikes relates.

"We have made so many dolls at such a fast pace, spending so much time making them it is like an addiction which we laugh about.

"It's only amusing in retrospect, but we have lost many nights' sleep to the production of our dolls. We have done many shows in which we drove there and back in one day, getting up at 3:00 in the morning, and getting back at 10:00 or 11:00 at night. We did this to avoid paying for a motel, which, fortunately we do not have to avoid anymore.

"Our children have had some interesting experiences, also, and there are some unorthodox aspects, I'm sure, to their childhood. Our attitude is -- it makes us all more interesting personalities."

Around 75 dolls are produced annually; each follows a similar plan. Bob details it.

1. I mentally draw a picture.
2. I do sketches on paper.
3. I make a front and side profile.
4. I make a cardboard pattern. Sometimes I make a clay model; not always.
5. I cut out all parts in wood on a bandsaw.
6. I carve the body parts.
7. I carve the head.
8. I carve the body joints and fit all parts.
9. I sand everything.
10. I recarve any necessary parts.
11. I paint the features.
12. I apply the finish.
13. I string the doll together.
14. A sketch is drawn for the clothing.
15. The clothing is sewn.
16. The wig is made and applied.
17. Accessories are added.

At this writing, Raikes Originals was producing the following dolls:

1. A large, approximately 26in (66cm) tall, all-wooden girl dressed as Little Red Riding Hood, Goldilocks, Gretel and a Turn-of-the-Century little girl with coat.

2. Elegant ladies. These are usually dressed in silk gowns, using antique lace fabric whenever possible. These costumes are researched. Among the group is a barefoot prairie lady, a medieval jester, the figure Faun (half goat, half man, all-wooden with attached fur), and an oriental lady in traditional all-silk kimono.

3. A series of 12in (30.5cm) fairies, each one different.

4. A gnome in different sizes.

5. A Victorian Santa.

6. A smaller, approximately 16in (40.6cm) little girl doll, introduced in 1985, who can touch her nose.

7. Three-foot-tall (91.4cm) figures, introduced in 1985, including an Indian, a king and a queen.

8. Woody Bears, which are described in detail in *Teddy Bear Artists; Romance of Making & Collecting Bears*, they, like the dolls, are a family project, one which has captured the fantasy of everyone involved.

Signed and dated on the back of the neck, the dolls and bears are sold at shows, a few shops and by mail directly from the artist, in his home-based doll-making studio.

What is a good doll to the modern Gepetto? "A good doll is a combination of talent, imagination, workmanship and the element of time and experience. Doll making for me is transferring ideas into material with creativity, expressing my feelings in the meantime."

Perhaps the reason Raikes dolls come to life is the feelings put into them by their creator.

Gretel, hand-carved, jointed wooden doll by Bob Raikes, undressed to show jointing. Approximately 26in (66cm) tall. Hand-painted face. 1984. *Photograph courtesy of Bob Raikes.*

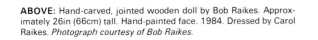

ABOVE: Hand-carved, jointed wooden doll by Bob Raikes. Approximately 26in (66cm) tall. Hand-painted face. 1984. Dressed by Carol Raikes. *Photograph courtesy of Bob Raikes.*

RIGHT: *Gretel*, dressed by Carol Raikes. *Photograph courtesy of Bob Raikes.*

ABOVE LEFT: *Rabbit Bride*, 19in (48.3cm) tall, by Bob Raikes. 1985. Costumed by Carol Raikes with fully-removable clothing including fancy undergarments and garter. *Waugh photograph.*

BELOW LEFT: *Rabbit Groom*, 19in (48.3cm) tall, by Bob Raikes. 1985. Costumed by Carol Raikes with fully-removable clothing. *Waugh photograph.*

BELOW: *Faerie Rabbit*, fully-jointed wood, by Bob Raikes. 19in (48.3cm) tall. Costumed by Carol Raikes. 1984. *Photograph courtesy of Bob Raikes.*

Medieval Jester, 23in (58.4cm) tall, by Bob Raikes. All-wooden, fully-jointed doll. Costumed by Carol Raikes. 1984. *Photograph courtesy of Bob Raikes.*

Faerie, 12in (30.5cm) tall, by Bob Raikes. 1984. Fully-jointed. Costumed by Carol Raikes. *Photograph courtesy of Bob Raikes.*

rebecca iverson

"Making dolls is a magical experience I greatly enjoy," says fabric artist Rebecca Iverson. "I may be inspired by a passage in a book, a child's face, a photograph or a remembered childhood moment and from there on it becomes my goal to transform this fleeting moment or impression into a tangible form."

Why cloth?

Rebecca says she began making dolls with cloth quite simply because it was available and inexpensive, but now she is thoroughly enamored of it as a medium. She finds it offers her freedom of expression though she admits many may question the notion of "freedom" with a flat piece of cloth. Cloth, she says, certainly does impose limits on a doll maker. It is easy to "mess up"...make it stiff, over painted or lumpy or saggy. It is unpredictable but, the challenge for her is in meeting and overcoming these limitations to finally achieve a smooth symmetrical and sculpted form.

Rebecca feels muslin doll bodies are beautiful because they are soft, bendable and imitate the human body. "Cloth works with you if you respond to it," she remarks, "if you can learn to understand it.

"Fingers and knees seem to emerge from the stuffing, formed by the cloth as I mold and stitch. I experiment with other substances, wax and Sculpey, but cloth and I remain the best of friends.

"Once my 'canvas' is prepared, I have *freedom* to transfer my mind's images to the dolls' faces with stitches and paint, unhampered by modeling."

Truth is, Rebecca Iverson's work is just not seen enough to suit the collector or to do her justice. Rebecca is not only a doll maker, but an "all rounder" in art. Only few artists have the ability to draw...whether they make use of it or develop it. Many would probably admit to wanting to at some point in the future, but most do not seem to get around to pen and pencil work because it seems so much more interesting to push, pull or model a material in three dimension. Rebecca has a highly developed graphic talent which she puts to use in making a number of printed items (paper dolls, note cards and stationery,) in addition to the sharp delineation of character in her fabric doll faces. She has done several excellent paper dolls of subjects and characters also portrayed in her dolls like *Caddie Woodlawn* (a wonderful girl's story which, unfortunately, is not read as much as it should be) and her own toy Teddy Bear and stationery designs.

Rebecca's figures in cloth, which mostly reflect her reading joys of childhood and really pluck the heartstrings, evoke the nostalgia of childhood and all its nice soft wonders. Her little girls

wear button boots or ankle strap shoes and hold their own dollies by the hand, often seeming to be lost in their own daydreams.

It is difficult to talk of Rebecca's dolls separately from any of her other creations. She, herself, says that her ideas move continually from one media to another, each borrowing from, being inspired by or sharing with each other to bring the ideas into being. Rebecca may call herself a needlesmith...(isn't that an absolutely perfect title for a professional fabric doll artist...it says it *all*,) but with an art degree, she is an accomplished artist in other media. She could, perhaps, be called "the complete" doll maker because all of her talents...painting, drawing, sewing, design and the needle arts themselves are used to create "full packages" of expression. That is, Rebecca seems to have a tendency to fill out. If a doll is made, it ought to have a bear or a dollie to go with it. Then, the dollie and its dolls probably ought to have a paper doll to go with them. And then, you could expect to see a handmade Iverson quilt with the set...and so forth...tidy treasures of total conception.

In "needlesmithing," Rebecca takes her time and applies all her various skills. She has done extensive work in quilting with embroidery, trapunto and piecing and these other crafts, all relating directly to the basic love of fabric, appear from time to time, well blended into a doll creation.

Each of Rebecca's dolls has a presence...a very appealing presence of its very own. She calls them primary all-cloth dolls and as Carol-Lynn says, they seem to be wistful introspective visitors from another world...a parallel world where all is peaceful.

One of our favorites is *Christopher Robin*. In this figure, Rebecca has captured the essence of the Milne character and the well-loved light watercolor impressions. Very simple in design, this boy stands with his bear...just thinking.

It would be impossible to speak of Rebecca's work without some mention of her bears. Bears take up a good percentage of her time...and like the dolls they often belong to, they have their own special character. One would not expect Rebecca to do bears that were like most bears. Her bears, naturally, are different. They have basically flat faces with a skillfully hand-stitched, needlesculpted muzzle and, very expressive, realistic, hand-painted eyes...these bears when done as characters often stand like the children, with paws together, gazing trustfully out at the world.

Rebecca's paper dolls are startlingly clear, black and white renderings in complex detail using several ink techniques so that the total effect is very like a woodcut or etching. We would have to say, without hesitation, that Iverson paper doll designs put her

Lill-Marta, a 15in (38.1cm) fabric doll designed as a contemporary Swedish child in navy and burgundy by Rebecca Iverson. *Photograph by W. Barry Iverson.*

Marcella and her *Raggedy Ann* by Rebecca Iverson, a needlesculpted impression of the little girl from the stories and, of course, everyone's favorite, the classic rag doll, *Ann. Photograph by W. Barry Iverson.*

amongst the top three or four amateur paper doll artists in the country. The paper doll collectors know this, of course.

Rebecca lives with her husband in a tiny brown house tucked amongst 40 acres of Wisconsin woods and fields. There they enjoy the activities and pleasures offered by all seasons, but also appreciate the long, incredibly fierce winters. "Winter" says Rebecca, "gives me all day indoors...we can enjoy the fire in the grate and I am seldom without a doll's petticoat, a bear's arm or a paper doll sketch in hand."

Grace, 20in (50.8cm), a contemporary fabric doll by Rebecca Iverson is dressed in a peach floral print dress and holds her blue gingham pony. *Photograph by W. Barry Iverson.*

Caddie, an interpretation inspired by the book, *Caddie Woodlawn, Caddie* carries one of Rebecca's very unique original Teddy Bear designs. *Photograph by W. Barry Iverson.*

"The Wonderland Three" — *Alice,* the *White Rabbit* and the *Mad Hatter* designed and constructed in cloth by artist Rebecca Iverson. *Photograph by W. Barry Iverson.*

patricia ryan brooks

"My dolls sell themselves. They are little people who, without any voices, say 'Take me home.'"

The way her art is developing, perhaps Pat Brooks' dolls actually will speak. Her hand-carved wooden dolls display an uncommon vitality and emotion that, from the start, caught the eye of judges and collectors. At her maiden doll show, in June 1978, she entered her first three original wooden dolls, and took home first prize and best of class on all three, as well as the Jill Johnson Memorial Cup for overall Best of Show.

At the time, the prizes and the doll show changed her life. Patricia Brooks became a doll maker. Looking at her life objectively, it seems almost inevitable she would take this path. Art and dolls were in her blood, even before she was born.

"For a number of years before I was born," she recalls, "my parents had a business making small, bendable latex doll house dolls, closing their doors with the onset of World War II and the scarcity of rubber for non-defense purposes. My earliest memories of playing with dolls were with these tiny Minikins left over from their business. I began collecting dolls when I was about five years old and made my own first rag doll when I was nine. I still have him.

"As far back as I can remember, I always wanted to be an artist. My parents were free-lance artists and worked in a studio in our home, so I absorbed art on a day-to-day basis.

Doll making helped Pat combine her goals.

She fell into it during an independent study project at college, where she was thrashing around, trying to find artistic direction. A 1977 issue of *McCall's* magazine, which showed the mechanics of wooden doll carving, set her on her path. The doll she made, following the plans, a lady, was one of the three blue ribbon winners. Her second, a miniature-scaled portrait of her daughter, dressed as the child in the Copley Family Portrait by Jonathan Singleton Copley, pointed the direction her future efforts would take.

Pat began making life-like wooden portraits of children. Show appearances and word-of-mouth spread her reputation, and she found herself flooded with orders.

Early Brooks' dolls were pouty-faced, until Pat's daughter, Stephanie, asked why they were so sad. From that day, the doll maker has striven to put joy, wonder and animation into her work. This animation is so convincing, people often ask if photos of the dolls are of living people.

Like real people, they are named after they are born, and the names usually fit them. However, one doll has an incongruent name, and a tenuous address.

"The only doll I've made in wood that is not listed on my catalog is one I made in the Spring of 1978, which I now refer to as *Trash Can Annie*. But she was not a "trashy" doll. She was beautiful, and I spent more than 120 hours making her. She ws a portrait doll of my great-grandmother, Anna Maria King Okey, great-granddaughter of Captain Philip Gidley King, third Governor of New South Wales. It was done from a photo of her taken in 1869, when she was 23 years old.

"Two days after I finished her she was accidentally thrown into the trash and is now buried somewhere in a dump in Santa Clara County, California. This mishap occurred because I did not have a box the right size to put her in. I stood her up in a brown grocery bag, all wrapped up with tissue paper. She was mistaken for a bag of trash and was taken out with the garbage!

"When I discovered what had happened, I cried and cried and cried. My daughter, Katie, was not quite four years old then and used to play in the courtyard in front of our house. That day she hung on the iron gate and told everyone who walked by that her mommy was crying because 'Daddy threw her dolly in the trash.'"

Both adult and child dolls are dressed in "real" clothing, which is removable, has facings, linings, snaps, buttons and whatever is necessary to achieve the proper look.

Children are most-requested, and form the greatest part of Pat's output. "My first dolls were adult, fashion ladies, but very early in my doll making career I discovered that I preferred to do children. Luckily for me, dolls of children sell very well. I still enjoy doing adult figures, but they are character dolls. More than 90% of the dolls I've made have been children, both girls and boys."

She averages about three dolls a month. They are done in comfortable-to-work-on sizes. Because of her medium, each doll is "from scratch."

"Of the three dozen or so dolls I make every year," Pat says, "every one is a one-of-a-kind doll and starts out with a block of wood. Some of them are limited series dolls that are costumed like previous dolls, but that is the only shortcut. Each doll I make is a brand new work of art."

For each doll she designs, she sculpts two. One is done with additive sculpting, the other with subtractive.

"Most often, before I carve a doll in wood, I make a preliminary model from Sculpey," Brooks states. "I always do this in the case of

ABOVE: *Gepetto*, 20in (50.8cm) tall, and *Pinocchio* by Patricia Ryan Brooks. © 1981. Carved basswood. *Collection of artist. Photograph by and courtesy of Pat Brooks.*

RIGHT: Close-up of *Pinocchio*, 7in (17.8cm) tall by Patricia Ryan Brooks. One-of-a-kind carved basswood miniature marionette. Carved head, hands and lower legs. Felt body. Carved-on hair and shoes. Fully strung and working marionette dressed in white cotton shirt, green suede cloth shorts with red suspenders, green felt hat. *Collection of artist. Photograph by and courtesy of Pat Brooks.*

a portrait doll or a doll that is doing something with its hands. *Geppetto's* hands had to be just right to hold the mechanism for the marionette, so I did him first in Sculpey and then had a good three-dimensional reference to carve from."

Pat often sees dolls in her head months before she makes them. Once she gets down to work, she uses detailed procedures.

"My dolls are planned on paper like blueprints and carved again and again in my mind until they seem just right, and then I make them. Mental practice is just as beneficial as the actual carving because it is the mind that guides the hands. In my case, my heart gets into the act, too! When an idea for a doll strikes me, I at least write it down, but usually I make a quick sketch and file it for later use. The ideas come much more quickly than I am able to produce the dolls. When I decide to make one of those ideas, I start creating the whole thing in my head, detail by detail, begin collecting the appropriate fabrics and materials for the accessories, and, generally get it all 'together'."

Pat works in a 12ft (3.65m) by 23ft (7.01m) room, which she describes as "organized clutter," filled with books, labeled boxes, fabrics, supplies, a sewing machine and sculpting tools -- the best she can find.

"Taking an early tip from my father, I have never skimped on tools and materials and buy the best quality. They last longer and will do a better job. My carving tools include knives, miniature gouges, surgical scalpels, X-acto® knives, wood rasps, and micro-mini files that are nearly 50 years old. I also have a wall-mounted Foredom miniature power tool with a handpiece that accepts everything from jewelers' drill bits to 3/16in (0.45cm) shaft grinders. I use this for detail sanding and finishing, but still do hour upon hour of hand sanding on everything."

When the clay sculptures are done, they are "filed" in her "reference department" for future use.

Brooks' dolls sport a number of body types. Pat describes her method of construction.

"Wire armature bodies are constructed of 14 gauge (18 gauge on miniatures) copper wire, wrapped with strips of resinated quilt batting. When it has been wrapped to the proper shape, the body is covered with a light t-shirt knit fabric, stretched skin tight and hand-sewn in place. Dolls that do not have stationary shoulder-heads have swivel heads."

Pat has tried other materials, but always goes back to wood.

"For a time I experimented with other media. I met NIADA artist Dewees Cochran and tried Vultex and I made a few finished dolls of Sculpey and Super Sculpey. In the fall of 1979 I signed up for a class in porcelain doll making that NIADA artist Jan Riggs was teaching. I entered the class with every confidence that I would do well, but my heart belonged to wood and I met with total frustration.

"Jan suggested that perhaps I just wasn't cut out for porcelain and I strongly resented it. I learned two valuable lessons from her class. First, that she was right, and second, how to make a very good mold. With porcelain out of my system, I made my biggest strides in wood in the year that followed and she urged me to apply to NIADA."

NIADA, the National Institute of American Doll Artists, accepts very few applicants, but Pat was chosen on her first try. One of the dolls submitted to the selection committee was her portrait of her father as *Geppetto*. While the NIADA board, and all her fellow doll artists, including the co-authors of this book, went crazy about the doll, he still was not fully understood or appreciated by collectors.

"The first time I exhibited *Gepetto* at the NIADA exhibit at the UFDC National Convention in St. Louis, he made quite a stir. One woman spent quite a long time looking at him and the four other wooden dolls I had on my table and then said, 'Do you make your own molds?' "

She does, and has begun series of dolls in latex composition. Chiefly, though, Pat experiments in wood.

When asked about this aspect of her work, she replied, "Experiments that failed? Are you kidding? As most people know, woodcarving is PERMANENT. Once a piece of wood has been cut off, it is gone forever. I just pretend I meant it to be that way and make it a smaller doll! A mistake is NOT a failure. As Thomas Edison once said, 'An attempt discarded is a step forward.' A mistake is

Katharine Hepburn, 19½in (49.6cm) tall by Patricia Ryan Brooks. © 1983. Carved basswood. Auburn human hair wig. Carved-on shoes with attached ornaments. Ivory voile blouse, black gabardine skirt, all-in-one "combinations" underwear, 4mm cultured pearl earrings. *Photograph by and courtesy of Patricia Brooks.*

always a success because one successfully finds out what will not work!"

Pat's dolls are primarily sold at shows. The orders she does fill are taken at such events. Dolls are marked variously, but always permanently and indelibly. Her customers are not only doll collectors but art collectors as well, and she is very proud of this fact.

"I consider my dolls art -- clothed sculptures -- and it is gratifying to have a few of my dolls in 'art collections,' rather than 'doll collections'."

Perhaps Patricia Ryan Brooks' dolls do not speak -- yet. But they do the next best thing; they allow her to express herself to the fullest. She puts it this way.

"Doll making gives me an opportunity to draw on most all of my art study and interests, utilizing sculpture, carving, sewing and designing, silversmithing, etc. I cannot think of any other one type of art where I could get to do it ALL."

ABOVE LEFT: *Red Riding Hood*, 15in (38.1cm) tall by Patricia Ryan Brooks. © 1983. Carved head, arms and legs. Wire armature body. Brown human hair wig. Black cotton floral print dress, ivory voile pinafore, cherry red acrylic fleece hooded cape with green grosgrain ribbon ties. Carved-on shoes. *Photograph by Jim Brooks, courtesy of Pat Brooks.*

BELOW LEFT: *Mary Lindsay*, 12in (30.5cm) tall by Patricia Brooks. © 1983. Carved basswood one-of-a-kind portrait doll of Mary Lindsay Miller at age two. Carved head, arms and legs. Wire armature body. Carved-on shoes. Dark blue painted eyes. Blended blonde English mohair wig. Doll stands next to miniature wicker chair with pink gingham cushion (chair by Cathryn-Marge Paul). Fleece fabric Teddy Bear and wrapped "present" on the seat of the chair. *Collection of Mr. and Mrs. Paul Felix Miller II, Raleigh, North Carolina. Photograph by Jim Brooks, courtesy of Pat Brooks.*

BELOW: *April*, 9in (22.9cm) tall by Patricia Ryan Brooks. © 1982. Carved basswood head and lower arms, polyester/wool jersey body. Blonde human hair wig with silk flower wreath in hair. Blue eyes. One-of-a-kind "Babes in Wood Character Child." Dressed in pink voile dress with lace and embroidery trim; matching panties. Lace-trimmed socks; pink leather shoes. *April* holds a 2½in (6.4cm) rag doll with needlesculpted face. "1982, Patricia Ryan Brooks, NIADA Certified" incised on head. "NIADA CERTIFIED DOLL" cloth label on body. Clothing labeled: "PATRICIA RYAN BROOKS." *Collection of Glenda Charkey, Fort Collins, Colorado. Photograph by Jim Brooks, courtesy of Pat Brooks.*

ABOVE RIGHT: *Little Lord Fauntleroy*, 14½in (36.9cm) tall by Patricia Ryan Brooks. © 1982. Doll No. 1 of limited series of three. Carved basswood shoulder head, arms and legs. Carved-on shoes. Wire armature body. Blonde shoulder length human hair. Blue eyes. Carved basswood stick pony with black mohair mane and red ribbon bridle. Doll dressed in blue-green velveteen suit with antique French lace collar and cuffs. Shoes have applied leather straps and buckles. "#1 of 3, Patricia Ryan Brooks, NIADA Certified" incised on shoulders. "NIADA CERTIFIED DOLL" cloth label on body. Clothing labeled: "PATRICIA RYAN BROOKS." *Collection of Kathleen Prunner, Arlington, Virginia. This was the first character in the artist's "Children in Literature Series." Photograph by and courtesy of Patricia Brooks.*

BELOW RIGHT: Close-up of *Tad* (companion to *Melissa*) by Patricia Ryan Brooks. *Photograph by Jim Brooks, courtesy of Pat Brooks.*

BELOW: Close-up of *Melissa* (companion to *Tad*) by Patricia Ryan Brooks. *Photograph by Jim Brooks, courtesy of Pat Brooks.*

kenneth von essen

At the International Convention of Original Doll Artists and Antique Doll Collectors held in Chicago, Illinois, in April 1984, one doll stole the show. A lifelike, nearly life-size fully-articulated lady doll won first place, best in category (originals) and best in show.

Kenneth von Essen, its creator, an optical systems engineer by profession, started sculpting about 1970. Initially self-taught, he became acquainted with the world-famous sculptor Rudolph Vargas of Los Angeles, California, and by 1984, had studied with him for a decade.

"I attempt to produce the realistic form of the human body in all of my sculptures," he says. "This desire for realism is transferred to my dolls' hands, feet, heads, proportions, etc."

He succeeds so well in his quest that von Essen dolls are almost unsettling to meet "eye to eye." They appear to be three-quarters human height and have such well-proportioned, naturally-positioned parts that they look a bit like Alice must have when she was experimenting underground with labeled foodstuffs. There is something too real, and not quite "dolly" about his work.

Definitely it is sculpture: masterfully-designed, expertly carved. The expressions on the faces of the figures are those of thinking beings, dreamers perhaps. The hands are as expressive as the inset glass eyes: graceful, fluid. They do things.

These are creatures from another reality, perhaps -- from a world of memory, of dreams, dressed in garments of bygone or half-imagined eras. A fairy dressed in pale peach tulle boasts carved wooden wings tinted with several delicate shades of lavender. Her Rossettiesque curls cascade past her shoulders as she raises her hand in greeting -- or is it in warning?

Of all von Essen dolls, she is the most doll-like. Perhaps it is because one seldom sees large winged fairies in the park nowadays, one tends to think of them as dolls. Intellectually, one must categorize these wonderful ladies as dolls, because they are constructed like dolls, with superb jointing, and they are intended as an artistic statement to be dolls.

Perhaps it is because their artistic statement is so strong, so well-wrought, that it is difficult to relate to them on the "dolly" level. They cannot be cuddled or easily dressed. Their proportions are excellent and do not take the liberties that are characteristic of many doll makers; no exaggeration or caricature comes through. Only beauty.

A von Essen doll is a challenge to the doll art historian. She refuses categorization. And she will never sit well on a collector's shelf. Made for public display, never-manikin-sized, but doll-conceived, she fits one niche nicely. She is fine sculpture, a superb example of the height to which doll artistry can climb.

Large-sized hand-carved fully-jointed wooden peasant lady doll by Kenneth von Essen. Painted features; inset glass eyes; human hair wig. *Photograph courtesy of Kenneth von Essen.*

Large-sized hand-carved fully-jointed wooden lady doll by Kenneth von Essen. This is the doll that won the armful of prizes in Chicago in April 1984. *Photograph courtesy of Kenneth von Essen.*

Articulated hand-carved wooden doll by Kenneth von Essen. Inset glass eyes; painted features. Costume of pale peach tulle. Wings are carved wood that has been tinted with several delicate shades of lavender. *Photograph courtesy of Kenneth von Essen.*

Articulated hand-carved wooden ballerina by Kenneth von Essen. Painted features; human hair wig; inset glass eyes. The shoes are carved onto the feet. *Photograph courtesy of Kenneth von Essen.*

ſuſan wakeen

"When I was a little girl," Susan Wakeen remembers, "I used to collect colored stones. For some reason I just loved them; I'm still not sure why. Each one was like a little treasure to me (I still have them somewhere). Once in a while I find a doll that makes me feel that way and I just buy it. That is how I would like someone to feel about a doll that I made."

Now a doll artist, Susan came to her profession through a circuitous route.

When she was younger, she wanted to study art, but, with four children simultaneously attending college, only one, her identical twin, Sandy, went to art school. Susan studied psychology, studied art whenever she could and ended up teaching special education at the Gaebler Children's Center in Waltham, Massachussets.

She took sculpting, portraiture, painting and illustration at the Art Institute of Boston, the New England School of Art and Design, The Graham Art Studio and Studio 39 in Brookline, Massachusetts.

"I have always been fond of dolls," Susan says. "I love my *Barbie* doll. I made my own clothes for it." It, therefore, was logical that her artistic investigations included, in 1981, a class in doll making.

"I knew right away I wanted to try it," she said of her art in 1985. "I love children, the ballet and portraiture. This is a way to combine all three. I started with reproduction dolls, but quickly began to believe that the future, if I was to have one, was in originals. Right away I wanted to try to combine my experience in portraiture with dolls and about three years ago I sculpted my first portrait. The biggest change in my work that I notice is dimension. I now am comfortable with a third dimension (depth). I was used to painting in two dimensions on a flat surface and for a short time I think that carried over to my first dolls."

Early Wakeen dolls were prettily dressed children, but, in 1984, she decided to concentrate on ballet dancers, calling her troupe, The "Littlest" Ballet Company." "I like to watch ballet dancers in rehearsal," she explains. "Also, I wanted to do something different from just an attractive child doll. I wanted my dolls to stand out, and, besides, most people know or have had a young girl who's attended dancing school. It makes people remember my work."

Susan's dolls, which stand approximately 16in (40.6cm) tall, are all-porcelain and fully-jointed. Portraits or composites of real children, they are done in a workshop-studio setting from her originals. She supervises a crew of five, works seven days (90 hours) a week at her work, in a studio consisting of three rooms. One small room is for sanding, one is for pouring and storing greenware and a third is used for sculpting, painting and teaching doll making.

"I love what I am doing and am committed and determined to be successful," she says. "I think I have been blessed with a certain patience and willingness to persevere. When you combine art with business, there is always a deadline to meet and working seven days a week is sometimes a strain. Family and friends don't always understand the commitment so sometimes I feel a little selfish about neglecting them. My desire to create is really deeply rooted and strong."

This commitment comes out in her attention to detail in her dolls. "I have been told that I am very protective of them, and maybe in a way I feel that I give each one the best part of who I am inside. And I really care how each one turns out. To me, sculpting is only a part of what I do, maybe the part I love best. But after sculpting comes mold making (an art in itself), designing the clothing and painting of the different body parts, not to mention the process of making the doll."

Her favorite doll is *Patty*, a portrait of her niece. "To me, she portrays the essence of youth and innocence," Susan says. She admires the work of Dewees Cochran, who also created animated doll-children.

Susan's dolls have lively faces and their bodies balance and pose nicely. It is hard to restrain one's self from reaching out and picking one up to play with it. With them, she is reaching out to her audience, in much the same way as a little ballet dancer does on stage.

"I guess I would like my dolls to be noticed by people of all ages and that people might see something, however small, of themselves -- past, present or future -- in them. Unfortunately, because they are made of a delicate material and are expensive compared to toy dolls, they are usually bought by collectors (adults)."

Since most of her time is spent in production, and her dolls are designed to reach a specialized audience, Susan does not sell her dolls directly; usually she works through her agent, Thomas Boland. Once in a while, though, she shows her work herself to selected shop buyers. Artists, by and large, are so involved in their work and deadlines, it is often better, however, that someone else does the selling. Susan recounts one such episode.

"I showed my dolls to the buyer at F.A.O. Schwarz in New York and, in the middle of the presentation, the buyer, after saying she liked the dolls very much, asked whether the quality would be consistent order to order.

Susan Wakeen sculpting a portrait of Abby Lynn. 1985. Note the turntable, sculpting tools and reference photographs, also the doll parts on the shelf at right. *Photograph courtesy of Susan Wakeen.*

ABOVE: *Patty* by Susan Wakeen. 1984. 15½in (39.4cm) tall. All-porcelain, jointed doll with glass blue eyes; brunette wig; black leotard; white tights; pink leg warmers and ballet shoes; white "pearl" choker. This doll, a portrait of the artist's niece, is her favorite. *Photograph courtesy of Susan Wakeen.*

BELOW: Close-up of *Patty* by Susan Wakeen. *Photograph courtesy of Susan Wakeen.*

"Well, I had just finished the new line and was rushed to get these samples ready for the presentation so I took some shortcuts --like gluing the pompons on the front of a clown costume. Just as the words were coming out of my mouth that, or course, I could consistently produce quality dolls, the buyer just touched one of the pompons. It dropped into her lap.

"Fortunately, she understood and believed me when I explained that they were usually sewn on, and I got the order."

Susan plans on changing her line at least every two years, with a limited production of each doll. A list of her work from 1982 to 1985 follows.

Abbey-Lynn. 1982. 10 made. 17in (43.2cm) tall. No longer available.

Joy (oriental). 1982. 25 made. 17in (43.2cm) tall. No longer available.

Le Ann. 1982-83. 14in (35.6cm).

Michael and *Michelle*. 1983-84. 11in (27.9cm) tall. 75 sets made.

Kristen (portrait). 1983. 14in (35.6cm) tall. 175 pieces.

Darlene (one-of-a-kind portrait). 1984. 15in (38.1cm) tall.

Patty. 1984-85. Dancer in leotard. 15½in (41.9cm) tall. Edition of 375 pieces.

Sandy. 1984-85. Clown. 15½in (41.9cm) tall. Edition of 375 pieces.

Susan is not done with her studies. "I want to continue to study portrait sculpture and apply it with the hope of being recognized as an important sculptress of ballet dolls," she says.

Although she had to scramble for her art training, Susan Wakeen is pleased with the direction it has taken her. For Susan, doll making touches a special part of her.

"The doll doesn't have to do anything," she explains, "and my feeling of accomplishment for any design or doll is just that, a feeling. It doesn't come to me in words. And when I do have that feeling, it may come to me at any point along the process."

With her work, she hopes to spread that feeling to the doll-collecting public.

ABOVE: *Sandy* by Susan Wakeen, 15½in (39.4cm) tall. 1984. All-porcelain doll with glass eyes; blonde wig; lavender and blue "clown" dancing suit with hat; white tights; ballet shoes. *Photograph courtesy of Susan Wakeen.*

ABOVE RIGHT: *Maxfield* by Susan Wakeen. 1984. 15½in (39.4cm) tall. All-porcelain doll with glass eyes; brown wig; cranberry and white satin jester dance costume; white tights; ballet slippers. *Photograph courtesy of Susan Wakeen.*

LEFT: Close-up of *Sandy* by Susan Wakeen. *Photograph courtesy of Susan Wakeen.*

RIGHT: Close-up of *Jeanne* by Susan Wakeen. *Photograph courtesy of Susan Wakeen.*

ABOVE: *Cynthia* by Susan Wakeen. 15½in (39.4cm) tall. All-porcelain doll with glass eyes; blonde wig; pink tutu and hat; tights; ballet shoes. *Photograph courtesy of Susan Wakeen.*

ABOVE LEFT: *Jeanne* by Susan Wakeen. 1984. 15½in (39.4cm) tall. All-porcelain doll with glass eyes; blonde wig; white sequin-trimmed tutu and tights; white ballet shoes. "Pearl" choker. *Photograph courtesy of Susan Wakeen.*

cathleen o'rork

"O'Rork Originals" combine classic materials and contemporary skills to produce a marriage of reality and fantasy. Porcelain dolls created by Tennessee artist Cathleen O'Rork, these largely one-of-a-kind sculptures explore illusory worlds: the worlds of Faerie and the theater. "My dolls," she says, "are a composition in silk and porcelain and paint. I consider my dolls art; certainly, sculpture. Not playthings: collectors' items."

Her first dolls, created in 1983, were fairies. 12½in (31.8cm) or 15in (38.1cm) tall, they boast wings with 15in (38.1cm) and 25in (63.5cm) wing spans, respectively. The wings, which set her dolls immediately apart, were a nightmare to develop. A combination of air-brushed silk and soldered, multi-coated hand-enameled wire, they emerge from an implant inside the doll's breast plate.

Early dolls were done in editions, from molds made by Keith Kane, husband of well-known doll artist Magge Head Kane. Catherine's only formal doll making training was a week's study with Magge. She terms herself "self-taught;" her professional training is in nursing, to the chagrin of her high school art teacher, who encouraged Catherine to follow a career in commercial art and fashion design. The dolls brought both together.

"A lot of people thought the nursing and the artistic ability were incompatible, but, to me, it seemed very compatible. The nursing has helped me tremendously. The anatomy, attention to detail and observation powers obtained from nursing have certainly helped me in the art."

She has worked in other media, but prefers clay.

"I do paint, and I draw; I do some block printing," she says. "But I enjoy the dolls because they're not an abstract art form. When you are painting, you are representing the three dimensional art object on a two-dimensional surface. When you are doing sculpture, it's reality. It has to look good from every angle.

"I really like to get my hands in the clay. I enjoy the texture of it. I enjoy the catharsis, and the purging of it; that is difficult to explain."

Working alone, Catherine developed her own ways of working with porcelain. She is known for her one-of-a-kind dolls, sculpted from solidified porcelain slip. Early on in her career, she decided that editions of dolls were artistically stultifying.

"I learned to sculpt in the porcelain slip so that I could continue to create on a daily basis," she says. "It gives me a chance to sculpt continuously, whereas if I do limited editions, I have to wait for a mold to be made and there's such an interruption in the creative flow. I want to create each time, and I have a real hard time doing anything twice the same way. I just found a need to do each one differently. And that's how I developed the process of the one-of-a-kinds."

The difficulties inherent in porcelain work challenge her; clay work brought her to doll making.

"It was the clay, itself, that held fascination for me, particularly the porcelain. Porcelain is not forgiving. It is not patient. But it's very plastic in appeal and I like the way it looks. So I'm willing to pay the price that it takes in order to do it. I'm really glad that I didn't have any formal instruction in doll making simply because I think I would have been told not to do a lot of things that I do. I sculpt in the porcelain slip when it's solidified, and a lot of people have told me you can't do that. Of course, I didn't know that you weren't supposed to be able to do it, so I just did it."

She describes her procedures.

"I pour the doll, and then I blank the features. I just take my palette knife or my hands and wipe the features off. It looks quite brutal. The first time I did it, I scared myself to death.

"Then I recreate the face. I change the shape. Sometimes I change the angles of the neck, the hands, or redo the entire doll each time. Only in this way is it something that pleases me. It can be a total creation each time.

"I work on, usually, two dolls at a time. I take them through different stages. I will sculpt two at the same time, working from one to the other because the porcelain slip is sometimes too wet and you have to stop and let it solidify and get a little harder. And then I go to the next one and work on it, until the stage where they're dry. Then I start on another two sculptures.

"The heads are cut open and eyes are hand-rolled, and the heads are put back together. The mouths are done the same way. The teeth are set inside in the wet state as the eyes are. The porcelain has to be very thick to do this and a Ziplock plastic bag is one of the main things you have to use.

"Sculpting with the solidified porcelain slip is very tricky. The failure rate is quite high.

"Sometimes it cracks so that you have to do it very, very carefully, and it must be fired very carefully or it cracks.

"I do heads in pairs, and kind of get them going in waves. I don't fire a massive amount in my kiln, not any more than four to six. I find that, when I do that, accidents happen.

"I hand-paint the eyes so I can get the colors to match the outfits, particularly with the clowns. I do the doll as a composition, and I like the costumes of the clowns and the color of the eyes and the color of the clown makeup to all complement each other. You

ABOVE LEFT: *Darcy* by Cathleen O'Rork. A sleepy pink porcelain child or baby clown dressed in pastel pink and aqua. Human hair; aqua eyes; blond hair. She sucks her thumb. One-of-a-kind. *Photograph by Becky Hall, courtesy of Cathleen O'Rork.*

ABOVE: *Sugar* by Cathleen O'Rork. A child jester dressed in pink china silk with marabou collar and imported blue beads. Cathleen's daughter, Tara, was the inspiration for this doll, one of the artist's favorites. Set in teeth and eyes. Done in pure parian porcelain. 15in (38.1cm) tall, but sitting. *Photograph by Becky Hall, courtesy of Cathleen O'Rork.*

LEFT: *Shanae* by Cathleen O'Rork. A French mime dressed in royal purple silk and satin with rabbit fur trim. 18in (45.7cm) tall, but seated. Set in eyes are shades of violet and purple as is her star burst makeup. Sculpted, glazed set-in teeth. One-of-a-kind. *Photograph by Becky Hall, courtesy of Cathleen O'Rork.*

can't do that with glass eyes. So, I paint them very carefully in colors like sea foam green and amethyst and gold, periwinkle blue, peacock blue. I build up the layers; sometimes it takes seven firings, sometimes as many as twelve. I have one doll I have fired the head 15 times to get just the right look in the eyes.

"The eyes are fluxed, sometimes two, three times to get a real shiny look. The teeth are fluxed. Everything is geared so it looks real."

Catherine strives for a blend of fantasy and reality in her creations. The fairies have very down-to-earth body constructions; the technical difficulties in creating the illusion of ethereality are vast. The dolls must look insubstantial, and yet alive. One solution the artist has found is to employ classic materials in the balance of the piece: leather, silk, real fur and feathers, gold and silver antique jewelry, and to underlie it all with a wire armature.

"After the doll is fired, it's taken to the dressmaker, Bea Goddard, a very talented artist in her own right. She drafts patterns from my sketches, does my designs and puts the body together.

"The fairies have a kid leather body with a double wire armature underneath — 18 gauge wire twisted together for durability. Polyfill is attached to the arms and legs. The leather is put over the wire armature and stuffed. Then the head is sewed to the body on the breast plate.

"The clowns are done a little differently. They have a conal shape button bottom. It's flat on the bottom and looks like a huge button, but it's conal. The wire goes in and out. That is fabric covered and it forms the doll's sitting base. It's a change; the arms and legs are floppy.

"Sometimes, though, the hands are wired so the doll can hold something or change position.

"Bea dresses the dolls. I pick out all the fabric and do the design and she works from my sketches.

"It's always a bit like Christmas Day when I get a doll back from Bea because she sometimes has to translate my designs into the limitations of the fabric. And, even though I have a very definite idea of how I want that doll to look, it always looks just a little different."

Besides the fairies, Catherine makes mimes, clowns and plans to do other fantasy creatures. Recently she has been asked to do quasi-portraits of children as fairies. She refuses to do them, however, as true portraits.

"I have been commissioned to do several portrait dolls, but what I tell my customers is that I will interpret a photograph for them. Most of the time people are very happy with the interpretation. They really like the sculpture. But I do not call them portrait dolls. I reserve the right to be an artist and my interpretation may be different from that of the individual looking at the doll."

Truth be told, most of the dolls are portraits — of members of Catherine's family. She uses family photographs — old and new — not to create portrait dolls, but to ensure that the dolls have lively, realistic expressions, to make them different each time. The early fairies were portraits of her daughters, as are some of the clowns.

"I guess," she states, "if there were anyone who inspired me to make dolls, it would have to be the children. Their photographs were the basis for making the dolls. But everything inspires me. I have a way of translating everything into dolls. Ideas come from everywhere. They come from nature. I'm very much a naturalist and nature is very much part of my designs. They come from photographs of wallpaper, the church windows, slides of pollen, a jewelry design — anything I see I have a tendency to translate into dolls."

Much of what Catherine sees has an aura of fantasy around it, and this fantasy speaks through her attitude as well as in her art work.

"A lot of times I find that the creation is a fantasy. The doll lives in my mind first. It's almost like giving birth. The fantasy, that creation your mind has, is unlimited and the fairies move and the clowns are animated.

"But the clay itself, the materials are themselves limited. So to bring that fantasy to reality is the trick.

"In a way my dolls are real; in a way they are fantasy.

"I think of them as creatures with kind of a special life of their own. Sometimes I think that, when I've walked into the room, I can almost notice that an expression changes — sometimes with different angles, the way the dolls are. Sometimes they look sadder, or happier and sometimes I notice, especially when I look in their eyes, something I didn't notice before.

"Sometimes I find myself talking to them. I get quite attached to, especially, the one-of-a-kind. I think of them as being my creations. My special little creatures.

"Fantasy is one of the things that makes reality easier to bear and makes it worthwhile. I think it's a blend of those two things —the fantasy and the reality, or a real fantasy — that makes my dolls work. They are fantasy subjects, but they are done very realistically. The marriage of those two things is the hallmark of O'Rork Originals."

Overcoming some of the technical difficulties in bringing fantasy to life led to another sort of marriage.

"The wings on the fairies were a great problem. We wanted them to look very large and light and gossamer, but they had to be sturdy so they would last.

"It took two years and many different people in different fields to finally come up with something that would work.

"Last January (1984), Lewis Beckendorf and I started working on the dolls together. I had gone out to speak with his father, who is in the plastics business. My dressmaker suggested I see him.

"We had been working for six months or so on impregnating silk with different glues and plastics and all kinds of stiffening, whipping the silk on a wire frame and trying very hard to get a satisfactory wing that would give us a very airy look, yet be something sturdy and butterfly-like.

"It took Lewis and me from January to April. It was only a week and a half before the Chicago doll artist show, my first show, that we actually came up with the soldered wire armature.

"There's an implant inside the breast plate. All of it's hand-machined and it's a very complicated process. I think the key part is that, out of all of that, and all the work, a relationship that started as a business one — like a fairy tale — has ended in a permanent relationship, with our marriage this January (1985) 19th.

"At my wedding, I'm going to decorate with my dolls, because they are such a part of the two of us together."

Cathleen's work is changing; she is new to the field and is bursting with plans and ideas — baby dolls, fashion dolls, creatures of dreams, but, mostly, creatures of imagination.

"I'm very excited about my work," she says. "It means being myself. I try to put my emotion into the dolls' faces, into their costumes. I want the dolls to have soul, to have feeling. In that way, they are real as well as fantasy."

Dolls have made Catherine O'Rork's life a real life fairy tale.

RIGHT: *Echelle*, 15in (38.1cm) sitting French mime. Face painted in mauves, pinks, burgundy and grays. Eyes are burgundy brown. Dressed in mauve silk satin with lace collar trimmed in antique costume pearls. She wears a turban of antique silk ribbon. Bare footed. One-of-a-kind. *Photograph by Becky Hall, courtesy of Cathleen O'Rork.*

BELOW: *Toby* and *Charity* by Cathleen O'Rork. *Toby*, 12½in (31.8cm) tall one-of-a-kind singing angel with red human hair; aqua eyes and open mouth with white set-in porcelain teeth. Inside of mouth is anatomically correct, all-porcelain. Dressed in white china silk with china silk wings; velvet pants; lace and pearl trim. *Charity*, 12½in (31.8cm) tall singing angel with honey blonde human hair; blue eyes; open mouth done in porcelain. White china silk dress, slip, panties, trimmed in lace and pearls. Bare feet. Hinged silk wings. One-of-a-kind. *Photograph by Becky Hall, courtesy of Cathleen O'Rork.*

BELOW RIGHT: *Victory*, a not-so-nice one-of-a-kind 15½in (39.4cm) tall fairy by Cathleen O'Rork. 1984. Dressed in full leaf costume air-brushed in yellows, reds, oranges and greens. Wings are orange Victory Butterfly design. Gold eyes. Inspired by comment John Noble made in Chicago, Illinois, April 6, 1984. *Photograph by Becky Hall, courtesy of Cathleen O'Rork.*

RIGHT: *Lacy*, a 12½in (31.8cm) tall fairy. Leather body; silk wings; aqua dress; brown eyes; blonde hair. Inspired by photos of Cathleen's daughter, Shanae, at age 7. Posable body and hinged wings. *Photograph by Becky Hall, courtesy of Cathleen O'Rork.*

BELOW: *Aisling the Ice Fairy* by Cathleen O'Rork. The name means ''fairy dream.'' 16in (40.6cm) porcelain breast plate doll with flesh fabric and wire body. Artist-designed two-piece cape dress of silk chiffon with gold and silver threads trimmed in marabou feathers sewn on one at a time. Blonde human hair; blue hand-painted eyes. One-of-a-kind. No shoes — this is a trademark. *Photograph by Becky Hall, courtesy of Cathleen O'Rork.*

BELOW RIGHT: Close-up of *Aisling the Ice Fairy*. White porcelain set-in eyes and set-in hand-sculpted teeth, glazed for shine. Blue eyes multi-fired. *Photograph by Becky Hall, courtesy of Cathleen O'Rork.*

ruth ann eckersley

Ruth Ann Eckersley may never produce a warehouse full of original dolls but this does not trouble her. She aims for each of her creations to be a work of art.

Threads of art have woven through her life since childhood, when she studied at the Baltimore Museum of Art. One of her paintings, done at age ten, remains in its collection. She dabbled in many media and, in high school, won a five-year tuition scholarship to art school, which she turned down in favor of nurse's training. "I was far more interested in drawing anatomy for my physiology classes than I was in acquiring skill in O.R. procedure, injections or post-mortem care," she admits.

No one art form satisfied her until, in 1979, she stumbled onto porcelain reproductions, while seeking replacement limbs for a relative's antique doll.

"It was instant intrigue for me and I signed up for a class. In a very short time I was so frustrated with the driving and inability to concentrate and curiosity about pouring, firing, etc. that I went to the bank and got a small loan, bought a kiln, supplies, books and some molds and began by trial, error, experimenting, reading, note-keeping and perseverance to make reproductions, then on to adaptations, and, originals."

Omnivoracious in her doll-related reading, Ruth Ann digested erudite tomes on china repair, and any and everything touching upon her new area of interest. She pushed the clay to its extremes, winning honors with her work from the start. Her originals were daring, combining arcane procedures, mixtures of clays and sophisticated themes.

She describes her methods.

"I tend to use a lot of combined techniques with porcelain on a doll. A single doll may be cast of white with all flesh coloring pounced, or it may be cast of mixed porcelains or double cast with different colors with a combination of bisque surface, glazed surface, draped surface and "sand" surface.

"I often add plasticized porcelain ornamentation to greenware after casting, both for the fun of it and to inhibit the future chances of someone feeling tempted to make molds of my work.

"I am interested in playing around with the use of glass, fiberglass resin, wood, and silver, gold and semi-precious stones for jewelry and other accessories."

Ruth Ann approaches her art with great seriousness and chooses subject matter after extensive research. Her dolls have an introspective beauty, an almost melancholy regal quality -- never frivolity. They are not toys.

"Dolls may be 'people' to others and dolls may be likenesses of people," she says, "but when I have finished researching a subject for a doll I have, figuratively speaking, 'been there' in that place or time and acquired a mini-education. It is like having taken a brief trip into that place or person's life. Therefore, the finished doll is more like an experience, a very personal experience!

"When I made *The Daughter of King Midas*, I checked out 12 books on mythology, and two books on medieval and ancient instruments -- 14 books, and I read them all!"

The Daughter of King Midas is a good example of Ruth Ann's work. A character from mythology (Ruth Ann does not do portraiture of living beings, preferring ideal types), King Midas' daughter is portrayed as both the "living child," in flesh tones, and after her father had touched her, "turned to gold." The latter doll, done in gold-hued porcelain with color-coordinated clothing, disconcerts some collectors, who prefer to see what might be termed "normal" dolls. For Ruth Ann, this work is an artistic statement; it conveys her message and it is beautiful to see, especially in contrast to its twin. She does not much care whether it has universal appeal. Her doll making has taken her beyond the need for positive feedback from the public; she is secure about its excellence.

"My doll work, for me, is an example of Abraham Maslow's theory of motivation," Ruth Ann explains. "There is a heirarchy of needs. They go through stages of development. There are deficit needs: for shelter, protection, etc. The fifth need is for self-actualization.

"This is a level you get to when you're beyond needing to derive your sense of self from others, when you're to a point where you develop self-confidence. A creative person starts to look inward for that. To be a well-rounded person, you have to be creative.

"I believe a person who never reaches that level is a slave to everyone around him; he's always doing for others.

"Doll work satisfies me; it fulfills me. When I'm creating, I'm on a level beyond the need for approval from others. I have total confidence; I do it for myself. Criticism does not threaten me at all. Critics have their own points of view, their own problems."

A gold doll for Ruth Ann is not outrageous. She plans to do one in blue porcelain -- a male dancer. And if no one cares for him, he will still please her; he will still be an aesthetic lesson. It is important that her work teaches.

"Not all, but a lot of the dolls have very didactic intent, not only in the subject matter chosen or expression being conveyed, but, hopefully, in the future; as I improve, my dolls will, in themselves, be

an aid to educating the buying public to cultivate a taste in discretion for quality and creative uniqueness when buying.''

Her public is self-selected.

''My intended audience is whomever is drawn to my particular style of artwork and subject matter. There are varying tastes in doll collecting, as there are to any form of collecting and one can't possibly expect his or her work to be everyone's 'cup of tea.' So, I appeal to whomever I appeal. I want to create dolls that will be an aesthetically stimulating, quality 'visual' experience -- that will help promote doll-creating as a serious art form.''

Ruth Ann's dolls accomplish this. Best seen in person, they combine subtle, sensitive sculpture with daring combinations of porcelain technique. Her subjects are idealized, drawn from history, literature, mythology, paintings and Americana.

She takes great pains to construct props, stands, clothing with as much thought and excellence as the sculpture, but she admits that the latter holds prime interest.

''I enjoy most the planning, designing and making of the doll. Clothing is hardest for me because it means depending on circumstances, some of which are not in my control, like the amount of time that goes into trying to find appropriate fabric or settling for less desirable substitutes and researching appropriate style and underwear.

''Good grief! I don't know where to go for answers to a question like 'What would a Greek Goddess of Mythology wear for underwear?' If you will pardon the mixed metaphor, I don't have a 'green thumb' when it comes to clothing. Some doll artists seem to just throw a little of this with a little of that and the effect is fantastic. I try to do that and it looks as though it will die on me.

''Come to think of it, speaking of undies, a Greek goddess of Mythology, probably didn't!''

Clothing and sculpting, designing and painting, all done with meticulous care, are the signature of Ruth Ann's work. Now that she has found her artistic medium, she works to express a lifetime-worth of images, eschewing redundancy.

''My philosophy is not to repeat any one thing to the point of boredom. If I do something which, through lack of public interest, or extreme boredom, is not likely to reach the filling of the edition, I will 'retire' the edition, maybe take it up at a later time.

''I do not work rapidly. The word 'rapid' is not in my doll related vocabulary.''

This attitude leads to a limited, high-quality output. Ruth Ann Eckersley's goal is not to fill the world up with her dolls, but to make those she does produce reach out.

Her greatest pleasure in her dolls is ''the satisfaction they give others, both in an immediate way and a lasting way, in that if any survive over the years, they may pass from one owner to another, one collection to another, one generation to another, pleasing and touching many people.''

Through the centuries, this has been the traditional goal of the artist.

Tribute to Pioneer Womanhood by Ruth Ann Eckersley. ©1981. Limited to 10. Approximately 16in (40.6cm) tall. Super Sculpey and acrylics. Wire armature; cloth torso. Bare feet; sculpted arms to shoulder. Mohair wig. Ceramic pitcher and bowl, both with blue resin "water." Dressed in cotton, wool and silk blends as Pioneer American. *Photograph courtesy of Ruth Ann Eckersley.*

Side view of *Tribute to Pioneer Womanhood* showing ceramic bowl and pitcher. *Photograph courtesy of Ruth Ann Eckersley.*

mary ann oldenburg

"I love creating children: any kind, any size, any age, any color."

Mary Ann Oldenburg's love for children is evident in her work. The Sheboygan, Wisconsin, doll artist's sculptures burst with life and personality. They embody the freshness of childhood, and veer from sentimentality and sweetness. One expects them to speak.

So does the artist.

"My dolls are real," she admits. "I talk to them. They talk to me. They always have names, right from the original sketch, although in the final product the names may change. They are my children, especially the first one, even if it's a prototype. They are not play dolls, but a form of art, sculpted art.

"When the sculpted head is everything I want, everything else falls right into place. When it's completed, it can't only talk to me, but it must invoke that reaction in others whose opinion I respect."

She expects the same from other doll artists.

"If a doll doesn't talk to me, I've always thought it was because the artist or creator did not put himself into his work. If the heart isn't in the maker, it can't be in the doll."

Mary Ann's dolls have heart. Although she has branched out to some adult figures, children dominate her production. Many of them are portraits of family members, but they reach a universal audience.

"What is my audience? -- The whole world? Why not?" She laughs. "I don't aim for a particular audience. Almost everyone loves children.

"When I do a souvenir doll for a convention and they have specifics, they want a certain kind of doll. Of course, I do what they want. But, in the creation, I still aim for the general audience. I aim for a general reaction that almost everyone will like."

Her children, which include an immigrant, Indian toddlers, babies and older boys and girls range from 6in (15.2cm) to 20in (50.8cm), and generally have porcelain heads and limbs, with soft bodies, sometimes armatured. Other media employed include polyform, sometimes wax-coated, and needlesculpture, but these dolls are personal, given as gifts.

Production dolls have limited editions of from 25 to 35; convention contract work at times reaches the 300 mark, but these dolls are not personally done, for the most part. Mary Ann sculpts the original, and, often her family will fabricate the balance of the project, or it will be done by a ceramics firm.

Several convention souvenir dolls are to Mary Ann's credit, including a Gibson Girl for UFDC Region 2's 1985 Conference. Production on these dolls takes years, sometimes. The Gibson Girl head was designed in 1982. Unlike many dolls with that name, the Oldenburg head seems almost vibrant. The eyes search to communicate with the viewer. She almost breathes.

Many of Mary Ann's dolls bring this reaction, which comes close to her goals.

"Because I create mostly toddlers, young children and babies, I guess I'd want the reaction to be the same as if it were my own child: "May I hold her?" -- you know. Nice and cuddly."

The first Oldenburg dolls appeared in 1973, and were inhabitants for a small-scale housing development. The doll house bug bit her, and she built eight of them, all bereft of inhabitants.

"I started experimenting with different media and ran into the doll world, fell in love with it, and never left it," she says.

A series of "Poem Tots," doll settings made of synthetic clay, illustrating poetry was an early project. Eventually, she studied porcelain doll making and centered her production in this medium.

Clay was an early inspiration to Mary Ann, although she admits to loving baseball far more than dolls as a child.

"When I was young," she says, "I lived only two blocks from Lake Michigan. Our summer days were spent lolling on the beach. There were clay banks near our home and we would dig the clay out and create things from it.

"I remember several baby dolls I made from the clay and let self-harden. Of course, they didn't last, but I remember that very distinctly.

"I also made paper dolls. I loved designing clothes for them. I'd cut figures from catalogues and design clothes for them, too."

Ideas for her dolls come from advertisements, illustrations, photographs, greeting cards and "real live children." She averages 35 or 40 hours a week at her work. "Not that I really want it that way," Mary Ann says, "but snowballs have a way of growing once they're pushed." She tries to complete at least two new dolls per year, and always dreams up new projects to enter into convention competition, because many of her orders derive directly from collectors' reactions to her entries, which always win prizes.

Sometimes the efforts involved in competition are frustrating.

"I did a doll once for competition and everything went wrong," she says. "I put the Sculpey into the oven. I thought I'd let the heat cure it after I turned the oven off. But you don't do that -- it's a no no and it came out charcoal.

"I scraped off as much as I could, filled in the creases and took away the bumps, gave it several coats of gesso, and painted it with several coats of paint. But I rushed the painting and it never dried.

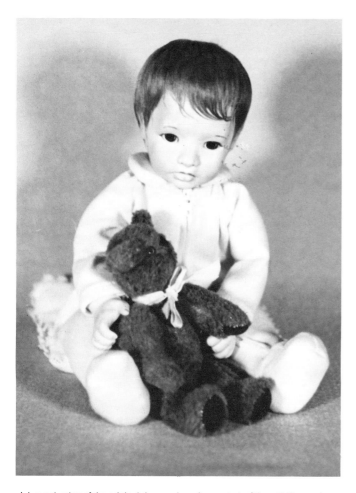

J.J., a reduction of the original *Jeremy Joseph*, a portrait of the artist's grandson, sold in kit form only. This version shows *J.J.* made up and dressed in a diaper, shirt, knit sleeper with blanket and a bear. *Photograph courtesy of Mary Ann Oldenburg.*

"So I had to remove all the paint and start all over again. Finally, I finished. I got it right and I really liked it.

"She was really turning out good, but I thought I would try something different, so I coated her head, arms and legs with several thin wax layers.

"She turned out beautifully. I finished her about 2 o'clock in the morning before we left, and we were leaving like at six.

"I packed her securely in the trunk of the car and forgot her. It turned out to be a heat wave. It was like 96 degrees F. We were in bed in the motel the first night of our trip, and all of a sudden I remembered, 'Oh, my God, the wax and the heat all day. The doll is ruined for certain.'

"I put my robe on, ran out, got her out of the trunk and -- surprise. She was unharmed. She ended up winning second place. I named her *Judith Alexandra*, after St. Jude, who was patron saint of lost causes."

At conventions and seminars, Mary Ann often teaches sculpture and other forms of doll making. She has developed a line of patterns, paper dolls, stuffed animals and Teddy Bears, which are available from her.

These are, however, ancillary to the sculpture. Working in a three-room basement studio, the Wisconsin artist, who trained in commercial art, delights in bringing three-dimensional children to life.

"Doll making is the first art-related activity that has given me complete satisfaction, to my complete, whole being," she explains. "It satisfies every aspect of imagination and creation. From the original concept or dream to the actual creation in clay, the design of the body, the clothes, the accessories, even the mechanical aspects of doll making -- I LOVE IT."

Anna Marie, a souvenir doll made for the 1981 International Dollmaker's Convention by Mary Ann Oldenburg; a limited edition of 300. The doll could be dressed by the owner with the patterns the artist designed (seven different ethnic versions) to match the conference theme of "An Immigrant Child." *Photograph courtesy of Mary Ann Oldenburg.*

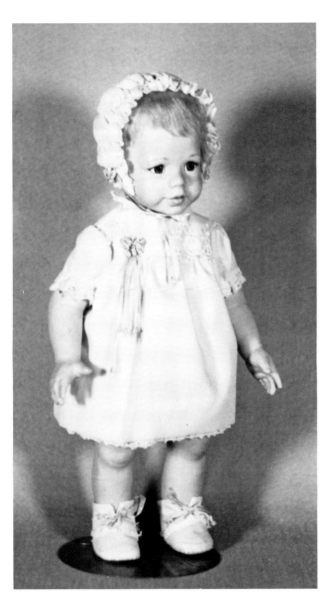

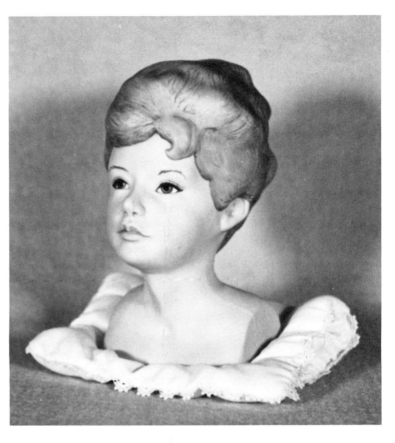

ABOVE: *Jennifer Marie*, a 12in (30.5cm) porcelain child created by Mary Ann Oldenburg as a portrait of her granddaughter at 18 months. *Jennifer Marie* wears a batiste dress and petticoat combination with an eyelet yoke and linen booties. *Photograph courtesy of Mary Ann Oldenburg.*

ABOVE RIGHT: The *Gibson Girl* head by Mary Ann Oldenburg was given as a United Federation of Doll Clubs Regional Conference souvenir in 1985. The head has sculpted and china-painted light brown hair and brown eyes and was produced as an edition limited to 750. Made up, the full figure stands 15in (38.1cm). *Photograph courtesy of Mary Ann Oldenburg.*

RIGHT: *Bré* as "Merry Christmas" by Mary Ann Oldenburg. *Bré* is a limited edition doll with porcelain head and limbs on a cloth body. The artist makes the members of this edition to order as various characters such as "Snow White" and "Cinderella" so that no two are alike. Each head is marked with the artist's initials, date made and copyright symbol. *Photograph courtesy of Mary Ann Oldenburg.*

ABOVE: *Best Friends*, a one-of-a-kind set sculpted of polyform by artist Mary Ann Oldenburg. This pair won a silver medallion at the 1980 International Dollmaker's Competition. *Photograph courtesy of Mary Ann Oldenburg.*

LEFT: *Judith Alexandra*, a one-of-a-kind, wax-over-Sculpey creation by artist Mary Ann Oldenburg. The body is fabric over wire armature and the shoes and stockings are sculpted. The figure wears a white batiste, lace-trimmed dress with blue accents and is seated in her own handmade chair. *Photograph courtesy of Mary Ann Oldenburg.*

debbie anderson

Along the waterfront, in Portsmouth, New Hampshire, Marcy Street snakes its way past Prescott Park. High above the doorway of a quaint old two-story shop, figurehead-like wooden sign of a gift-bearing doll indicates the Marcy Street Doll Company. The doll, whose name is *Molly*, was one of Debbie Anderson's early one-of-a-kind felt artist dolls. She is not available for sale. But Debbie's other work is -- here, and nowhere else.

Debbie's artistic felt children were inspired by a Lenci doll. She traded a hand-knitted sweater for it to her cousin, Ann Barden. "I loved that doll and wanted to make one like it," she admits. Ann, a doll lover, provided her with a copy of Catherine Christopher's book, *Doll Making and Collecting*, which tells how to make a felt doll, and with encouragement.

Debbie experimented and developed her own felt doll-making methods, drawing on an extensive crafts background. "I made dolls in the beginning to earn money to buy a knitting machine," she says. "Now I do it mostly for pleasure and because people want them."

Indeed they do. In 1978, Debbie and Ann combined forces and opened the Marcy Street Doll Company. Debbie designed and made the felt dolls; Ann dressed them. They averaged a doll per week: charming, all-felt toddlers and children with molded faces and sweet, lively, sometimes pouty expressions, hand-painted by Debbie. Her technique for eye painting affords the dolls with a special spark. "I like dolls to be 'alive'," she says. "That is--life in the eyes! I look for good workmanship as well as good design."

The dolls range from 11in (27.9cm) to 21in (53.3cm) tall. Their heads are molded felt, the bodies disc-jointed felt. Most of the children are from two to eight years old. "I love children and couldn't go on having them forever so this somehow compensates," she states.

Debbie describes her doll-making techniques.

"I start by sculpting a mold in air-drying clay. That can take a week or two to get it just right. Then I varnish the mold a number of times to seal the clay. I use at least 50% wool felt and like 80% even better. One-hundred percent wool felt is very expensive. I dye the felt a flesh color.

"When I'm ready to 'try' the mold, I dip felt in starch and coat one side of felt with thick wallpaper paste. I put a thin coat of vaseline on the mold. I also spray lightly with "Pam." Now, I spread the felt on the mold, playing with it and gradually it conforms to the mold. It takes about 24 to 36 hours for the felt to dry completely.

"I paint the features with acrylics.

"I use iron-on interfacing bonded to felt for the body. For stuffing I like cotton. It packs firmer. Also sawdust for body and head.

"I attach limbs with buttons on small dolls and "Teddy Bear" joints for larger dolls.

"The clothes are designed for each doll, coordinating eye and hair color so everything goes together."

Debbie and Ann's collaboration ended several years ago. Now Debbie works alone, creating 30 to 40 dolls a year. "I probably spend about three days on a doll," she says. Debbie makes most everything, except wigs ("the French wigs are so nice," she comments), and some shoes.

The dolls' expressive faces, that seem intelligent, and lost in thought, have to be seen in person to be appreciated. And they have become so much in demand that Debbie finds it difficult to keep up with orders.

Over the years, her dolls have improved tremendously. The early dolls were charming, doll-like. Current dolls seem to have an inherent life to them, as if they are portraits of dream children. But

ABOVE: *Molly* by Debby Anderson. © 1978. Early felt doll with molded face, jointed body, painted features. Auburn French human hair wig. 15in (38.1cm) tall. Dressed by Ann Barden. *Waugh photograph.*

Debbie does few portraits. One of the finest is that of her daughter, Siri. She was commissioned to do a portrait of her daughter's mother-in-law as a child of six. "It was great fun!" she says. But portraits are unusual.

The emotive quality of the dolls is outstanding. "My husband maintains he can tell my mood by the expression on my dolls' faces," she reports. "I must admit the two I have done here on the island have pleased me very much. They look very contented."

In August 1984, Debbie and her family moved from Portsmouth, New Hampshire, where her daughter, Marcie, now runs the Marcy Street Doll Company, on a small island off the coast of Maine. They had never visited a coastal island; it was love at first sight.

Within a month the family bought a house and transferred operations to a spot of land only accessible by occasional ferry. "I moved to have more time to make dolls and be with my kids. I also hope to get into sheep raising on a small scale," she says.

The solitude of the new location seems to bring out the best in Debbie's abilities, as is the case with many artists who work in Maine. She only misses one thing: her Marcy Street studio.

"My work room used to be a delightful room above the shop looking out over the gardens of Prescott Park and the Piscataqua River. Now I'm back at the dining room table in North Haven, Maine."

Anderson dolls, marked with an ironed-on tag on the doll's back, with the doll's name, number, year and Debbie's signature, are sold at only one location, the shop on Marcy Street, Portsmouth, New Hampshire. The original *Molly* no longer lives on Marcy Street; the wooden sign is a silent reminder of her existence. But, every so often, when the roads are good, she makes the 200 mile round trip down to Portsmouth, from her home in Winthrop, Maine.

Close-up of *Marika*. *Photograph courtesy of Debbie Anderson.*

LEFT: *Marika* by Debbie Anderson. One-of-a-kind 13in (33cm) toddler doll. Molded felt; blonde human hair; brown eyes; felt body. 1981. *Photograph courtesy of Debbie Anderson.*

ABOVE: *Baby Elizabeth*, one of Debbie Anderson's first dolls, made circa 1973. Fur hair; blue eyes; pink floral dress; green sweater; booties. One-of-a-kind molded felt. *Photograph courtesy of Debbie Anderson.*

LEFT: Siri Anderson, age five, with her one-of-a-kind molded felt doll, *Siri*, made summer of 1984. 21in (53.3cm). Blonde hair; blue eyes; lavender smocked dress. *Photograph courtesy of Debbie Anderson.*

margaret hickson

Margaret Hickson's dolls are a celebration of color, texture and panache. They knot together the myriad of tangents that led her to doll making.

Educated at the Royal College of Art and Crafts, she studied design, particularly textiles, for seven years. Moving to London, she created original clothing for an exclusive boutique. "Most of the clients were wealthy and connected with film and theater so it was almost a continuation of my art training with plenty of scope for experiment," she notes.

An interest in teaching led her to the "Club of the Three Wise Monkeys," a finishing school for wealthy and aristocratic girls from many countries, where she produced an annual fashion show from the work in her dress design and dress making classes. Because of the students' backgrounds, the clothing was sophisticated and used expensive and exotic materials.

The "club" folded; she helped run a craft workshop in Henley-on-Thames and started making dolls for sale. Made of many substances, "some were just of paper, others of cloth, and many of mixed media." They varied in size and design.

Teaching and doll making continued on parallel paths, one feeding the other. "It was a useful stimulus," she says. "The contact with young people certainly made sure I kept abreast with all the latest crazes and ideas."

The resultant product combines many loves -- a love of color, texture, theatricality, luxurious and rare fabrics, contemporary, up-beat thought and design and a lifelong love of black dolls.

"As a child, black dolls were my favorites," she says. "I suppose it was only natural for me to turn to making them. Dolls have always interested me -- to play with as a child and to make when older. My choice for both has always been for black ones."

Her little people -- and she thinks about them that way -- "I do think of my dolls as people, just as I often see people who would make good dolls" are usually 15 to 20in (38.1 to 50.8cm) tall. They have elongated bodies and stylized faces, and a bright, upbeat air, and breathe fresh air into the concept of the "black doll."

Margaret describes her motives.

"At the moment, I seem to be specializing in black dolls, especially modern ones in theatrical or dancers' costumes. So many dolls are of the old black mammy type but I prefer con-temporary and even futuristic styles. My training and experience combined with my great interest in theater and dance, as well as the love of ethnic and folk arts, obviously affects my choice of subject."

Her subject ranges from disco girls and dancers of all kinds to Southern Belles and mermaids. Hickson's definition of "black" includes Indians, both eastern and western: royally garbed ladies fit for a pasha's harem and squaws with papooses.

Her output is integrated, though, reflecting her personal doll collection. "My collection," she says, "is mainly of ethnic or folk-costumed dolls. I would like to have modern examples but rarely see any! Indian work attracts me as the colors are so beautiful." To limit her own designing to dark-skinned dolls closes out possibilities. "I like to experiment," she says, "so still do not confine myself to just one kind of doll."

Outstanding, surprising color and texture combinations and a command of a lexicon of needleworking techniques are the hallmarks of Hickson dolls. Her "people," obviously, are a labor of love and very absorbing.

"I am just beginning to work full-time making dolls," she explains, but feel I can produce about 20 a year. All are one-of-a-kind. Each doll takes a long time: doing research, searching for the right materials (or making them) and spending hours planning and designing."

The artist appears to delight in all these pursuits. One feels that, if her dolls were not so all-encompassing, so challenging technically, she would not make them.

"Why do I make dolls?" she asks. "Many reasons. They involve so many things: modeling, painting, textile arts such as weaving, embroidery, needlecrafts, all of which have been practiced by me during my training and in my career.

"Above all, one can design and be creative using color, texture and imagination. My dolls are, to me, works of art. I like to be as original as possible with craftsmanship -- as good as I can achieve. If the enjoyment I have when making them shows through, that is very satisfying. If they can attract and look 'different,' so much the better."

Margaret works at home. "I have a work area in my bedroom and share a small studio with a friend." She describes it as "neat before starting, messy while working, but back to neatness at the end of the day! All tools and materials are ready, in place, for resuming work." In these locations she produces almost everything she needs.

"I like to make all accessories, shoes, wigs, etc., though I have used a few items, found or bought, if they are appropriate and objects that would be difficult to make. I have used a tiny printed leather bound book and various small pieces of jewelry."

She describes her doll making procedure:

"I usually prepare sketches and notes and jot down thoughts and ideas all the time.

"My major medium is soft sculpture, but I also have used papier-mâché, clay and mixed media, and hope to use wood so have recently been carving some heads and hands.

"I make a flexible armature which I cover with soft padding and cloth. I make 'real'-removable clothing.

"Hair can be made of anything from hemp, fur, wool, etc. I paint with acrylics as they are so durable. I enjoy all parts of the making but especially the clothes."

A member of the British Doll Association, Margaret regularly shows her work, mainly at museums, and attends doll shows. "It is an ambition to have my own show when I have made enough," she admits. "One needs a large number to really make an impact. But I am working on it!"

The idea of commercial production appeals to the Bournemouth, England, designer, but she feels her current styles are far too detailed. "If there ever was a chance to have a design mass-produced, I would create a simple style for that purpose," she states. Perhaps, though, the streamlining of her dolls would take away their very essence, the mixture of media and rare materials that attract them to a select audience.

Her work, she feels, appeals to the buyer who is open to new artistic concepts, alternative ways of viewing dolls. She describes her patrons as "people with progressive ideas, who are not only looking for reproductions of the past, but are young at heart. If they regard the dolls as artistic creations, I would be really pleased."

BELOW: *Eastern Beauty* by Margaret Hickson, 25in (63.5cm) tall. One-of-a-kind. Hands and head of papier-mâche. Acrylic paint. Hair of wool. Dress of silk, satin, lamé and taffeta. Jewelry of various types -- some from the 1920s. Organza turban. Made in 1983. *Photograph by Betty Lorimar, courtesy of Margaret Hickson.*

ABOVE RIGHT: *Disco Girl* by Margaret Hickson, 30in (76.2cm) tall. © 1984. One-of-a-kind. Head and hands of papier-mâche. Acrylic paint. Body is soft sculpture over wire armature. Beaded velvet leotard. Silver net tights. Silver jacket. Silver material boots. *Photograph by Betty Lorrimar, courtesy of Margaret Hickson.*

RIGHT: *Southern Belle* by Margaret Hickson, 20in (50.8cm) tall. One-of-a-kind. Hair of wool. Body is soft sculpture over wire armature. Head and hands are clay with acrylic paint. Clothing employs antique lace over satin. Hat made of straw with flowers and feathers. Leather shoes. Seed pearl necklace. Removable undergarments. Made in 1983. *Photograph by Betty Lorrimar, courtesy of Margaret Hickson.*

Black girl with baby by Margaret Hickson, 30in (76.2cm) tall. © 1983. One-of-a-kind. Head and hands of papier-mâché. Acrylic paint. Hair of wool. Body is soft sculpture on wire armature. Hand-woven wool apron over woolen skirt trimmed with antique paisley material. Sheepskin jacket over jersey blouse. Brown velvet hat. Brown leather boots. *Photograph by Betty Lorrimar, courtesy of Margaret Hickson.*

moments in time — the portrait figure

Artists who create portrait figures are those who are finely tuned to the individuals and personalities who have shaped and influenced the history of mankind and they find great pleasure in making those people come to life for us in doll form.

To reproduce the figure and facial features, or even a recognizable impression of some one who lives or has lived, is an exceedingly challenging task and in setting that challenge to themselves, portrait artists automatically accept a stricter critical factor. Their work can be, and often is, compared to the existing reality -- the person, other portraits or photographs. With a mission for authenticity, their reconstructions are only begun after extensive research in pictorial archives, biography and works recording the history of fashion. They undertake the execution of extremely exacting detail in sculpture and costuming and the figures that result from their diligence never fail to strike us deeply with their vitality, presence and realism.

They bring life to the dry pages of history. They reacquaint us with our heritage and they teach us gently with the most delightful of examples...the doll.

charlotte zeepvat

"Two things started me on portrait dolls: a love of history and a desire to produce better portraits."

Charlotte Zeepvat's historical portrait dolls attest to her attainment of that goal. Meticulous in detail and exactly in scale, they faithfully reproduce personages of the past and present.

Made of air-hardening clays with wire armatures or of bisque fired earthenware, they are generally 2in (5.1cm) to 1ft (30.5cm) scale, and are intended as "display dolls." "The ceramic dolls could be played with," she says, "but I don't know if anyone does."

The English doll maker has made dolls since she was five but never had art or design training; instead, she read history at University and possesses a M.A. in the subject. This specialized knowledge shows in the treatment she gives her miniature people. A knowledge of historical research techniques is vital to the accurate depiction of personages. And, in Zeepvat dolls, every detail is correct.

The one-of-a-kind portraits are specially ordered and the artist encourages input from clients. "They are often things I wouldn't have thought of," she says. "I welcome this -- it widens the range of subjects I attempt. For myself, I'm usually started off by pictures which capture a particular expression or position, or by a wish to make a portrait of someone who interests me."

Once the concept for the work is settled on, the artist collects reference pictures. "Often a good deal of research is necessary; I like to know as much as possible about the subject and need to check the accuracy of appearance, costume details and accessories," she says. "When I 'know' the subject, I begin the modeling of head, hands and legs, which takes two to four days. Drying takes ten to fourteen days and I return to them several times during this period to make alterations and smooth the surface.

"Then they are painted with acrylics, the wires of the armature are joined and padded and the dolls are dressed. I design the appropriate patterns to fit the body, make the clothes separately and sew them onto the body. The hair goes on last."

The above description hardly does justice to the painstaking detail that goes into Zeepvat dolls. The portraits are sensitive and capture the feeling of the tintypes and paintings from which they are derived. The bodies stand, weighted, with convincing realism. This is often a fault of portrait dolls. Even if they have reasonably convincing miens, they often slump awkwardly and look, well, like dolls. Zeepvat's work looks like miniature people. She tells her secret. "Position of the figures requires a good deal of thought, but I'm more inclined to try the position myself to see if it's comfortable

(or possible!), to see how the weight is distributed and how it looks from different angles, and then try it out on the doll."

Proportion on these figures is, again, exact and the artist has developed a tool for this. "I have drawn out proportion charts for myself which show the comparative size of people at different ages, in 2in (5.1cm) to 1ft (27.9cm) and 1in (2.5cm) to 1ft (27.9cm) scales. These are an invaluable aid to modeling."

The success of Zeepvat figures in scale comes from a trained eye for historical detail and an unerring ability to recreate costume. The clothes fit and drape naturally (identically if subject is done from a picture); buttons, belts and braids are exact recreations. Hats and shoes are replicated and even small socks are knitted to fit. These dolls have no wigs. The hairstyle is built-up on the head. Furnishings and settings are constructed with a miniaturist's detail to harmoniously blend with the dolls.

Old Bill, a World War I private from the Warwickshire regiment is an example of Charlotte's total attention to detail. The figure, derived from a contemporary cartoon, sports the correct uniform with webbed belt, large and small packs, bayonet, water bottle, entrenching tool and SMLE #3 rifle (made by the artist in wood, brass and Fimo). To top him off, she carved a wood pipe and made a copy of the then-current magazine, *Fragments From France*, to tuck under the straps of the pack.

"A doll has to look lifelike -- and also be a good likeness if it's a portrait," she explains. "If a doll is in uniform or special costume, I look for accuracy."

The accuracy of her depiction stands out in her portraits of the royal family, which are generally done from photographs. Her grouping of the Prince and Princess of Wales with their family in 1870 is outstanding. Each member of the group of seven figures of assorted ages, stands or sits realistically -- or, as realistically as a portrait photographer would permit in those days. The little *Prince Albert of Wales*, 6in (15.2cm) tall, leans against the fence in a pose familiar to perusers of old family portraits. His kilt, buckles, buttons, socks, shoes and hat seem fairy-wrought, and his expression can only be expressed as "19th century Daguerrotype."

Queen Elizabeth the Queen Mother possesses a pair of Charlotte's portrait dolls, *Queen Mary* with her infant son, *Prince Albert,* presented to her in 1978. It is displayed in Windsor Castle, near Queen Mary's Dolls' House.

Contemporary royal portraits include *Prince Charles* and *Princess Diana* in wedding attire. All are done from photographs, when available. By 1984 the artist had completed approximately 50 portrait dolls.

She never makes identical portraits. "If asked to repeat a doll, I make a point of changing something. There are no molds for these dolls, so an exact repeat wouldn't be possible anyway," she says.

Ceramic dolls are larger than the portraits, and are done in multiples. Thirteen inches (33cm) tall, they are soft-bodied with head and limbs in bisque-fired earthenware. More dolls than figures, they have real hair wigs and removable clothes, and are a bit more experimental and less tied to historical recreation, although one ceramic portrait doll of Prince William of Wales has been produced.

"Ceramic dolls also start with an idea," Charlotte explains. "I model the head and limbs in clay and make plaster molds. The doll parts are then poured in earthenware slip, smoothed and fired.

"The earthenware slip I use was a chance discovery but I like the color very much. It's warmer and more lifelike than porcelain. I've thought of trying these dolls in porcelain and may do so, but I rather like the idea of working in a medium which most doll makers don't use."

Made since 1980, earthenware dolls, known by names such as *George, Elizabeth, Peter* and *Mary,* are signed and numbered, but not limited formally. "In practice, they are limited by the fact that I work alone," she says.

The exception to this rule is the portrait doll of Prince William, done in an edition of 25 only, each signed, numbered and dated.

Dollhouse dolls, in 1in (2.5cm) to 1ft (30.5cm) scale, are Charlotte's last category of dolls. "I've been told that some of my dolls' house dolls are in a museum in Japan," she says. "But I have no detail (or proof)." Sold exclusively through Michael Hunt's shop, The Dolls House, in Covent Garden, London, under the name, "Perfect People," these are the only Zeepvat dolls not directly available from the artist.

The historical figures have been displayed in exhibits of the British Dollmakers Association, to which Charlotte belongs, and have won awards, both in England and America.

A long waiting list of orders attests to their popularity. Orders for family portraits as well as for dolls of famous people are welcome, and Charlotte is amenable to visits from collectors, by arrangement.

Earlier portrait dolls are marked: "C.M. Zeepvat," embroidered in white on the petticoat or some place out of sight. Newer dolls are signed: "C. M. Zeepvat" or "C.M.Z" on the sole of the shoe.

The ceramic dolls have:

> C. M. ZEEPVAT
> Name of doll
> Number (in Roman numerals)

on the back of the head or shoulder plate.

The artist also uses ⟨mark⟩ as a mark.

In spite of her 25 years of experience in the field, Ms. Zeepvat states, "Doll making is still a hobby. My work has changed as any work does, with experience and practice and is still developing and improving (I hope!). There are lots of subjects I would like to make, just for my own amusement."

With her training in, and love for history and dolls, Charlotte Zeepvat has the potential for creating, just for her own amusement, some of the most accurate portrait dolls available to the collector.

Old Bill by Charlotte Zeepvat. One-of-a-kind 11½in (29.2cm) tall figure. Made of air-hardening clay with padded wire armature. Painted eyes, hair and moustache are applied artificial hair. He wears the uniform of a private soldier of the Warwickshire Regiment in the 1914-1918 War (British Infantry). Correct webbing equipment including large and small packs, bayonet, water bottle, entrenching tool and SMLE No. 3 rifle (made from wood, brass and "Fimo"). The pipe is carved wood. Under the strap of his pack is a tiny hand-painted copy of the contemporary magazine *Fragments from France.* Leather boots. Signed: "C.M. Zeepvat 1982." Derived from the First War cartoon character drawn by Bruce Bairnsfather. *Private collection. Photograph courtesy of Charlotte Zeepvat.*

Prince Albert Victor of Wales, (single doll from group in previous photograph) by Charlotte Zeepvat, 6in (15.2cm) tall. Costumed in dark green jacket and kilt in Stewart tartan. Leather shoes. Buttons, buckles and badge in "Fimo." *Photograph courtesy of Charlotte Zeepvat.*

Kaiser Wilhelm II with his son, *Prince Wilhelm* by Charlotte Zeepvat. One-of-a-kind dolls made of air-hardening clay with padded wire armatures. Painted eyes and applied (artificial) hair. Father seated on sofa holding standing child. Wears uniform of the Prussian Life Guard Hussars. This particular uniform was designed to be worn about the house, at a court where uniform was the ordinary daily wear for men. The tunic is red with gold lace and the trousers a very dark navy. Leather boots. The child wears a typical white lace dress with pale blue underskirt, sash and shoulder ribbons and black leather shoes. Signed: "C.M. Zeepvat 1983" on soles of feet. *Artist's collection. Photograph courtesy of Charlotte Zeepvat.*

Queen Victoria with her great-grandson, *Prince Edward of York* (the Duke of Windsor) by Charlotte Zeepvat. 1982. One-of-a-kind dolls made of air-hardening clay with padded wire armatures. Painted eyes. Wooden sofa with padded satin upholstery. Clothing of cotton, silk and lace with leather shoes. The child has pale yellow sash and ribbons. Derived from old photographs. Signed: "C.M. Zeepvat" on sole of foot. *Artist's collection. Photograph courtesy of Charlotte Zeepvat.*

Mary and *Peter* by Charlotte Zeepvat. Bisque fired earthenware dolls 13in (33cm) high. Ceramic arms, legs and shoulder plates. Soft bodies. The heads turn. Blonde real hair wigs. Painted blue eyes. Unlimited edition; each doll numbered. *Mary* wears cotton dress with a pink floral print and pink smocked neck. Cream-colored leather shoes, white socks and vest, and lace-trimmed knickers and petticoat. *Peter* wears pale blue cotton suit with white collar. This has a hand-embroidered blue and white edging. Matching blue leather shoes and white socks. In his pocket is a brown toy rabbit. Signed: "C.M. Zeepvat, 'Mary' or 'Peter'" on back of neck, with number of individual doll. *Mary* © 1983. *Peter* © 1981. Available separately. *Photograph courtesy of Charlotte Zeepvat.*

RIGHT: *Prince William of Wales*, 13in (33cm) tall by Charlotte Zeepvat. Bisque-fired earthenware doll with ceramic limbs, shoulder plate, head which turns and inclines and soft body. Molded hair. Painted blue eyes. Two teeth. 25 dolls only. Wears white vest and nappy. White cotton romper suit with hand-smocking in pale blue and white, white lace trim with blue and pearl buttons. Second romper suit also available in apricot and cream, with apricot-colored smocking. Signed: "C.M. Zeepvat 'Prince William' no.   ? 1983 (or 4)." Made in 1983 and 1984. *Photograph courtesy of Charlotte Zeepvat.*

LEFT: King Charles II, 12in (30.5cm) tall by Charlotte Zeepvat. One-of-a-kind doll made of air-hardening clay with padded wire armature. Derived from contemporary portraits. Painted eyes. Artificial hair. Wooden walking stick. Holds King Charles' spaniel (made of air-hardening clay with hair coat). Brass and aluminum sword. Clothing from the late 1660s. Black and gold coat, black "velvet" breeches and leather shoes. Wears Order of the Garter star and ribbon. Signed: "C.M. Zeepvat" on sole of foot. 1982. *Private collection. Photograph courtesy of Charlotte Zeepvat.*

marilyn stauber

A funny thing happens when we talk about doll artists...we tend to want to put them in neat little boxes according to the type of medium or the thematic treatment they use -- a very dangerous thing to do, that is. Again and again we run perilouslessly close to making over generalizations. An artist is an artist and, if good at one art endeavor will be good at many others...and will bring skills and experience acquired in one field to another with ease and this is just the case with Marilyn Stauber.

Chosing times at random in the last 20 years, we could have looked at what Marilyn was doing and said she is an interior designer (15 years ago), she is a painter (10 years ago), she is a fiber artist (maybe 8 years ago) and she is a miniaturist (6 years ago). At every point we would not have been off at all because at each period of time Marilyn was involved with exploring all the possibilities of each of those art expressions. This does not mean that she did each one of these things, completed all she wanted and moved on. It means that she extended her knowledge and skill in a widening circle with each area. You can go to Marilyn's house any day and see a portrait commission in progress, a doll house in perfect scale under construction, a stack of fabrics being incorporated into a wall hanging, a hoop with an embroidery or trapunto work going and a doll of her own design being costumed.

When Marilyn decided to try doll making a few years ago (because the doll house was obviously going to require a population), she had all these other art experiences plus a super sense of scale, proportion and design to put into the work. Naturally, the first dolls were very good and the ones after that were superb.

Her first tries in doll making were done in Sculpey but it did not take long until she knew she had to try making her sculptures in editions (too many costuming ideas!). Where many would have been defeated by the prospect of learning a whole new technically demanding process, Marilyn approached it with her usual boundless enthusiasm, figuring that it was a challenge.

These first figures were all-jointed porcelain ranging between 6 and 8in (15.2 to 20.3cm) in size because the porcelain did not always reduce as desired. The basic figures were made from one original sculpture, which, by subtle variations (not always planned!) created a series of elegant fashion ladies. Each one was carefully costumed to scale with intricate detailing. For example, the costume for an Empire Period lady has a skirt where delicate hand-embroidery has been incorporated with tiny seed pearl detail and a bridal costume of the 1850s has a skirt with trapunto-like puffing. Gibson ladies have fabulous furs and hats that are feathery concoctions and *Marie Antoinette* has been done with ribbons and laces -- all the fripperies that can, and did, go straight to the doll collector's hearts.

Soon, Marilyn was widening her range of fashion subjects to include a series based on film stars and Erte design inspirations and also added a male figure, *Clark*, and some children.

Artists who specialize in costume spend hours in research and Marilyn finds that a good part of her source material comes from historical portraits...mostly of the rich or royal class since they were the most interesting and financially able to have their portraits made. For Marilyn these portraits not only provide information as to the actual dress of the period but also the type of face and figure that was most admired (portraits would often show the person in the "look" of the era even if the person really did not meet the requirements in looks).

In order to recreate a period of history in a doll, it is necessary to find out just what was in the minds of the people -- just what female qualities were felt to comprise beauty. Today's look, for example, is the "skinny" figure; whereas, in the 19th century women went to exceeding lengths to achieve a plump and well-rounded look... adding corsets which pushed out, pads that added to and bustles to puff up...all to change the female silhouette to conform to a look based on "classical" sculpture.

Social and economic factors also must be discovered in order to understand why certain costumes would become in the mode for a particular period. For instance, the short skirt of the 1940s was the reaction of the fashion designer to the wartime fabric shortage. The invention of analine dyes in the 1850s for commercial use led to a whole new palette of hot, bright colors in fashionable frocks.

Marilyn was no sooner off and running -- literally seeing the figures off to collections as soon as finished -- when another challenge came along. The Eugene area doll clubs had undertaken to host the 1985 United Federation of Doll Clubs regional conference and invitations to bid on the design and construction of the conference souvenir had been extended.

As noted, most doll artists are mentally several dolls ahead in their thoughts and, also, quite often think in terms of groups or series. Marilyn's interest in the fashion figures had led her thought towards the eventual design of a series of female dolls which would portray the idea of beauty in the major fashion eras of history. The souvenir bid offered the opportunity to begin at least one figure for the projected series.

In just a few months, Marilyn sculpted a figure, designed and constructed a prototype fabric body and produced three finished and dressed figures. The doll, named *Eugenia Lane* for the conference host city and county and the first figure that Marilyn had done in a larger size, was totally irresistable to the souvenir selection committee -- the contract was hers on the first vote!

A souvenir doll contract -- often calling for the production of 300 to 2000 dolls in a three year period -- is a large and fearful undertaking for any doll artist, particularly when one is to do it without the back-up of mass production facilities and personnel. In the first place, a figure has to be designed, as Marilyn's was, to suit the conference's designated theme. Next, the figure has to be designed so that it will be efficient and economical to produce. Molds have to be made -- at least one for every 50 pieces cast. Then there are hours and hours, days and days, and months and months of working on the same thing over and over again...and maybe doing that thing all over again if a problem comes up. When something goes wrong in a large batch, the difficulties and corrections are multiplied by tens and hundreds rather than ones! A mild annoyance in an ordinary edition becomes a major catastrophe in an edition of 500!

Did she know what she was getting into? While most artists would have run the other way as fast as possible, Marilyn undertook the fulfillment of the contract with her usual healthy curiosity and optimistic response to a challenge. Said she, "I have always wondered if I could be a cottage industry and this will be my chance to find out."

In order to make the shift from individual studio artist to a "cottage industrialist," Marilyn approached the project in a series of well-organized steps. To begin with, the basement of her home was converted into a *porzelinfabrick*. Before any pouring was done and while the molds were being made, racks for storage and drying were built, the sewing room became a polishing area and upstairs rooms were turned over to painting and sewing. Husband, neighbors and friends' teenagers were trained to help with the various parts of production. Some came in to work on scheduled hours and some did "out work" in their homes.

At the time of this writing, the souvenir doll project is not yet completed, but it has surmounted a number of unexpected delays and mishaps with Marilyn's concentration on problem solving. She has found the job a terrific learning experience...and typically, Marilyn, she has put every problem to work for the best advantage of the production. For instance, in working out a difficulty in firing, she discovered a new finish which she felt bettered the work. She has tracked down supplies from odd corners of the country and has learned new china painting techniques -- all of which will enrich her future work even more.

The Stauber powers of organization are legend amongst her local colleagues and we were not surprised that while most doll artists would find such a contract left no time for other activities, Marilyn has been able to keep up with her self imposed schedule and still have time to sculpt other figures, dress several figures and enjoy the recreational pursuits that are so much a part of her life. (So far, the one free day a week has produced a new pattern series and a prototype for a rather unique paper doll.) At this point, she is unsure about becoming a "cottage industry" on a regular basis -- time will tell, but she knows now that she can do it.

Let us keep our fingers crossed that Marilyn might find her next challenge to become an author and publisher...goodness knows we could all benefit if she would produce a book based on her experiences in porcelain work and costuming!

Eugenia Lane, 5¾in (14.7cm) porcelain 1985 UFDC Region 1 souvenir bust designed by artist Marilyn Stauber. The artist chose an auburn color for the hair of acrylic roving to harmonize with the red-orange tints of the china paint and to set off the big blue eyes. *Photograph by W. Donald Smith, courtesy of Marilyn Stauber.*

RIGHT: These four plaster sections join together to make the production mold for the doll bust. To make an edition like this one, numbering 500, several sets of these complex molds must be made. *Photograph by and courtesy of Marilyn Stauber.*

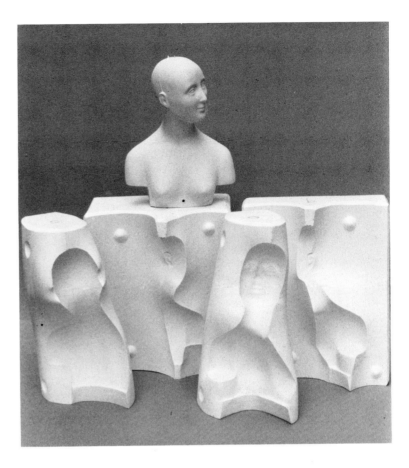

RIGHT: Three *Eugenia Lane* busts. The one on the left is finished, the larger bust in the center shows the uncleaned greenware and the one on the right shows how much the greenware shrinks when it is fired to cone 7. *Photograph by and courtesy of Marilyn Stauber.*

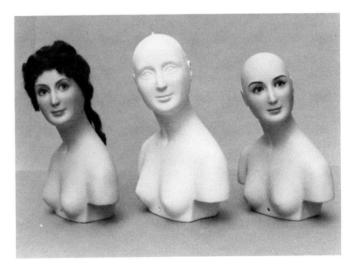

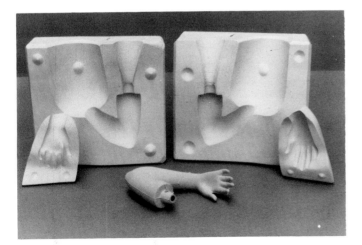

LEFT: The *Eugenia Lane* arm mold. Shown is a four-piece plaster mold which is joined together to form the right arm. In the foreground is an uncleaned greenware arm that was cast in this mold with porcelain slip. *Photograph by and courtesy of Marilyn Stauber.*

LEFT: In making the body for *Eugenia Lane* four layers of fabric are laid together with the flesh colored cloth in the middle and a layer of muslin on either side, allowing the bias cut leg pieces to go directly into the sewing machine without further handling. Dual duty thread and small stitches make the body strong enough to resist the pressures of tight stuffing with polyester batting. *Photograph by W. Donald Smith, courtesy of Marilyn Stauber.*

BELOW LEFT: This view of *Eugenia Lane* shows how the arms are jointed onto the porcelain bust and indicates how they can move around horizontally. The arms are held snugly to the bust by elastic which runs through a carrier on the top of each arm up over a wooden dowel which is inserted in a horizontal position inside the head. The bias cut, double layered cloth body is stitched to the bust through two holes in the back and one in the front. *Photograph by and courtesy of Marilyn Stauber.*

BELOW: *Eugenia Lane* by Marilyn Stauber dressed in the costume of the 1770's. *Photograph by Marilyn Stauber.*

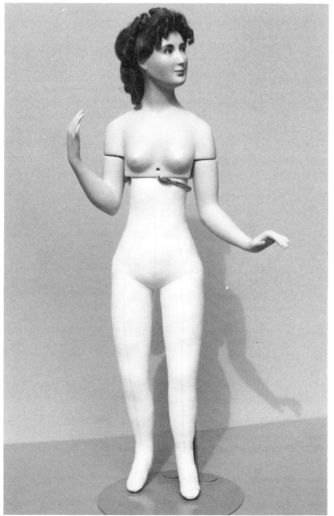

RIGHT: The completed 19½in (49.6cm) souvenir doll is part of a series showing 19th century ball gowns. The costume is a composite of ideas taken from fashion illustrations of about 1850 and is of a soft peach color with brighter flower accents. The weight of the outfit is lightened by a stiffened hoop skirt so fewer petticoats are required to achieve the wide bell look that was admired at the time. *Photograph by and courtesy of Marilyn Stauber.*

BELOW: *Eugenia Lane* costumed in the fashion of the 1820s. Note the detailed hand embroidery work. *Photograph by and courtesy of Marilyn Stauber.*

BELOW RIGHT: *Dancing Betty,* a 6½in (16.5cm) miniature porcelain doll, is a member of the "Hollywood Series" by Marilyn Stauber. In this series the artist may attach various heads to the body in whatever position she desires during the greenware stage. This process allows the creation of a variety of effects as well as personalities. Pale peach silks are employed in this dolls' petal skirt, a style which enjoyed popularity in 1929. *Photograph by Leo Stauber, courtesy of Marilyn Stauber.*

cecilia rothman

A few years ago a friend of mine said "the only doll maker I know in San Francisco is the Mushroom Lady."

Mushroom Lady??

The only doll maker I knew in San Francisco was Cecilia Rothman.

With a few more questions, I found that Cecilia and the Mushroom Lady were, indeed, one and the same person. It turns out that Cecilia, who has a lively curiosity and the ability to follow up, had decided to paint mushrooms, which are, of course, rather popular in the decorative arts. Cecilia, however, was not content to just paint whatever mushroom shapes that came into her head. She made an in-depth study of mycology and became so precise in her renderings of that species that her paintings were purchased for reference and teaching purposes by expert mycologists.

The little episode of the mushroom tells a shorthand version of Cecilia Rothman, her life and work. When Cecilia takes up a subject, she learns it thoroughly!

Cecilia Rothman has been making dolls since she was a girl...since she was laid up for a year as a teenager recovering from rheumatic fever. To keep her mind occupied, her mother supplied her with a steady stream of art books. Cecilia may not have had formal art training but she did begin with a good knowledge of the best there was.

Even then her doll making turned to portraiture. The first person she chose to depict in three dimension was, of all people, the enlightenment philosopher Voltaire. This was not exactly the obvious choice for a high school girl, but one that certainly did reflect Cecilia's excellent educational and family background.

With time out for side excursions into other areas of art (from mushrooms to marionettes and teaching the blind), Cecilia has continued to make portraiture her main focus in doll making.

The thing is that in her portraiture, Cecilia, true to the original example of Voltaire, has always done only the people who had a special meaning for her as individuals -- people whose lives influenced or changed events, even minor events. She does not do portraits of the "historical superstars" as a rule, but picks out those people who, in their way, are important to her for their own particular contribution to the course of history.

Many of Cecilia's studies have been of native American people, especially those who lived and made a mark on California history and she is open to suggestion from collectors about native American portrait figures to try. One of her recent choices has been Sara Winnemucca who pleaded with the people of California, the government, and even President Hayes for the preservation of the ancestral lands of her people in California and Nevada. Sacajewea, the bird woman, who accompanied Lewis and Clark's expedition is another figure who has caught her attention. Both of these figures have thoroughly researched and accurate costuming...and if that means extra hours of beading, then it is done.

Two favorites among Cecilia's portraits are undoubtedly her studies of John Muir, the famous conservationist, and Teddy Roosevelt. The figure of John Muir shows him in old age, taking his ease in the Yosemite wilderness he loved so much. By no stretch of the imagination is John Muir one of history's glittery celebrities; yet, Cecilia gently shows us how much we owe to him for making us work to save the natural beauty of our country. Even in this figure, Cecilia has taken extra lengths. In order to fill out the illusion of the nature setting, she had to find a rock of appropriate size, take a mold from it, pour it in latex and then paint it to look like a real rock.

Teddy Roosevelt is brought to life by Cecilia just as we have always imagined he must have been...right down to the pince nez glasses, both feet planted firmly, wearing rough and ready outdoors clothing, eyes straight ahead to the current goal he had in sight.

Along with John Muir and Teddy Roosevelt, Cecilia has also taken up figures of people who have been leaders, ground breakers or workers for good causes. She has done dedicated ladies like Salvation Army founder Evangeline Booth, Soujouner Truth and Miss Jane Pittman...quietly courageous women who put themselves on the line for things they believed in.

Cecilia can be sneaky with her portraits. Sometimes real people are disguised in traditional doll themes. The first one she did for show was a study of her beautiful daughter. However, Cecilia did her first as a lovely fairy-tale princess, *Lovelia*, in a specially built castle interior room setting -- absolutely breathtaking. Another version of her daughter in doll form was done as a turn of the century beauty in Gibson costume and yet another as a bride.

It should be added that in the year 1974 when *Princess Lovelia* was shown at the IDMA convention in Reno, Nevada, Cecilia took ten dolls to exhibit and went home with twelve ribbons including Best of Class and Best of Show. Then, the following year, her tiny, jewel-like *Gypsy* dancer took the first.

Another figure who has been circling in her mind for some time is the, as yet unattempted, Ishi. Ishi, a lone survivor of the stone age Yahi Indian way of life was found living by himself in the mountains of northern California near the turn of the century. Anthrolopogists brought him to the University of California at Berkeley where he

RIGHT: *1776 Sailor Boy.* Wax on wire armature figure with celastic flag and patriotic setting made by Cecilia Rothman in 1976. *Photograph courtesy of Cecilia Rothman.*

BELOW RIGHT: *Bridgit,* a 7in (17.8cm) all-porcelain girl dressed in a costume of the 1920s. Note the fine features and delicate hands Cecilia Rothman is able to achieve in such small scale. *Photograph by W. Donald Smith.*

recreated his habitat and customs of the wild. Many older people in San Francisco have memories of actually visiting Ishi and, others like Cecilia, have certainly been influenced by his story. To bring Ishi into form as a doll portrait figure, however, presents several construction problems for a doll maker. Ishi would have to be shown in his brief native dress. How could Cecilia, working in porcelain and wanting to show movement, show Ishi looking natural? How could she manage joints and yet cover them with something that would make the appearance of skin over bones and muscles? This is a particular problem that the doll maker has...especially one who wishes to do an accurate portrait. Every once in a while Cecilia comes back to the problem, studies a bit more, gives a bit more thought to materials and methods that might solve the problem, and probably, in doing so, learns a few more techniques which are able to be applied to other figures.

Cecilia is not one to "go by the book" even if there was such a thing as an absolute rule book for doll artists. Most who work in porcelain make a sculpture in wax or clay and from there make a mold and pour porcelain slip. Cecilia, on the other hand, makes a base head that can be poured from a mold and on top of that sculpts each head out individually (carves, in her word), adding porcelain clay and sculpting to suit for each head. This essentially makes members of her editions one-of-a-kind figures.

Cecilia also comes at the construction of a body in her own unique way. Though some of her work is in the traditional all-porcelain form, much of it is done as heads, hands and legs of porcelain built onto a wire armature body. That is just her porcelain work. Cecilia also does figures in papier-mâché and of carved wood and all have the same delicately carved faces and limbs.

This is all not to say the Cecilia does not have some fun with her doll making, too. Her reading is not all "heavy" stuff; she has done two versions of *Alice in Wonderland*. It is not all portraits either. She does a delightful series of whimsical elves and gnomes (seated on absolutely scientifically exact mushrooms!) and she has an open series of nymph-like maids which can be made to represent the state flower of your choice. Altogether, the "Rothman roster" must include 50 or more individual characters including clowns, babies, dancers and fashion figures, but because of her painstaking methods of making, not too many of any one type has been made.

Cecilia Rothman's work is understandably rare and very much in demand by the collector but, as one collector said, well worth the wait. Cecilia, herself, works every day and tries not to get too bogged down in filling orders...she always needs to have time to think, imagine and start the exploration of a new interpretation of character.

All of these wonders come up out of the Rothman basement where Cecilia spends hours oblivious to the world and time, working in the necessary delicate details under magnification, firing in double kilns and doing whatever is necessary to bring the proper bit of "life" to each personality that comes under her fingers.

ABOVE: *Voltaire* by Cecilia Rothman, 16in (40.6cm) tall. Papier-mâché head, with hands and feet built over a copper wire armature. Cecilia made this figure while still a high school student. *Photograph courtesy of Cecilia Rothman.*

ABOVE RIGHT: *Balinese Dancer* carved of wood by Cecilia Rothman. This figure is one of several the artist made to show the grace and color of this dance form. *Photograph courtesy of Cecilia Rothman.*

RIGHT: *Chief Truckee* and *Sara Winnemucca*, porcelain and wire armature figures by Cecilia Rothman depicting two significant native American figures. Costumes are researched for authenticity and hand-sewn by the artist. *Photograph courtesy of Cecilia Rothman.*

RIGHT: *Jasmine,* a country bride 11in (27.9cm) tall of sculpted porcelain on a wire armature. *Photograph by Margory Novak, courtesy of Cecilia Rothman.*

BELOW RIGHT: A portrait of United States President Theodore Roosevelt in his "rough and ready" garb. *Photograph by Dorothy Aspinwall, courtesy of Cecilia Rothman.*

BELOW: *Loquol,* a harloquin, 16in (40.6cm) standing. *Lequel* has a porcelain head, hands and feet constructed on a wire armature body. He is seated on a large wooden "treasure" box filled with such mystrious emphemera as a crystal ball, a gold key, beads and feathers. Cecilia made this figure as a helper for the 1984 convention of the National Institute of American Doll Artists. *Photograph by Calvin Rothman, courtesy of Cecilia Rothman.*

ABOVE: Close-up view of John Muir by NIADA artist, Cecilia Rothman. *Photograph by Dorothy Aspinwall, courtesy of Cecilia Rothman.*

LEFT: A portrait of conservationist John Muir, 16in (40.6cm) tall, porcelain on wire armature. *Photograph courtesy of Cecilia Rothman.*

gillian charlson

"Dolls are more personal somehow than a sculpture. My dolls are sculptures with life in them."

Gillian Charlson's dolls are, indeed, lifelike. Her medium, wax, produces probably the most realistic dolls available, which is why establishments like Madame Tussaud's use it for their sculptures. Its translucence and malleability enable it, in the right hands, to produce sculptures which seem to breathe. Gillian Charlson's hands are such a pair.

Maybe it is their sheer size -- her dolls run largeish, and maybe it is the sculptural technique which can be best described as a combination between nostalgic and photographic, with a dash of the romantic to give it flavor, but Gillie dolls are unforgettable.

As they are in shops, collections and museums in many countries, the peripatetic doll fancier will most likely encounter one in his/her travels. This writer has met them in New York and twice in Paris. Each time the response was the same: fascination. The dolls forced one to edge away from the present and enter their other-timely world.

Their glass eyes probe with a calm, patient, knowing stare, and their often semi-melancholy smiles wait for a response.

Many are portraits. The artist has done three of her daughter, Nina, at different ages. But even these combine verisimilitude with a quality that I can only describe as a feeling for the 19th century. By this I mean that the dolls somehow have a patina on them; they do not look contemporary, or late 20th century. There is nothing brash, hard-edged or "modern" about them. They are gentle, flowing, nostalgic, contentedly out-of-step with the times.

Again, the medium from which they are made has much to do with this aura. But a lot has to come from the personality of the artist, too, and from her artistic sources.

When she was young, Gillian Charlson had few playmates and spent much of her time with her dolls, sewing and caring for them. As she matured, she mastered many crafts and kept her love for dolls alive by experimenting with many doll making media, and visiting doll exhibits and museums.

At one such exhibit, she encountered a Montanari wax doll. She was 16 and knew she could never afford one, so she began a campaign to learn how to make her own. After much experimentation, at the age of 20, she had perfected her wax doll making technique. From her results, she must have kept alive the mental image of that museum doll, because Gillie's dolls embody the same 19th century aura as the originals, but with a 20th century subject matter. The combination works.

So does the artist.

"Doll making is fulltime and a half for me," she says. "I must learn how to relax. Doll making is my work and my relaxation. In my spare time I sleep. I think you can get too involved at times."

Their maiden exhibit was at the first English doll convention in 1976; everything sold within a half hour. The artist went home with eight months' worth of orders and decided to trade in her teaching job for fulltime doll making. Since that time, her husband has followed suit. He now casts the heads and makes the molds, and performs numerous other tasks.

But the invention and artistry comes from Gillian, who has had five years' art training and has worked as a costume designer, teacher, painter and jewelry maker, all of which are utilized in doll making.

In the early 1980s, Mrs. Charlson added porcelain to her repertoire and does designs in both media. Dolls range from 3in (7.6cm) to 28in (71.1cm), have cloth bodies which sometimes have wired armatures, and wax or porcelain heads and limbs. "I like both media just as much," she says. "I like to have a change from one to the other."

Gillie dolls are dressed in fine fabrics: natural fibers, if modern, antique if available. All accessories are handmade and wigs are generally of human hair, occasionally inserted into the wax, depending on the style of doll.

The collector has a wide range to choose from because, Gillian says, "I like to make something for everyone. What I make depends on my mood."

When she speaks of dolls and doll making, Mrs. Charlson chooses words with sentience: "A good doll is one that stirs up some emotion in you when you look at it. To catch a mood in a doll or to get a very good likeness in a portrait is important. I like my dolls to remind people of happy memories or people they know, or to make them think of a story to the doll." Her dolls do seem to express these intentions to the viewer.

Every once in a while -- not often enough -- a new doll will come from the Charlson studio, which Gillian describes as "organized chaos." "I would make more new ones but I have to keep up with orders for dolls I have done before," she explains.

Sold by mail order and wholesaled to shops all over the world, Gillian's wax and porcelain sculptures are reaching out to new passersby all the time. They, too, stop and are for a moment transported to another, quieter level of existence. This is why so many have found their way into doll collections. They are sculptures with life in them.

ABOVE: *Nina*, 22in (55.9cm) portrait doll at age 12 years by Gillian Charlson. Made in wax and in bisque with limbs of the same. Cloth body. Glass eyes. Human hair wig. *Photograph courtesy of Gillian Charlson.*

RIGHT: Gillian Charlson's tag. *Courtesy of Gillian Charlson.*

Original hand-made wax and porcelain

"GILLIE" DOLL

ABOVE: *Anna Pavlova*, 16in (40.6cm) tall, by Gillian Charlson. Bisque head and limbs. Glass eyes. Mohair wig. Organdy dress. *Photograph courtesy of Gillian Charlson.*

RIGHT: Gillian Charlson working on a wax doll. "This is the heated ball I use to make the eye sockets inside the head." *Photograph courtesy of Gillian Charlson.*

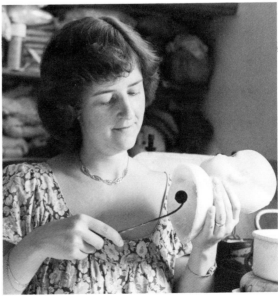

ABOVE: *Rebecca* by Gillian Charlson, 25in (66cm) tall. Wax head and limbs. Cloth body. Glass eyes. Human hair wig. This doll won best of class and first award of the show at the International Doll Makers Association 1980 convention. *Photograph courtesy of Gillian Charlson.*

LEFT: Gillian Charlson inserting the hair into the wax head with a hot knife. "I only do this on baby dolls that do not have much hair as it is a very tedious job." *Photograph courtesy of Gillian Charlson.*

don anderson

Doll artists naturally come from a wide range of backgrounds, but the story of a boy growing up in a Wyoming ranching community where he enjoyed the out-of-doors, was a soda jerk, and managed a dance hall, does not prepare the reader to expect him to become a fashion designer and doll artist in a glamorous place like Hollywood. However, after serving in the Air Force's Pacific campaign from the Aleutians to Iwo Jima, that is just what Don Anderson did become.

Don studied fashion design and illustration at Los Angeles' Choinard School of Art, but, as is so often the case, a lack of jobs in the field forced him to put his talents and learning to new and better uses. After finding employment scarce in the fashion world he had trained for, Don began making his own men's shirts and casual wear for several of the better known Hollywood men's shops and, eventually, went into a shop of his own on the famous Sunset Strip. His sportswear became very well known and many movie world personalities sought him out for his unique work. After several years, he decided to close up shop and spend some time decorating his home. But in the midst of painting and papering, the phone kept ringing with clients wanting special orders so, in the end, Don remodeled one of his two-car garages into a convenient home workroom.

And that is the way it went until Christmas of 1974 changed his whole life. He was planning Christmas decor for the house and decided to build the theme around a doll, but, alas, no commercial doll could be found that quite suited his idea. Don made his own. Naturally, as you might expect from a person who has a lifetime experience with fabrics, costuming and tailoring, she turned out to be a fabric doll.

She was floppy, he says, a limp lady with yarn hair, but he gave her a romantic Scarlett O'Hara dress of pink satin with a lace overlay, corsets and petticoats. She was beautiful...and he was hooked on doll making!

Don so enjoyed the challenge of that first doll that he dug out his old art school costume drawings and selected a few to try with dolls. He experimented with the body design -- applying his sewing experience to streamline and improve the design and construction -- and he designed a good doll stand to hold them erect. He continued to experiment, to improve and to make more and more of them.

Soon, there were about 20 of these dolls, as Don recalls, just sitting around the house looking beautiful. Then, a visiting friend recommended him to the Broadway Stores who were looking for ideas to be used in public displays. They were immediately delighted with Don's ladies and set up a fabulous exhibit.

There, for the first time, Don met other people interested in dolls and was encouraged to continue with the doll making. It did not, however, happen all at once. He found himself doing a stint of costume design for theater productions before he could open a doll shop of his own.

Since beginning there, he has made about 200 figures and costumed many others for customers. His dolls have found homes with celebrities like country singer, Bobby Gentry, and television personality, Don Berry, as well as the Boston Museum and Santa Barbara's Ruth Dougherty Museum. Also, shipped around the world, Don's dolls have been seen in many shows where their displays have invariably drawn crowds and won ribbons.

Don's creations are generally representative of that type of doll we call the fashion mannequin; however, they have the added attraction of being representative of historical experience. Don's goal is to educate the viewer -- in a most gentle way -- by constructing costumes just exactly as they were made for everyday wear in bygone days.

He is a stickler for correct detail and to achieve it he has done considerable research in the history of fashion and clothing construction. "I look for ideas in books, papers and magazines," he says. "I have acquired a great number of books on the history of clothes and am constantly adding more. Authenticity is a must in my approach -- no matter how much time it takes." Indeed, his figures are authentic -- so much so that if you could shrink down to fit the doll's clothes, you might find yourself transported back into history -- corsets, bustles and all!

Many doll artists start out working in a corner of a kitchen and very often stay there, but, even so, each one develops systems and arrangements which make the work progress in the best way possible for themselves. Anderson's workroom may be atypical, but it is an example of what most doll artists would like. With his many years in the business of making clothes, his workroom, most professionally, includes a padded top cutting table, a professional steam iron, five (yes, five!) sewing machines for various uses, a button covering machine, and efficiently planned storage areas so that all fabrics, laces, trims, beads and buttons are ready at hand as needed.

His approach to the construction of the figure, itself, is unique. Basically, he constructs a head and a trunk in one unit, separate arms with hands incorporated in the form of gloves and legs with the shoes seamed in. The process is essentially a very unusual,

BELOW: Back view of Don Anderson's lady in the green brocade promenade dress. Note the extremely fine and very authentic tailoring of the bodice. *Photograph by Elyn F. Marton, courtesy of Don Anderson.*

BELOW: Detail of French gown showing the stomacher and over bodice. *Photograph by Elyn F. Marton, courtesy of Don Anderson.*

BOTTOM: Don Anderson's creation of a fashionable lady in promenade dress of green brocade with leg-o'-mutton sleeves. She has a white lace jabot and a black velvet ribbon and pendant at her throat. Arms, legs and body are of cloth. *Photograph by Elyn F. Marton, courtesy of Don Anderson.*

BOTTOM: "A La Francaise" gown in pale green with soft yellow flowers. Trimmings are gray silk and cream lace. Don was inspired to make this costume by a period gown displayed at the Los Angeles Museum. True to the original styling of the day, Don has even fashioned a stomacher under the bodice. *Photograph by Elyn F. Marton, courtesy of Don Anderson.*

individually developed version of the fabric/rag doll.

It almost goes without saying for this designer/clothing builder that all parts of the dolls are made of various types of fabrics. Cotton-like sateen drapery linings (no doubt familiar from his work in theater costuming) are used for the bodies and this is the only phase where one could say "mass production" is used. Layers of fabric are spread out and the patterns arranged and marked. The head and body are of double thickness and about 30 dolls are cut out, snippety-snap, at one time!

After all the complexities of body building are accomplished, finally comes the fun part. "I like making the clothes and accessories best," says Don. "The stuffing, assembling and hair application is most the tiring and time-consuming part."

After the costume is made -- all costumes, by the way, are removable and may be laundered or dry cleaned -- the doll's face and shoulders are sprayed with a flesh colored acrylic paint. The features are drawn on and painted to make a face as lifelike as possible. Now the hair can be arranged in the chosen style and sprayed with a clear lacquer for permanance.

At last, the clothing goes on. Jewelry and accessories appropriate to the period and the costume design are added. Dressed, signed and mounted on her own stand, the doll may be kept or sold, but, by all means, it is loved!

BELOW LEFT: This demure lady created by Don Anderson wears a gown of 1874 straight from the fashion pages of *Harper's Bazar.* The costume is made of black and white pinstripe satin with neatly contrasting backgrounds. A white lace jabot front finishes the costume. Most of the Anderson dolls are about 27in (68.6cm) tall to show off the detailing of the costume. *Photograph by Elyn F. Marton, courtesy of Don Anderson.*

BELOW: A Don Anderson doll in "My Fair Lady" costume inspired by the Cecil Beaton sketches for the stage production costumes. The dress consists of black crepe skirt draped and split down the left side front and a blouse of white corded lace. Completing the outfit is a white taffeta cummerbund and hanging panel trimmed with white silk flowers. *Photograph by Elyn F. Marton, courtesy of Don Anderson.*

paul crees

Dollmaking for Paul Crees is a by-product of a theatrical career. Crees' interest in the stage began in childhood. "I did not play with dolls," he says, "though I did like making miniatures -- furniture and buildings. I also made a miniature theater which had small figures. Maybe that's where the interest came from."

As an adult, he does not play with dolls, either. He works six days a week, creating charismatic dolls perpetuating the legends of ladies of the silver screen.

Mr. Crees studied stage design at London's Mountview Drama School. A career as a theatrical designer and scenic artist lasted from 1971 to 1979. He designed sets and costumes for The Royal Shakespeare Company, Glyndesborne Opera, The Royal Ballet, The Northcott Theatre and the Bristol Old Vic, among others, and freelanced costumes for the BBC and independent television companies.

Among the plays Crees worked on was "The Changeling," for which he designed a full-sized Madonna figure which flew onto stage among clouds of smoke, and stood praying. "Every night," he says, "people believed it was a real live actress suspended there. I got really excited about that. As I had so enjoyed making the figure, I decided to experiment with a much smaller figure in the likeness of Marlene Dietrich."

The choice of Marlene Dietrich as subject matter was deliberate. The artist had met her on several occasions and is an ardent fan of hers, possessing a cache of stills from her films.

"The first (*Dietrich* doll) I made created a lot of interest", he reports, "and a lady who came to see it said 'I want one!' I didn't believe she would ever come back. But she did. Two months later. By then I had completed three different *Dietrich* dolls and she chose the most expensive one at 250 pounds. I realized, then, there was a market for them."

This was in 1979. Once word got around that he was making the dolls, people snapped them up, and the theater designer embarked on a new career.

An ever-growing cast of silver screen ladies crowds his small apartment-workshop in Bath, England. Approximately 29in (73.7cm) tall, they include *Greta Garbo, Tallulah Bankhead, Marilyn Monroe, Judy Garland, Jean Harlow, Jane Russell, Olivia De Havilland, Vivien Leigh, Diana Ross, Joan Crawford, Jayne Mansfield, Bette Davis* and British television star, *Marti Caine*, the latter commissioned by the BBC. "*Marlene Dietrich* is my favorite," he says. "I have always admired her greatly, as a beauty, a movie star and as a woman."

These "portrait dolls" portray larger-than-life legends, but the only "real" portrait he has done was that of Marti Caine. "It doesn't really interest me," he says. "My own works are portraits anyway, and that takes up enough of my time. I'm not interested in any other ladies except actresses. There's still a lot to do yet without resorting to Mrs. Smith of Pittsburgh."

"Mrs. Smith" can't compare with the glamour and fantasy of the ladies of the film. "I am inspired most by the actresses, themselves. I don't like Jean Harlow but she does have a wonderful face. Certainly not a wonderful face but a good one to model and paint."

Mr. Crees' early dolls were carved from polystyrene and covered with muslin for strength and realism, then given three coats of plaster of paris. The bodies were carved as one with the legs, feet and shoes, unless the figure was seated. The arms were soft and stuffed, the hands plaster of paris. Head and hands were sanded and painted, wigs fashioned from dolls' wigs, restyled.

The first *Dietrich* dolls, shown at the initial British Doll Association exhibit, at Bethnal Green Museum of Childhood, in the East End of London, in 1980, were an instant hit.

Crees' dolls reach a public different from that of many doll artists. Iconic figures, they appeal to a wide crossection of the populace. "I have no specific audience," Paul states. "My audience is everybody, I hope. They are not aimed at a particular market, i.e., movie buffs or dedicated fans. All sorts of people, from all walks of life, for all sorts of reasons have bought my work, and I'm quite happy with that...People can like them or leave them. It doesn't bother me."

He works for only one critic. "My dolls have to please ME. They also have to be beautiful, elegant and charismatic and faithful to the actress they convey. I think of my work as art dolls, and they are frequently referred to as works of art. My dolls are definitely not 'play dolls,' but collectors' pieces."

Current "collectors' pieces" are fashioned from wax. The artist describes his procedures.

"I make my own plaster molds. I do all my own modeling.

"The molds are soaked in cold water.

"Colored molten wax is poured into the molds. The wax components are then cooled in cold water and the excess seams trimmed with a surgical knife.

"The head is attached to the body with molten wax.

"The body is then covered with stockinette and a transparent covering of flesh color on top of that. The legs are covered in the same manner.

RIGHT: *Greta Garbo*, 29in (73.7cm) tall by Paul Crees. Wax doll with painted features, human hair wig and inserted eyelashes. Costume designed after the one worn in the film *Camille*. Black chiffon evening dress trimmed with silver beads, diamonte and sequins; black lace headdress. Edition of 50. First made in 1981. *Photograph courtesy of Paul Crees.*

BELOW RIGHT: *Marlene Dietrich*, 29in (73.7cm) tall by Paul Crees. Wax doll with human hair wig, painted features and inserted eyelashes. Clothing based on a cabaret costume worn in a performance in Rio. See-through black chiffon draped around the body; black see-through body stocking and tights; black shoes; diamonte trim. Edition of 50. Signed on neck. Numbered certificate of authenticity. First made in 1984. *Photograph courtesy of Paul Crees.*

"The arms are covered in the same way and then attached to the body by sewing. The legs are also sewn on.

"The face is painted with artists' oils and eyelashes inserted."

Before wigging, the doll is painstakingly costumed. The doll artist relies on an extensive library of film books, movie stills and other photographs. One particularly useful volume details Hollywood's best known costumes. Countless hours go into each design, which must faithfully recreate the garment in question.

"For a new design, my partner, Peter Coe, and I spend many hours studying film and research books," Paul states. "Costumes are then scaled down and paper patterns are made. We often work from videos of the particular films. Real costumes are made -- but often figure-hugging dresses are sewn directly on the doll. All beaded dresses are made by hand and bugle bead costumes require a minimum of 50 hours to complete."

Dolls are then wigged with human hair. "This is the part I hate the most," he says.

Accessories are handmade -- from handbags to cigarettes. Each doll is one-of-a-kind. Editions are small. "I doubt if more than 100 of a particular doll will be made. The largest number so far is 13."

The dolls come to life in a small flat and outside workshop in Bath, England.

"Every room in the apartment is a small workshop in itself. The kitchen is used for pouring the wax, the bathroom for soaking the molds. The bedroom is used for storing the dolls and doubles as an office. There are two sewing machines in the workshop. Fabrics are stored there. The sitting room is used for hand sewing and the hairdressing. During the summer the garden and patio are also used as working areas."

Most Crees dolls find their way to the United States. Britons seem more intereted in antique dolls, according to the artist.

"In America, the doll collecting public is very well informed and imaginative in its outlook. With antique dolls overreaching the market in price, the Americans have, over the years, recognized many fine original doll artists and have invested in their future. This is a very healthy attitude and breathes new life into the doll collecting industry.

"In Europe, the attitude is more stagnant and remote, in particular towards English doll artists who are often ignored in this country. There is an abundance of original doll artist talent in England, but often the main markets are abroad, particularly the States."

Unaware of the doll subculture until he was part of it, Mr. Crees now belongs to the British Doll Association and participates in exhibitions and sales. Sometimes the reactions of the public are comical.

"I once had a lovely *Dietrich* doll at a London fair, dressed in black sequins and feathers, and a rather stupid child thought it was Cruella de Ville (from *A Hundred and One Dalmations* -- the Disney film).

Such occurrences are rare. Crees dolls' calling cards are the universally recognizable personages they depict. These by-products of a theatrical career offer the collector art, glamour, fantasy: the sirens of the cinema in miniature.

ABOVE: *Vivien Leigh* 29in (73.7cm) tall by Paul Crees. Wax doll with human hair wig, painted features and inserted eyelashes. Costume based on that worn for Ashley's party in the film *Gone with the Wind*. Claret-colored velvet dress studded with red stones; trimmed with wine-colored tulle shawl. Edition of 50. Signed on nape of neck. Numbered certificate of authenticity. Made since 1982. *Photograph courtesy of Paul Crees.*

LEFT: *Greta Garbo*, 29in (73.7cm) tall by Paul Crees. Wax doll with human hair wig, painted features and inserted eyelashes. Dressed in a copy of the costume in the film *Queen Christina*. *Photograph courtesy of Paul Crees.*

Close-up of *Marilyn Monroe* by Paul Crees costumed as she appeared
in *Gentlemen Prefer Blondes*. Photograph courtesy of Paul Crees.

ABOVE: *Diana Ross*, 29in (73.7cm) tall by Paul Crees. Wax doll with human hair wig, painted features and inserted human hair eyelashes. Wears white and silver evening dress with batwing sleeves, oversewn with bugle beads; diamonte trimmings; black stockings; silver shoes; white flower in hair. Edition of 50. Signed at nape of neck. Signed and numbered certificate of authenticity. First made January 1984. *Photograph courtesy of Paul Crees.*

LEFT: *Judy Garland*, 29in (73.7cm) tall by Paul Crees. Wax doll with human hair wig, painted features and inserted human hair eyelashes. Wears costume fashioned after that from the film *Get Happy*. Signed on nape of neck. Signed and numbered certificate of authenticity. *Photograph courtesy of Paul Crees.*

ann parker

Ann Parker's historical dolls are real. The British artist has spent so much time creating each character, she knows his foibles, fashions, mindset, hairstyles and the set of his shoulders -- not to mention historical data and catty gossip.

She speaks about them with fondness derived from intimacy, often as if the dolls were living beings. For example, below, she writes about the derivation of *Princess Charlotte*.

"The *Princess Charlotte* figure came into being because I wanted to do one of those regency silver dresses; however, she turned out to have a most interesting history. Her husband, Prince Leopold, was heartbroken when she died, but devoted himself to helping to bring up Queen Victoria. (Later he became King of Belgium and father of the Princess Charlotte, or Carlotta, wife of the Emperor Maximillian, who was shot in Mexico.) Princess Charlotte's father and mother were both rather notorious characters; a contemporary jingle about her mother runs:

'Oh gracious Queen we thee implore
To go away and sin no more.
Or if that effort be too great
To go away at any rate' "

Ann's dolls have a fine lineage. Their creator was a fashion artist and illustrator on Fleet Street, London, for a dozen years, and is adept at pastel portraiture. A jack-of-all-trades, she resisted returning to work as an illustrator after a hiatus, because of the limitations of working in black and white. A chance comment from her husband, that one of his patients, a toy agent, was looking for a doll dressed in Sussex costumes, for sale to airports, clicked off a mental explosion.

"I felt as though a large brick had hit me between the eyes. I knew, instantly, I was about to embark on something successful and I felt that my whole life had been geared to this moment of realization."

Months of trial-and-error ensued, culminating in a two-week period, in 1973, in which she had the house to herself.

"That was the most exciting fortnight of my life. I dashed off to Southampton to buy fibreglass resin and rubber molding material. It cost a quarter of today's prices, otherwise I could never have afforded to experiment in the way I did. By the last evening, before the return of my family, I was dancing round the kitchen shouting 'Eureka!' I knew then, for certain, I could do it."

Ann developed a casting resin with an ivory-like texture to reproduce her sculptures. As her methods were born in the kitchen, this is where, to this day, her dolls are produced. When asked to describe her doll making studio, she wrote: "kitchen table, drawing room chair, dining room table, bedroom, etc. Some neat. Kitchen's become a bit grim, especially with mold making mixed up with the cooking."

From her sculptures, carved in plaster originally, now done directly into resin, she makes rubber molds in the kitchen. "This is a bit tricky and nerve wracking," she states. "I usually take the first few casts to work on and make the clothes, and then hand on the molds to one of the ladies who casts and assembles the figures for me in between household tasks. The figure is then passed on to the lady who does the hair, (although I do some of the hair myself, particularly *George*, who is a perfect nightmare) and then comes back to me so that I can paint the face. We have a tremendous number of rejects, unfortunately."

Ann now works with a group of about a dozen carefully chosen women who perform various doll making tasks for her. In the beginning it was just her and her mother who did some of the sewing. Every step of the way, though, the dolls are checked. She finds, sometimes, this to be infuriating. "It's hard to keep my cool when things have been sewn wrongly."

Ann puts the hats on, at just the right angle, mounts the doll on the stand and sorts things out. "There is usually a good deal of gnashing of teeth at this stage I fear, but I do it once a week when one of my ladies comes in to help me twiddle the wires of the stands and pack up dolls for the mail, etc."

With the assistance of her helpers, ten dolls a week, about 300 a year, are produced, not necessarily at an even pace. "We have a lot of weeks' holiday!," Ann says. She now spends only 30 or 40 hours a week doll making; at the beginning, it was more like 100. Each doll entails at least 40 hours' work.

From the start, they were historic figures. Ann tries to make one new doll every year, in January. She totally immerses herself in the subject and his or her era, as she seeks knowledge that will produce a true portrait -- not only visual knowledge, but verbal, and sensory; she needs to feel his presence, to know that the subject will cooperate with her. When they do not, things never work. Sometimes subjects just will not sit, will not be captured. Ann describes such an occurrence.

"*Jane Austen* (1775-1817) was my second portrait figure, being my favorite person. Unfortunately, there is no authentic portrait, other than an unfinished scrawl by her sister, Cassandra, on which the two well known engravings are based. I feel fairly certain that she disliked having her likeness taken, as she has

BELOW: Close-up of *Beatrix Potter* by Ann Parker, 11in (28cm) tall. Solid resin. Wool crepe hair in very light brown. Pale turquoise-colored bustle style dress. Beatrix is holding a furry rabbit. She was very round shouldered and became quite humpy in old age. *Photograph courtesy of Ann Parker.*

LEFT: *Henry VIII* by Ann Parker, 11½in (29.3cm). Solid resin. Painted hair and beard but mohair moustache. Red velvet cloak with imitation fur; black velvet hat. *Photograph by Nick Nicholson. Courtesy of Ann Parker.*

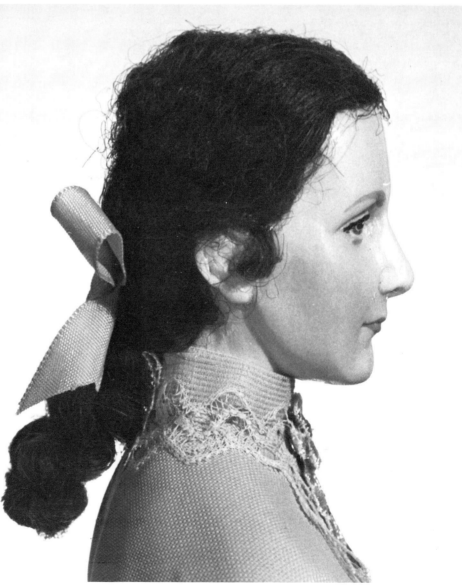

definitely been fighting back. Everything goes wrong with *Jane*. However, I'm hoping she's thrown in the sponge, as we seem to have a lull in the hostilities since the stamps came out in her honour in 1975.''

Constructing a three-dimensional sculpture of an historic figure from two-dimensional sources is difficult. Often, portraits are only available in full-faced or, at best, in three-quarter views.

"Naturally, one can only get good results where there are good portraits available. This makes the Royal personages so tempting to do. I usually bank up 8 or 10 pictures of the subject if possible, but there's always ONE extra special one.''

Reconstructing a profile necessitates a lot of skill and luck. In the case of *Lord Nelson*, she was able to work from the death mask -- at least, from a photograph of it. Often though, death masks are misleading, as they can be taken at odd angles and Ann believes that the set of a person's neck determines his whole persona.

"Sometimes when I've got a figure half finished but still with no features, people can tell who it is even then,'' she states. I get quite surprised when people think I stick a selection of different heads on the same figure, or suggest that I rationalize production by doing so.

"There are some interesting funeral effigies in Westminster Abbey,'' she says "which were taken from death masks, and they are extremely misleading because the angle of the head is wrong. These include Henry VIII, Queen Elizabeth I and Charles II and don't look a bit like them. If I could get my hands on them and pull their chins down...''

Like *Jane Austin*, Ann's *Henry VIII* has a mind of his own. He asserted his personality, even as he was being designed.

"A letter written at the end of his daughter's, Queen Elizabeth I's, reign describes a portrait of Henry as being so lifelike that it was impossible to look at it without feeling frightened. He certainly frightened me as he took shape. As he began to be nearly finished, I became quite terrified of him; however, I feel I've really done him justice, by some fluke. He looks noble and dignified and rather dashing, as well as frightening. However, he continues to be rather a trial to us, mainly because he's so heavy. He fights his way out of boxes and breaks the ladies' hands if you let him get too near.''

Sometimes a doll just will not let itself be born and a different one emerges, changing Ann's plans. Such was the case when she tried to sculpt Winston Churchill.

"There were lots of books about Sir Winston Churchill to celebrate the Centenary of his birth. I bought most of them with the idea of getting down to the sculpture of him. Most of the busts, etc. on the market don't really catch his impish look.

"However, I ended up doing Jennie Jerome instead (the celebrated American beauty and mother of Sir Winston Churchill 1854-1921), and am still thinking about Sir Winston.''

Beatrix Potter was a delightful subject to study, but rather difficult. She was so depressed during the first half of her life, when various little animals seem to have been her only friends, but after writing her books, marrying and becoming a prosperous farmer, she became a very jolly old lady with twinkling eyes.

"She wasn't a bit interested in clothes and sometimes wore old sacks, so I chose the charming photograph on the cover of her most interesting and delightful journal (written in code in her late teens) and tried to represent the dress she wore -- undoubtedly chosen by her mother.''

Another lady writer asserted her will. "Agatha Christie was unusual, looking quite different at different ages; I intended to portray her at 60 but in the end it was the dreamy picture taken in childhood that caught my eye.''

Ann's aim is to bring her subject to life with as much fidelity as possible, to put herself in contact with, as it were, the spirit of that person, and let it transmit itself to the clay through her hands.

"What I want to do, more than anything else,'' she explains, "is to capture the REALITY of the person. I have no ideas at all of self-expression; the whole concentration goes to the subject (or should I say object). Any preconceived ideas of mine are nearly always wiped out by some intuitive process that seems to grab the reality of the sitter. I'm nearly always surprised by the result and, of course, disappointed, like most artists. I see it so intensely after a

"Where I work. It's very handy as I can do the cooking at the same time.''
Photograph courtesy of Ann Parker.

few weeks' work that the result really couldn't possibly compare with what's in my mind. When the vision fades, THEN I sometimes QUITE like the resulting doll -- usually a few months later.''

Her dolls, when done, are packaged, and marked with the BDA silk label in their clothes, as of late 1982. They carry a swing tag at wrist. But they are not signed or dated in any way. One does not emboss one's friends.

"My dolls certainly are people, and I have resisted ALL advice to mark my figures in any way. Numbers, initials and trademarks make them seem like concentration camp victims, tattooed with numbers. Quite shuddery.''

One feels that even King Henry would approve of her sentiments.

ALICE

JANE SEYMOUR

ABOVE: *Alice in Wonderland* by Ann Parker, 8¼in (21cm) tall. Mohair hair. This version of *Alice* is not based on the real Alice Liddell but on Tenniel's famous drawings. She wears a blue dress and carries a toy pig made of pink felt. *Photograph courtesy of Ann Parker.*

RIGHT: *Ann Boleyn* by Ann Parker, 11in (28cm) tall. Solid resin, with the exception of wires in the upper arms. Mohair hair. Black velvet dress. *Anne Boleyn* was completed some years ago, but has only recently been joined by the other five of Henry's wives. *Photograph courtesy of Ann Parker.*

ABOVE: *Vivien Leigh* by Ann Parker, 11½in (29.3cm) tall. The costume alludes to Scarlett but is not a replica. Solid resin. Painted eyes. Mohair hair, black net snood, white organza dress with crinoline hoop. Most Ann Parker dolls have lavish lace-trimmed petticoats and *Vivien Leigh* is no exception. *Photograph by Andrew Macmillan. Courtesy of Ann Parker.*

RIGHT: *Queen Victoria* as an old lady by Ann Parker, 10in (25.4cm). Solid resin. Black silky dress. Several petticoats. Long white drawers. Painted eyes. Mohair hair. *Photograph by Sylvia Hays. Courtesy of Ann Parker.*

sheila wallace

When Sheila Wallace displayed her wax historical dolls at the Folger Shakespeare Library in Washington, D.C., they reached a cross-section of the populace. People who knew nothing about original dolls came, marveled at their lifelike quality and meticulous dress, and made comments.

"The elderly gent who worked as parking attendant made a point of telling me that he'd seen the dolls, and how much he admired them," she remarked. "He said, 'My favorite is *Raleigh*. Boy was he some dude!' I don't know if Sir Walter would have appreciated the comment, but it brought home to me that dolls, being little versions of ourselves, are a great denominator. I've talked to people from other countries, men and women, kids, old people, etc., and they are all fascinated with these 'little people.'"

Sheila, a doll artist since 1973, works in a special bleached beeswax formula derived from one used by 17th century wax workers, and creates one-of-a-kind portraits of historical figures and idealized fashion types that bring the past to life. This is her goal.

Her dolls are the end product of extensive research and intensive craftsmanship, and involve a knowledge not only of anatomy, sculpture, painting, wig making and wax techniques (many of which she picked up from Madame Tussaud's), but an almost total immersion in the life styles, culture and personages of the era she represents. Working on a doll, for her, is a bit like a trip in a time machine.

"I guess I have gotten so totally engrossed in the creation of my dolls that they have become very real to me. I don't mean that the wax and cloth figures themselves are real, but the people they represent are terribly real and very, very human.

"My research for a doll covers not only portraits but other incredibly fascinating things. I've read books on the history of cosmetics and learned of the horrible concoctions people put on their hair and faces in the name of beauty. I've read biographies of many individuals and learned such things as Queen Victoria's nickname. Her German-born mother called her 'Vickelchin.' Plus the fact that she (Victoria) didn't like children in what she called their 'frog stage,' that is as babes in arms, but she and Albert were good parents otherwise.

"I've learned that Sir Walter Raleigh wrote poetry to the aging Elizabeth, comparing her to the moon; thus, she wore many gowns of white or silver to try to live up to his imagery.

"Katherine, the Great was nicknamed 'Fyke' and as a girl she was also quite a tomboy.

"I've also read books of a more general nature and learned what everyday life was like in a medieval castle, about witchcraft and medicine (not always easy to tell apart!) during the Restoration and endless bits of 'useless' information -- unless to most people, but vital to me and my work!"

Sheila's passion for her work is evident. She treats each portrait doll as if it were real, dressing it from the inside out, according to the conventions of its era, in an attempt to recreate the proper silhouette, which depends upon the proper underpinnings.

"I firmly believe that the underwear must be correct in order that the finished costume look right. I remember trying to watch a T.V. movie about a girl who finds an old dress from the turn of the century and sees the same dress on a lady in an old painting. Whenever she puts on the dress, she becomes the lady in the picture and relives the past. I couldn't figure out why that beautiful dress looked so terrible on the actress until I realized that she was not wearing the correct straight-fronted corset of that period."

Wallace dolls wear whatever corsets their time-periods dictate, as well as appropriate makeup and hairstyles (sometimes these are interchangeable wigs to show more than one design). Their body postures as well as their physiognomy reflect those of the poeple and their place in society.

Heads and limbs are sculpted from wax, around wire armatures. Each finger is formed about a tiny wire for reinforcement. Hair, eyebrows and lashes are inserted into the wax. The rest of the body is fabric.

When groups of figures are executed, interacting parts are carefully balanced, as are comparative heights, fabrics and colors.

Props and jewelry are made to scale and these include amazing items -- swords, rings, earrings, daggers, plate armour, purses, handkerchiefs, parasols, walking sticks -- whatever is necessary to the composition.

Sheila learned many of the skills necessary to create these items while an art student in London, where her family was stationed during a decade; her father was with the United States military. Like Winston Churchill, and her fellow doll artist, Ann Parker, she studied at the Heatherley School of Art, where Queen Victoria once had her portrait painted. The curriculum included painting, drawing, anatomy and sculpture.

"I fell in love with sculpture and when I went on to the City and Guilds of London School of Art, I specialized in this course. While at City and Guilds I was able to attend the anatomy lectures at the Royal Academy School of Art, which included a visit to the

LEFT: *Gibson Girl* by Sheila Wallace. Limited edition doll designed exclusively for Kimport Dolls in 1983. She is 13in (33cm) tall and dressed in striped white cotton with yellow straw hat elaborately trimmed, and she carries white "kid" gloves and a parasol. *Photograph courtesy of Sheila Wallace.*

BELOW: *Gibson Girl in Evening Dress* by Sheila Wallace. One-of-a-kind doll approximately 19in (48.3cm) tall. She wears a mint green off-the-shoulder evening gown with long train and chiffon overdress, trimmed with ecru lace. The ribbon shoulder straps and gathered belt are of dusty purple. She carries a tiny beaded bag and feather fan which Sheila made (it can be folded). She also has a short evening cape (not shown) made from midnight blue patterned taffeta. Made in 1979. *Photograph courtesy of Sheila Wallace.*

BELOW LEFT: *Late 18th Century Gent with Wardrobe of Wigs* by Sheila Wallace. He has a leather-covered storage box to both contain and display his various wigs. His long tail coat is russet velveteen, his breeches green suede and he has a striped waistcoat trimmed with white fringe. He carries a long walking stick. One-of-a-kind, approximately 19in (48.3cm) tall, he was produced in 1978. *Photograph courtesy of Sheila Wallace.*

dissecting room of a major London hospital."

Her career as a doll artist really began after returning to Pennsylvania in 1974, where she combined her extensive art study, a love of costume, history and of doll into sculpted figures, ranging in size from doll house scale (1in = 12in: 2.5cm = 30.5cm) to an average of 18 to 20in (45.7cm to 50.8cm). Most are individually done, although some limited editions employ wax castings from her clay models.

Wallace dolls are not toys; Sheila is delighted they are considered art.

"Obviously, my dolls are not playthings, but I admire people who design and create dolls which are. My passion is history and historic costume, but I also admire those who make modern dolls, that is dolls which represent contemporary characters or subjects," she says. "I like to think of my dolls as 'art' or mixed media 'sculpture.'

"I am always very flattered to be called an 'artist.' My training was in England where the term 'artist' is a very narrow one, confined to fine art: painting, sculpture, etc. There, I would be considered a 'craftsman.' However, I think that is changing."

Craftsman or artist, she is content in her work.

"I feel that I am not only doing what I want to do, but what I SHOULD be doing. Looking back, I realize that all my past experiences -- traveling and living in Europe, the influence of my parents and the type of art education I had all 'conspired' to lead me to making the type of dolls I now make. I love wax as a working medium, but have also done some carved wooden heads and am always willing to try new materials. However, any new medium would still be tried with an eye to creating a 'Historic Costume Doll.'"

Although the dolls are done with identical care, Sheila does admit to favorites. This is because the dolls come to life to her. She feels the force of their personalities and hopes to convey this to viewers.

"I was told by one of my instructors at art college that good art makes the beholder feel what you felt when you created it," she explains. "I think any doll should do the same. Naturally, all the technical points should be correct: anatomy, construction, suitable use of materials, etc, but the entire 'feel' or 'mood' of a doll should be complete of itself.

"Hopefully, anyone who sees my dolls will feel what I felt in creating them. I would hope that, perhaps, people would become interested not just in the figures themselves, but in the people they represent, and would realize that these people were really people and just as human, in their way, as any of us today."

Sheila certainly reacts in this way. Certain of her creations have spoken distinctly to her.

"Elizabeth I, to me, was a very dynamic lady -- one of the original 'women's libbers!,'" Sheila says. "She ruled a powerful nation at a time when women were very much second class citizens. I have read somewhere that men such as Shakespeare and Johnson gathered in the coffee houses to discuss such topics as 'Do Women Have Souls?' So, you see, Elizabeth came a long way, baby!

"Marie Antoinette is another favorite, not just because of her lavish taste in clothing, but because I think she and Louis were rather misjudged. They were not particularly evil people, just found themselves in the wrong place at the wrong time, so to speak. I tend to think of them with more sympathy than anything.

"Henry VIII is a character for which I get many requests, and although I do not like him as a person, he is quite a lush, fantastic figure to create and costume. Actually, if you can put yourself in his place and think as the people of his time thought, one can almost forgive, and can certainly understand some of his actions regarding his wives."

At one of her recent exhibits, Sheila overheard a mother speaking with her son, who was eight or ten years old. They were reacting to the lifelike quality of her figures, one specifically. She describes the scene.

"The mother pointed out *Henry VIII.* Her son mis-heard her and asked why he was called 'Henry the Ape.' By our standards, his physical appearance and actions would warrant that he be called "Ape," but, as I said, we shouldn't judge him too harshly!" He might just come to life.

Henry VIII by Sheila Wallace. One-of-a-kind doll approximately 20in (50.8cm) tall. This is the third version of *Henry* Sheila has done. Because of the way these dolls are produced, no two versions of the same character are ever alike. This close-up shows the fur reverse of his black velvet gown, his slashed and gold braided doublet, heavy neck chains and the typical feather-trimmed "court bonnet" of the period. His body construction is typical of Wallace dolls, but he has both composition lower and upper legs. They are jointed at the knee. Sheila often uses this method of producing legs for men who will wear either very tight breeches or, as in *Henry's* case, long hose or "netherstocks," which will show the contours of the legs. *Photograph courtesy of Sheila Wallace.*

LEFT: Close-up of *Queen Victoria* and *Baby Edward* by Sheila Wallace. One-of-a-kind. She is dressed in pale yellow striped silk with a deep frill of the same material around the hem of her dress. Her cap is lace-trimmed and the ''pelerin'' around her shoulders is also of antique lace. Her body construction is the same as all Wallace dolls, and the baby has a wax head, arms and legs attached to a polyester-filled body. His clothing includes the many layers of underwear a Victorian baby wore, plus the long, lace-trimmed christening robe and two caps. The outer cap is lavishly trimmed and has a blue ribbon rosette on the left side to indicate that he is a little boy. *Photograph courtesy of Sheila Wallace.*

BELOW: *Princess Victoria* by Sheila Wallace. Cast wax, limited edition doll, 13in (33cm) tall, the first doll Sheila produced which had the chubbier proportions of a ''play'' doll. Modeled from a portrait of Queen Victoria as a little girl, the doll's costume shows the type of dress a little girl would have worn ''for best'' in the 1840s. It is made of off-white batiste and trimmed with laces which Sheila dyed herself, and has a pink satin sash. The cap is of batiste and is worn under a dusty mauve satin bonnet. There were 24 in the completed series. *Photograph courtesy of Sheila Wallace.*

BELOW LEFT: Close-up of *Princess Victoria*, Sheila Wallace's first cast-wax play-doll style sculpture. *Photograph courtesy of Sheila Wallace.*

LEFT: *Empress Eugenie* by Sheila Wallace. One-of-a-kind doll stands approximately 18in (45.7cm) tall. She wears a cream taffeta ball gown with huge hoop and petticoats. Her dress is trimmed with flowers and antique black lace. Body construction is basically the same as for all Wallace dolls, but she wears short sleeves, thus has full wax arms, not just hands. Produced in 1978. *Photograph courtesy of Sheila Wallace.*

BELOW: *Godey Lady of 1876* by Sheila Wallace. One-of-a-kind doll standing approximately 19in (48.3cm) tall with hat. Her face was taken from one of Mr. Godey's illustrations and she has the large dark eyes and dark hair popular at the time. Her lavish costume shows the "cuirasse" body popular after the collapse of the bustle. She wears a long corset and lavish petticoats underneath and her outer costume consists of the long-trained dress and draped overskirt, both of which are made from man-made silk, but many of the trimmings are of antique fabrics or real silk. Her body construction is as usual, except that her wax hands and arms have long kid gloves fitted over them. *Photograph courtesy of Sheila Wallace.*

BELOW LEFT: Disassembled parts for *Admiral Lord Nelson* by Sheila Wallace. Composition legs with finished stockings and shoes. Directly modeled head with face completed and hair implanted, fingernails cut and painted and veins indicated. Produced in 1977. *Photograph courtesy of Sheila Wallace.*

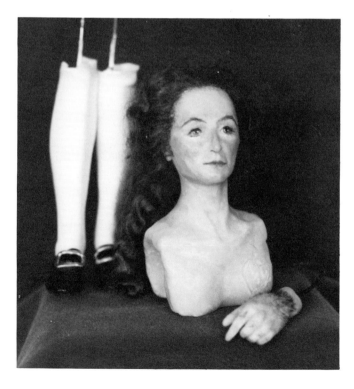

june gale

June Gale's portrait dolls reflect her personal philosophy of doll making. While they capture the essence of the subject and are recognizable, both in dress and physiognomy, they are definitely dolls -- not rarified sculpture. Their features have what the artist calls a "dollified" look. Unlike most portrait dolls, they are "real" dolls, with swivel heads and soft bodies that can sit down. Their clothes are removable; they are potentially playthings.

The Kent, England, artist currently specializes in portrait dolls of British royalty, contemporary and past. The series of *Lady Diana* and *Princess Diana* dolls is perhaps the most popular of her work, attracting attention from the United States, Japan, Italy and Australia.

Starting with an engagement portrait of Lady Di in her famous blue outfit, she followed with *Diana*, bride, which was complete except for clothing on the Royal wedding day. Before its end, June had fully costumed her creation. A portrait doll of the little bridesmaid, Clementine Hambro, soon followed.

Prince Charles, she reports, has been the most "challenging" of the current Royal family to recreate, but his first son has inspired more than one portrait doll.

The second *Prince William* was done from official photographs of the Royal family's tour to Australia, and is 10in (25.4cm) high. As June feels most doll collectors prefer glass eyes, he is one of the few dolls she has made with painted eyes. They give him an extremely lifelike look -- much more so than the glass-eyed dolls, even though she refers to him, also, as "dollified."

Glass eyes, while desirable to doll buyers, must be kept in their place. "I often carry pocketsful of glass eyes around with me," June states, "which has proven somewhat unnerving to the general public. But this is the sort of thing that happens to most doll makers, I'm sure."

Her favorite portrait doll is that of *Princess Mary Stuart*. "There is a nice mixture of childish innocence, sensitivity and vulnerability in her face, which is, at the same time, that of a Royal Princess. This pleases me."

She tries to bring the personalities of her "sitters" (she works from paintings and photographs) to life, to make them recognizable as portraits, and yet remain dolls.

"In making dolls my aim is to produce a lively, real personality; to give the illusion that there is a tiny brain and character in those little porcelain heads. I hope that some of this comes across to the people who like my dolls and that they are aware of the qualities I try to endow my dolls with," she explains.

They vary in size. Many adult dolls are 18 or 19in (45.7 or 48.3cm) tall, and the child dolls are from 10 to 12in (25.4 to 30.5cm). "I do not work to any particular scale," June states. "I would probably feel very restricted if I tried to."

Early Gale dolls were child dolls and "lady" dolls. From the first, they were originals, but, because she was working in a vaguely nostalgic style, sometimes her work was not understood by the public. Most infuriating was *Miss*, a lady doll discontinued, as she puts it, "mostly because people kept on thinking she was a reproduction doll, which -- after all my hard work on the modeling --was very hard to take!"

A reproduction doll she chanced to spy in a shop window sparked interest in creating her own, the first of which, made of pottery clay coils and glazed, were rather crude. Since then Gale has amassed what she terms a catholic collection, but dolls were hardly her childhood companions.

"Oddly enough, I came late to the love and appreciation of dolls," she reports. "As a child, I was never very interested in them, apart from the paper ones. Not for me the sweet-faced darlings other children wheeled proudly about in their doll prams. My doll pram contained either a very large, furry Teddy Bear, tightly wedged in under the covers or -- far more exciting -- our very obliging family cat! Both Big Ted and Timmy Shang'hi suffered the indignity of being dressed in baby bonnets, booties and bibs, but happily both survived the ordeal. Timmy lived to a ripe old age and Big Ted is still with me, living in dignified retirement in Beckenham."

After experimenting with directly-sculpted glazed heads, producing some rather peculiar early attempts, she progressed to earthenware slip-casting sculpted models and began to make molds for them.

"This was quite an experience as I used the mold-making techniques I had learned for life-size sculpture and found myself enthusiastically throwing wet plaster, handful by handful, at the small modeled doll heads.

"Consequently, we lived, for some time, almost up to the eyebrows in plaster.

"I will never forget my first attempt to make a mold of an arm. It took exactly seven attempts to achieve a reasonable result. With grim determination I carried on and on! In those days -- about six years ago, today being 1984 -- I was unaware of any books available on the subject of mold making and casting, although I believe there were some available in the U.S.A. I had to learn through trial and many errors!"

Most doll makers, even those who have had classes -- and there are few of those -- learn in a similar way. For many, their processes, although individually developed, echo June's.

"Inspired by a painting or by a real child or a famous personality, I set to work, armed where possible with a large variety of photographs, and model my doll in either plasticine or clay. I prefer to work in clay but because time is always at a premium with me and clay dries out so quickly, and because there is much more refinement in modeled plasticine, I have to use that medium more than clay.

"This is the most time-consuming and, for my part, enjoyable part of the whole proceedings. When satisifed that I can go no further with the modeling (and I am never ever satisfied), I go on to make the dreaded molds. I hate this part of the business exceedingly. Then comes the slip-casting in porcelain and the exciting moment when the first casting is made.

"The porcelain is then fired in my small test kiln (I really ought to buy a bigger one), rubbed down, painted and re-fired as necessary. I go on to design and make the body and clothing, including the shoes, hats and other accessories, and, as often as not, make my own wigs.

"I am never too sure what my dolls are going to turn out like. They sometimes take over their own development and until a doll is completely finished and has lived with me for a while, I am not even sure what I think of it."

Many doll makers, this writer included, have makeshift kitchen "studios." June describes her studio's particular lure for her -- and for her family.

"Most of my work is done in the kitchen. It is a large, pleasant room, but unfortunately for me it seems to have irresistible attractions for the home hobbyist, of which our family boasts more than one.

"My husband has a penchant for restoring old furniture, boxes and frames and brings them into my 'workroom' to deal with them, whilst my son uses the water supply for washing his prints (he is a keen photographer). Both of them are also keen winemakers.

"Over the years I have grown accustomed to making dolls to the accompaniment of bubbling demijohns, running water, hissing pressure cookers and the sound of sawing wood, but a more ominous turn has recently been taken inasmuch as my son is developing a powerful interest in restoring car engines.

"Several car parts (including one whole, complete engine) have surreptitiously found their way into the kitchen during the past few months, and if you add to these intruders the congregating furniture, doll making equipment (kiln, clay, plaster, sewing-machine, fabrics), books, typewriter and the occasional visitor (who always insists on being where the action is), you will have some idea as to what my 'workroom' looks like most of the time!"

Besides porcelain, June has worked in wax and needle-sculpture, but always returns to clay.

Considering her working environment, it is no wonder that in a good year she produces perhaps a dozen dolls, which are marked "Rose Gale." There have been some "doll poor" years. Editions are limited by circumstances, and are never large. Often designs are one-of-a-kind, and most work is commissioned by people who read about her or see her dolls at shows.

"I am not at all businesslike," June states. "I just make the dolls as and when I can. Not one of them has been made in large quantities. I feel the need to move on to new subjects, to improve and not to become stale."

Fortunately, variations on the theme of British Royalty are boundless. An artist has generations of images from which to choose, a full range of "sitters," eras and attitudes. As others have averred, the field is not without its difficulties, and June thrives on them.

"The thing that has helped me most in doll making," she says, "is the constant, ever-increasing challenge -- the challenge to capture beauty perhaps, or charm, an elusive personality, a fleeting expression -- and also the challenge to do better. There is such a lot I want to do."

The Princess of Wales and *Bridesmaid* by June Gale. The *Princess* is 19in (48.3cm), the bridesmaid 13in (33cm). Porcelain. Six variations of the *Princess* made, two similar bridesmaids. *Princess* has a swivel neck on a shoulder plate. *Bridesmaid* has a flange neck. Cloth bodies. Both have porcelain lower arms and legs. *Princess* has wired arms. Both have blue glass eyes and synthetic fair hair. Both dressed in pure silk trimmed with lace and embroidered with pearls and sequins. 1983. A pair of dolls similar to these can be seen at the Lilliput Museum on the Isle of Wight. These two are in the artist's collection. *Photograph courtesy of June Gale.*

Close-up of the heavily-embroidered lace on the wedding gown of the *Princess of Wales* doll by June Gale. The lace is embroidered by hand by the artist with tiny pearls, in strings and separately, and also embroidered with tiny transparent pearlized sequins. "It takes forever!" the artist says. The train is embroidered in the same way. *Photograph courtesy of June Gale.*

ABOVE: *Prince William*, 18in (45.7cm) tall by June Gale. Summer 1983. One-of-a-kind. Porcelain head and limbs on cloth body. Painted eyes. Swivel head on shoulder plate. Hand-made synthetic wig. Dressed in white shirt and peach rompers. Marked: ''Rose Gale. 1983.'' A ''dollified'' version of Prince William dressed in clothing he wore on the New Zealand tour. The artist is working on other versions of Prince William at other ages. *Photograph courtesy of June Gale.*

RIGHT: *Prince William*, 7in (17.8cm) tall by June Gale. 1982. Only two dolls made. Flanged-neck porcelain head. Porcelain arms and legs. Fabric body. Painted eyes. Satin christening gown with lace over, based on the royal christening gown. Matching pillow. Marked: ''Rose Gale. 1982.'' A ''dollified'' version of the Prince on his Christening day. Dolls in private and artist's collection. *Photograph courtesy of June Gale.*

ABOVE LEFT: *Miss Annabel*, 18in (45.7cm) and *Hannah*, 13in (33cm) by June Gale. Porcelain heads, lower arms and legs; fabric bodies. Both have glass eyes. *Hannah* has synthetic hair. *Miss Annabel* has real hair. *Miss Annabel* is dressed in pale yellow cotton trimmed with yellow satin. *Hannah* wears pale pink sprigged cotton, a voile apron and a matching bonnet. *Hannah* has removable shoes. *Miss Annabel's* are modeled onto her feet. *Miss Annabel* is a version of June's "Miss" dolls, of which about ten have been made. *Hannah* is typical of her "child" dolls. © 1980. *Photograph courtesy of June Gale.*

ABOVE: *Clementine*, 18in (45.7cm) tall by June Gale. Three dolls made to date. Poured wax head and lower arms and legs. Fabric body. Blue glass eyes. Synthetic handmade wig. Dressed in a white voile Kate Greenaway-style dress with a blue sash. Antique lace on her bonnet. Long petticoat and pantalettes. White leather shoes. No markings. 1980. "This doll was my first attempt at working in wax, and is still in my collection. Two similar wax dolls have been made with different hair and eyes. The other two are in private collections." *Photograph courtesy of June Gale.*

LEFT: *Lil*, 32in (81.3cm) tall by June Gale. One-of-a-kind all-fabric doll with wired arms. Synthetic wig. Bead eyes. Dressed in glittering turquoise evening gown, gold lace gloves, dark brown fur wrap, smothered in paste diamonds. No markings. 1983. "Made for fun. Kept in my own collection to accompany me on my doll 'talks.'" *Photograph courtesy of June Gale.*

margaret glover

"I feel I have been given the final accolade now. Madame Tussaud's has sent me some restorations and tomorrow I am being shown round their workrooms," reads a postscript to a letter from Margaret Glover in February 1984.

Her wax dolls have won numerous prizes over the years and are on display at Pollock's Toy Museum, Bethnal Green Museum and similar institutions in Britain and elsewhere. Noted for fine coloring, expert finishing and attention to detail, they attest to Mrs. Glover's uncompromising approach to doll making.

"The wax has to be perfect and a good color," she says. "The total effect, including the costuming, has to be as perfectly conceived and made as possible. I do not like short cuts of any kind like wigs or bought clothes. My dolls are not touched by anyone else and I make everything for them from hats to shoes. If anyone else had a hand in my producing my dolls, I should not feel that they were my own work."

Doll making came, not out of extensive art training (although her family included gifted amateur painters and musicians, and she did fine sewing, knitting and crochet from an early age), but out of a search for an occupation a bit more sedentary than restoring old cottages and boats.

She describes her varied careers. "I have been a farmer's wife, boat builder, glider pilot, house restorer, aeronautical engineer, nurse, hairdresser, secretary, language teacher, writer, broadcaster, wife and mother, not necessarily in that order, and amateur archaeologist."

A friend who had been trained in a waxworks showed her how to handle his medium and Margaret began to make wax dolls as a hobby, using techniques basically unchanged from the days of the Pierottis and Montaris in the mid 19th century.

Her interest in the subject led her to restoration work on antique dolls, which affords her invaluable experience handling the work of her predecessors. In this way, she learned that the skin tones on Pierotti dolls were far more lifelike than heretofore imagined, and was able to replicate their techniques on one of her own designs.

Glover dolls often are inspired by literature or art. *Claudine*, a 10in (25.4cm) girl with rooted gold-blonde hair, poured wax head and limbs and brown paperweight eyes, was based on the Renoir painting, "Les Parapluies." All the colors in the costume are as nearly as possible those in the painting, and the costume replicates that of the small child on the right of the painting.

The dolls come to life in a small work room with a large south-facing window under which stands a venerable gateleg table. Here, the process begins.

"First I make a model in clay or wax, from which I take a plaster mold. This is the basis of all my dolls -- the mold is used for making a poured wax shell with which I work. The bodies are made to an old design, strong cotton or calico stuffed with kapok or sawdust, to which the wax limbs are attached. All the clothes are real, made from natural or old materials, and are removable. I design and make the complete costumes, including hats, shoes, parasols, flamingos and anything else which is part of the design. No one else has any hand in producing my dolls."

Hair, including lashes, is rooted in the wax with a needle. Paperweight glass eyes are used. Bodies are fashioned from kapok-stuffed cotton.

Over 50 different dolls have been designed but no more than ten of any design are done. Each, even though mold-born, is unique because of the nature of the medium.

Mrs. Glover is opposed to mass production of her dolls. "I should never allow such a thing," she says. "Rather poor from what I have seen."

And she is modest about her achievements, stating that her creations are "just dolls. They are not play dolls, but I think that to describe them as art or sculpture would be presumptuous. I am not concerned with the art world. Dolls are just dolls. The dictionary definition is 'a puppet or small image in human form for the amusement of children' and although they have now taken on a deeper significance and possibly another dimension, they are still only dolls. I think many people take the whole thing too seriously, but this may be due to the fact that antique dolls have become collectors' items and so much finance is now at stake."

Her work, while it uses antique methods, has a distinctive style and signature to it. Glover children have pensive, sad, introspective faces. "One reaction which I did enjoy very much," she states, "was that of a lady who said she had never liked the antique wax dolls because she found them ugly, but she did like mine."

Dolls are available directly from the artist's London studio, by mail or by appointment. Often, customers offer her accolades, as the doll maker relates: "I sold several dolls to some Japanese gentlemen who said that if I were a Japanese, I would be given the official title of Intangible Cultural Asset or better still, Human National Treasure and a pension from the government to back the title up! I liked that very much."

LEFT: *Claudine*, 17in (43.2cm) tall by Margaret Glover. © 1979. Poured wax. Edition of less than ten. Rooted, needle-inserted gold-blonde hair. Brown paperweight eyes. Rooted lashes and brows. Poured wax arms and legs. Cotton-stuffed kapok body. Lace-trimmed pantaloons and petticoats. Coat of lace-trimmed brown velvet with eight large pearl buttons. Pleated blue wool edging to coat. Hat has blue, cream and brown frills trimmed with tiny flowers; gold-brown ribbon ties. She carries a hoop and stick. Black stockings and black leather slippers. All sewing done by maker. Marked: "Glover/date" on shoulder plate. This doll was based on the painting, "Les Parapluies," by Auguste Renoir. She is the small child on the right of the painting. All the colors in the costume have been made as close as possible to those in the painting. *Photograph courtesy of Margaret Glover.*

BELOW: *Cherry Ripe*, 17in (43.2cm) tall by Margaret Glover. © 1979. Edition of less than ten. Poured wax. Rooted red-gold hair, needle inserted. Inserted eyelashes and brows. Blue paperweight eyes. Poured wax arms and legs. Cotton-stuffed kapok body. Fine cotton pantaloons and petticoat. White silk stockings and pink satin slippers. Overdress of hand-embroidered muslin (Edinburgh work), lined puff sleeves with top shirring, handmade lace fichu. Wide pure silk satin sash with bow at the back. Mob cap of cotton-trimmed lace and satin ribbon. Black lace mittens. Marked: "Glover/date." This doll is based on the painting, "Cherry Ripe," by Sir John Everett Millais. *Photograph courtesy of Margaret Glover.*

OPPOSITE PAGE: *Emmeline* by Margaret Glover. © 1977. Head only 4in (10.2cm) high. Wax: double poured. One-of-a-kind. Needle-inserted child's blonde hair. Paperweight blue eyes. Whitework fichu. "Glover" incised on back of shoulder plate. "This head was made to illustrate how wax dolls used to look in their original state. Many collectors do not believe that the wax always had a matte finish when it left the maker's hands. I tried to reproduce the finish found on a mint *Pierotti*, still boxed." *Photograph courtesy of Margaret Glover.*

Bubbles, 17in (43.2cm) tall by Margaret Glover. © 1973. Poured wax doll. Not more than six made. Rooted red-gold hair, needle inserted. Paperweight blue eyes. Poured wax arms and legs. Cotton stuffed kapok body. Dressed in an olive green velvet suit, silk shirt and silk ruffles. Green socks to match green leather shoes tied with green silk ties. He is seated on a log holding a clay bubble bowl and pipe. There is a small tablet of Pears soap at his feet. Marked: "Glover/date" on the back of shoulder plate. This doll is based on the painting by Sir John Everett Millais used by the Pears Soap Company as an advertisement. *Photograph courtesy of Margaret Glover.*

Alice, 18in (45.7cm) tall by Margaret Glover. © 1977. Poured wax doll. Edition of less than ten. Rooted hair, needle inserted. Blue paperweight eyes. Poured wax arms and legs. Cotton-stuffed kapok body. Carries a scarlet flamingo under her arm. Underclothing: pantaloons and petticoat made from old materials and hand-embroidered. Dress of blue nunsveiling trimmed with handmade lace. Pinafore of white cotton trimmed with hand-embroidered edging; one pocket, large ties at the back. Striped cotton socks and black slippers. The costume is an exact replica of that in the original Tenniel drawings. Marked: "Glover/date" on back of shoulder plate. *Photograph courtesy of Margaret Glover.*

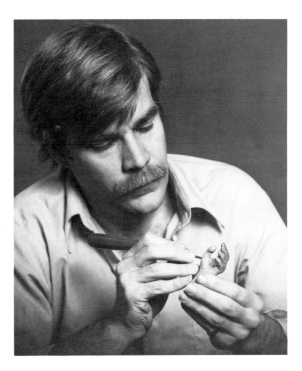

michael langton

Can you believe a carved rolled hat brim?

Can you believe a hat that has been carved so that it is absolutely undetectable from a real woven straw hat?

Can you believe cowboy boots carved with such detail that they are impossible to tell from tooled leather?

Probably not...at least not until you reach out and touch.

One of the absolutely most frustrating problems...one that recurs again and again for artists, collectors and photographers is managing to get a good, true picture of a doll.

When we first saw photographs of Michael Langton's work, it was pretty obvious that the pieces were especially fine, but it was not until we were literally "eyeball to eyeball" with the actual object that all of the wonderous detail could be seen and truly appreciated for what it was.

Michael is a wood sculptor and we say sculptor advisedly -- these are in no way just whittlings of a New Hampshire rustic sitting on his front porch in a summer's evening. (Although that may be just <u>where</u> and <u>when</u> he does do <u>some</u> of his sculpture.) They are works of art...one-of-a-kind pieces which evoke an immediate emotional response and awe for the technical skill and detail expressed.

When you do get the first-hand experience it is all you can do to keep from reaching out and reassuring yourself by feel that what you see is actually what has been done.

A lot of doll artists might have some reservations about people "pawing their work," but Michael believes that his figures have the potential to actively participate in the moods of their viewers or owners. He wants you to feel them and move them to reflect any mood you might have or feeling you see that the character could have. This capacity to be manipulated and to illustrate the viewer's ideas is just about directly opposite from solid sculpture where the pose is set by the artist to transmit one attitude or a limited range of attitude. Furthermore, his figures are meant to move easily and are also, being wood, durable and, are in addition, simply and sturdily costumed.

Michael's achievement in wood is the ultimate blend of the major aspects and potentials of the art. He can create a carved figure that moves...score one for the art and craft. But he can also put into his carving the recreation of personality strength and individuality. He makes a study of a particular character type and makes it real to the viewer.

"My dolls are definitely people...they have had lives, fears, pressures, successes and failures. I try to illustrate in the dolls the balance of pressure between the internal emotional and intellectual pressures and the outside worldly pressures of friends, enemies, jobs, families, etc."

To do this, Michael tries to represent as much detail as he can see, feel, smell, to give reason for that person's existence.

Transcending the material is one of Michael's favorite definitions in art. He feels that the making of the figure, itself, is only secondary to the feeling it can create in the viewer.

"If a person reacts towards a piece and is sensitive to the feelings I have tried to interpret, then it is a successful piece."

Now, after making dolls for four years, he is working a ten hour day, six day a week schedule. An individual figure takes about 200 hours to make...which, he says is relatively equal to his attention span... "any longer and I would find myself bored and unable to keep up the level of enthusiasm needed to finish the work."

Michael repeats what a lot of other artists have discovered and that is that a high degree of self-discipline is required in order to cover creative ground while the inspiration is being experienced. Michael sees this "creative horticulture" as the responsibility to have a clean work space and sharp tools so that one's thoughts on how to realize the vision are not cluttered, nor is the energy required compromised by unnecessary chores.

Also, he says, "It's a rush and it's exciting...addicting."

To make a doll, Michael selects a piece of wood for the head...a certain attitude for character is all there is to work from at this point...just an idea in *his* head.

"I leave the wood, itself, to influence the development of the character as much as it wishes. If the wood takes over and dictates, a character separate from what I had in mind may evolve. If so the piece is set aside until later when the head is worked to a point where it is believable, credible and the attitude visible."

By attitude, Michael refers to something like the bravado of a matador or the concentration bordering on fanacticism (fisherman) or the macho (cowboy) or the controlled power (a wizard) or the humility (an Arkansas farmer) that can be expressed in a character.

Once the head is done and it reflects the attitude desired, then the hands are carved. They must be done in a way that reflects the attitude in the head. The whole reading of a person is regulated by the hands. They can reinforce the image and make it all work or they can cancel the whole mood if they contradict the head...for instance, it would be very hard to illustrate utmost concentration in a character, if the hands were in a relaxed, loose position. Concentration takes energy and in order to reinforce that you would

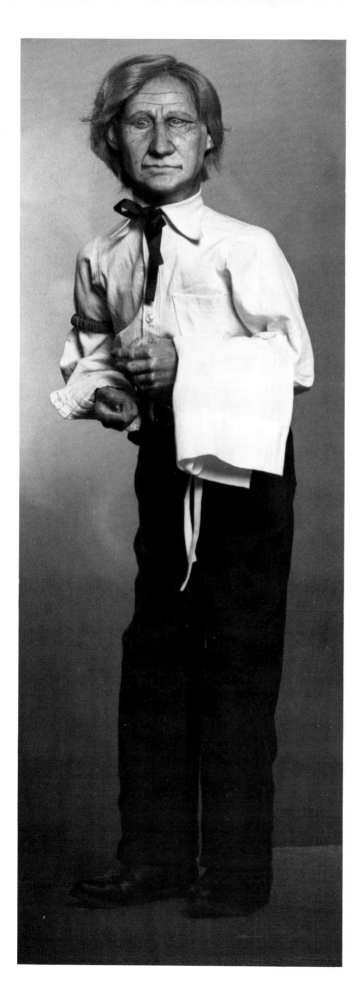

LEFT: *Walter-the Waiter* by Michael Langton. A fully-articulated wooden figure with polymer boots. Sewing by Barbara Itchkawich. *Photograph by Thom Hindle, courtesy of Michael Langton.*

BELOW: *Walter* by Michael Langton -- profile view. *Photograph by Thom Hindle, courtesy of Michael Langton.*

have to make the hand tense. Not only should the flesh be tense but the gesture should illustrate the use of energy.

"Once I have a pair of hands, a hat corresponding with the hands and the body is carved. The posture of the body has to correspond with the attitude that has been established in the head and hands. There are ratios in the body that have to be considered like the straightness of the shoulders relative to the thinness or heaviness of the abdomen and hips."

When the body is built (well over 50 parts), the footwear is designed, again, to reflect the character and reinforce the attitude... for instance, a dirt farmer would naturally have worn down shoes. The detail has to be taken for granted. It must be there but it cannot take over.

When the wooden structure is completed, the clothes are designed and sewn. If necessary, they are stressed to show age or wear. The hair is applied, colored and cut. Whatever other accessories that are necessary are built... like a saddle of hat or glasses, and, Walla! it's complete!

Well, not quite.

Michael's excellent worksmanship and artistry soon brought him face to face with a problem. Problem was: supply and demand. Many more people wanted the figures than he, himself, could provide and many people were not able to afford the amount for a product of so many hours.

The problem of mass production...or even assisted production is a major difficulty for any artist. Most find they must give up the idea or that their work is unsatisfactory when not done entirely by themselves. Mass production in porcelain has been overcome, but mass production of a hand-carved item? It seemed impossible.

Where there is a will there is a way and during 1984 Michael worked diligently to find the way to make his work affordable and available without loosing any element of the quality.

He experimented and achieved several breakthroughs in this direction. The first development was in discovering a faster way to make the multi-pieced hand-carved shoulder/rib joints. Now he can do them in about a fifth of the time it used to take.

As we noted above, Michael is no simple New Hampshire rustic. He, before turning to wood carving, had experience in several fields of art and graphic design. Next, he took experience gained in the production of metalwork in a local foundary and applied it to setting up a production system where the increase in demand would be met with no decrease in quality.

Most people tend to think that if a piece is worked on by more than one person, its value is somehow decreased. "Not so," says Michael. A group of talented, well qualified people, whose intention it is to do the best they can are capable of working jointly on a common project...and it is to the betterment of the project. It gives the buyers of the product a better investment. So, he has proceeded to develop a business on the concept of the guild system.

By late 1984, Michael had gone on to experiment with new combinations of products. He obtained and experimented with polymers for making cast versions of his carved accessory parts... such as the boots. He was looking forward to being able to offer three levels of product...the totally one-of-a-kind original, the combination of hand-carved, machine-produced and cast parts and one that was totally mass produced. Each one would fit some collectors budget and would still be a product of his imagination.

In February of 1985, Langton and Company...artists, production chief, costume designer and business agent... presented their eminently unique line at the famous American International Toy Fair in New York, New York.

Michael had taken a risk, but achieved a goal.

All of this has not gone unremarked. In December of 1984, Michael received a rare accolade for both his art work and his business organization. He was selected for the 1984 *Esquire Magazine Register* of the Best of the New Generation: The men and women under 40 who are changing America. From a beginning field of 60,000 outstanding candidates from all walks of life, this selection is made from a field narrowed first to 5,000 and then, finally, to 250.

What pleased Michael most was that they called him a <u>doll</u> maker.

Calhoun, a cowboy sculpted by Michael Langton in wood. The artist has also constructed the very accurately detailed leather western saddle. *Calhoun's* hat is also carved from wood. *Photograph courtesy of Michael Langton.*

BELOW: *Pierre-the Lumberjack*, 21in (53.3cm), wooden doll with cast polymer boots and gloves, one-of-a-kind, series of 20 by Michael Langton. The costuming is done by Barbara Itchkawich and the axe is by bladesmith Don Fogg. Hands and boots are hand-carved by Michael for the first original or prototype. Michael then makes a mold of these parts and uses the cast boots and gloves for the limited series members in much the same way as another artist might use shoes made by others. As each head in the series is hand-carved and all parts are constructed by him, his type of production is still essentially a <u>series of one-of-a-kind figures which look alike</u>. *Photograph by Thom Hindle; courtesy of Michael Langton.*

RIGHT: Side view of *Pierre* by Michael Langton. *Photograph by Thom Hindle, courtesy of Michael Langton.*

BOTTOM RIGHT: Close-up of *Pierre* by Michael Langton. *Photograph by Thom Hindle, courtesy of Michael Langton.*

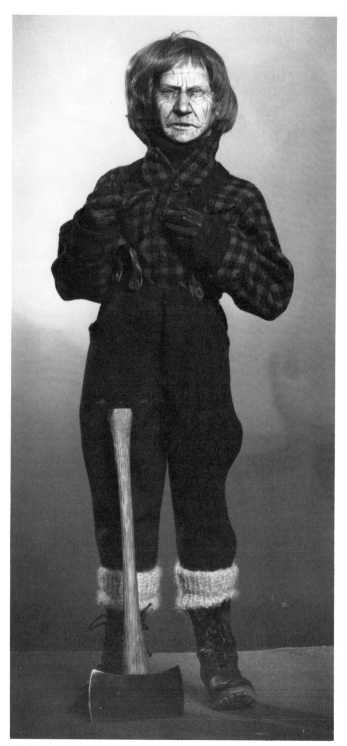

150

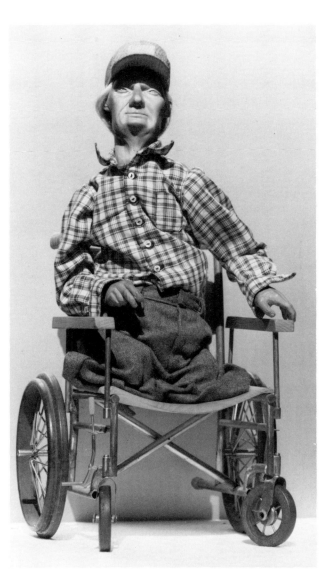

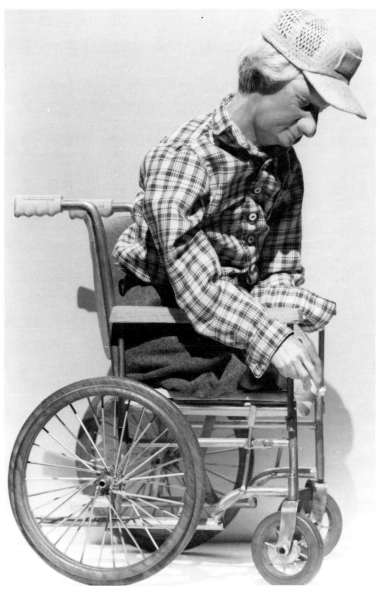

ABOVE: *David,* a 14in (35.6cm) tall wood figure sculpted and carved by Michael Langton. Michael also constructed the accurately detailed wheel-chair. The chair, itself, is carved pine, with walnut wheels and brass spokes. *Photograph courtesy of Michael Langton.*

LEFT: *David* from a different angle showing how the flexible joining allows very realistic positioning of Michael's figures. *Photograph courtesy of Michael Langton.*

flights of fancy —
the character figure

Not bound by the realities of the world around themselves, the artists who create character figures put together the odds, the ends, and the not normally associated parts of life to explore the outer limits of the possible for mankind and then, just as often, take us one step beyond by creating new possibilities.

They make things with wings, things with tails and things that live only in the imagination. They sense the extremes -- the sublime and the ridiculous, the extraordinary and the pathetic. They exaggerate, they manipulate and they rearrange. All this usually requires them to invent and develop new techniques to bring their mind play into a tangible, visible reality.

Knowingly or not, their work is often geared to create an intense reaction. They want us to laugh or cry or become angry...or, at the very least, to consider and to think about their conceptions of personality. They remind us, often with tongue in cheek, that all is not what it seems to be or as we would wish it to be. They are the innovators, prophets and visionaries of the doll world and we cannot do without their comments, messages and directions if we wish to realize our full potential.

152

edna ∫haw dohl

"My goal is to create a pleasure that will last," says Edna Shaw.

Edna sees her work as creating three dimensional pictures of ideas...something that one can hold, and turn and identify with. For her the most exciting part of the doll making process is creating a piece that pleases the eye and touches the heart of the viewer.

Another way to describe a pleasure that has lasting value is a museum quality piece. Edna's approach to an art museum is typical of her reaction to her own art and the art of the world as it relates to her own. First, she enjoys every minute detail of the exhibit of miniature rooms, but agrees with her companion that they would be just a bit more real if there were people shown living in them.

Then, she zips rapidly past the modernists with their abstract and cubist forms but begins to slow her pace through the medieval exhibits...pausing to marvel at intricate carvings in ivory and Gothic sculpture. At the Renaissance she begins to linger and dally as she admires the sculpture and the beginnings of modeling and painting.

She comes to dead stop at the work of the Baroque and Roccoco masters. Here, Edna's enthusiasm begins to get the better of her. In her desire to identify with the artist who produced this work or that, she longs to touch and run her hands over the lines and curves so much that she attracts the concerned attention of the guards who are afraid she might dare to lay a finger on the work. This is just exactly what she wanted to do just to be able to sense something of the original creator's experience...if she had not been caught!

The parts of the museum that attracted and held Edna's attention were those where art like her own was shown. Her attitude to the works of these famous masters was not one of reverent awe; it was one of fellowship and equality...of an understanding and identification with the way they held their hands, their tools, their brushes. If Edna could have had her heart's desire at any time while enjoying these works, it would have been to be immediately transported back to the studio of a Michaelangelo or a Raphael to work right next to the master himself and to share his experience of modeling the human form and the many ways in which the planes and curves work together. When Edna said, "Look what he did here," she did not mean "how marvelous." She meant look how he has really <u>moved</u> the material.

The modeling of form and innocence of expression found in the works of the masters is reflected in her own graceful sculpture. Edna's figures are rounded, they are unmistakably living, breathing flesh occupying space. Muscles are defined and dimples appear in a series of curves and rounds that flow together in an unbroken symmetry that can only be called classic.

As for type, Edna's dolls were once described as "whimsical" and immediately six other artists snorted and said, "whimsy, indeed!" What they were expressing was the fact that the element of fancy is only a very small part of what makes her work vibrant. The one word hardly does justice to the dolls in actual fact.

While it is true that Edna, herself, appears to be a very natural and artlessly unsophisticated person who certainly does appreciate whimsy, she is really quite a sophisticated artist and a very dedicated one who pursues perfection in every detail. Whimsy, yes, if you mean Edna is a person who is open and sensitive to all kinds of influences and not afraid to follow her imagination. She does, certainly, have the ability to love what she sees, to make it part of her, and to somehow express the possibilities she can imagine.

When you come right down to it, all doll artists are illustrators. Edna Shaw, however, is one of the few doll artists to actually identify herself as an illustrator.

Both the real and the imagined are seen in Edna's work. For example, illustration of the imagined is seen in her figures of the *Maids in Waiting* (and the reader can judge for himself whether a word like whimsy is sufficient to describe these pieces...woefully inadequate it seems to us).

The ladies are the result of her own visualization of the literal translation of the expression we all know from reading history and fairy tales. Edna said that she had heard the term in stories, but had never been sure just what it was that those ladies did. Typically, she did not go out and research court custom. Instead, she let her mind play around with the idea of ladies waiting.

Waiting for what?

How were they waiting?

As a consequence of this imaginative probing, the ladies that evolved were not the stiff, formally posed and overly dressed figures that might have been closer to a representation of real ladies in waiting. They were ladies, of course,...pretty, delicate, young ladies. They were posed in graceful attitudes of light slumber, lips smiling at pretty dreams or yawning langorously. What did they do while they waited?

They <u>napped</u>!

To emphasize the overall impression of napping, the composition is colored in muted grays and blues with hints of beige and rose. (And the maids have elegant coiffures which result from Edna's background as a cosmotologist.) To look at them is to feel you might be in Marie Antoinette's Petite Trianon playhouse when the shades

Wax studies for peddlers which will be produced as all-jointed porcelain bisque figures in three different sizes. Here Edna has been working out design possibilities for the costume. *Photograph courtesy of Edna Nell Shaw.*

were drawn on a warm summer's afternoon. The maids were originally intended to repose, each on her own nest of pillows; however, in order to carry them around easily, Edna put them together and the resulting composition, accidental as it may be, intensifies the idea of a sunny, sleepy afternoon being gently dozed away.

Even better, Edna invites you into her work with this composition. It becomes easy to fall into her mood and you begin to project scenarios of who they are and what they are waiting for -- probably waiting for handsome princes to ride up on dashing white chargers and carry them away to "happily everafter." These are the ladies in waiting that live in the fantasy court that Edna created so that we can all glimpse another interpretation of a thing we <u>thought</u> we knew about.

It was not all that long ago -- just about ten years ago -- when Edna began making fabric draped costume figures built on commercial figurines she had molded and remolded. There must have been a strong element of her potential even in these early figures for artists who saw her pieces strongly encouraged her to make her own originals.

Once she had her hands on a piece of clay, nothing else counted. Her development in doll art in a few short years is nothing more than a pure study in mastery of technique...most all of it learned on her own from methods described in books along with helpful hints and suggestions from other artists. She was able to master the complexities of porcelain, the methods of china painting, and additionally, find time to experiment with and develop her own special wax medium in record time. Few have built so rapidly, diligently and solidly in such a short span.

In all of Edna's figures, motion, movement or the implication of motion is a strong element. Many doll artists choose to create the illusion of movement by building a figure and arranging it in a given pose. There is a great deal more involved in the sculpting of a figure and jointing it...and it requires even more ability to engineer joints such that the figure is able to move smoothly from one position to another which is what Edna's figures do...often assuming very unusual and seemingly difficult postures.

Notice a child figure that sits with one leg tucked under the other...that figure is not a solid figurine type of a piece. It is not a wire armature that has been bent in that position. Its hips and knees have been <u>sculpted</u> and engineered to assume that very natural, yet very unusual position for a doll. Some might think that this is going a bit farther than is really necessary. Edna, however, wants to make <u>dolls</u> and dolls <u>move</u> in her definition. If complex joint mechanics are required to make the illustration move, then that is what Edna does...sometimes combining three different jointing techniques in one figure. It does not matter that the doll may never be moved, the fact is that it <u>can</u> be moved.

Edna said that for years she "felt artistic but didn't know where it was coming from." Although she had been sewing since she was a small child (dressing her cats and dogs because dolls didn't have enough action), it took several wasted years before she realized there could be more to life than making beds and scrubbing floors. Now, like most artists, she is going full speed ahead knowing that "there will never be enough days to accomplish all the ideas in her head."

Edna spends much of her day working on her dolls and depending on the part of the process, daily activities can include working on the original clay or wax model, mold making, china painting or costuming. Every part of a figure is given equal attention and Edna never hurries or shortcuts. Her figures are produced in limited edition series averaging about two or three finished figures a month and in a good year about two or three new models... pleasures well worth waiting for!

ABOVE: Close-up of two of the very delicate *Maids in Waiting* by Edna Nell Shaw. *Photograph courtesy of Edna Nell Shaw.*

RIGHT: Close-up of the yawning *Maid in Waiting*, porcelain sculpture by Edna Nell Shaw. *Photograph courtesy of Edna Nell Shaw.*

BELOW: *Maids in Waiting* by Edna Nell Shaw, a set of porcelain sleepy heads in all attitudes of languid repose. Each figure is individually sculpted and each wears a variation of mid 18th century costume in muted blues and mauves. *Photograph courtesy of Edna Nell Shaw.*

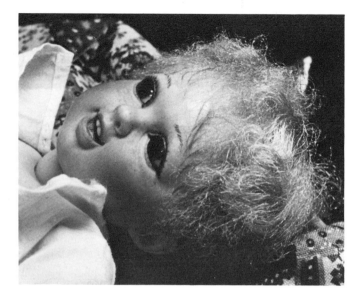

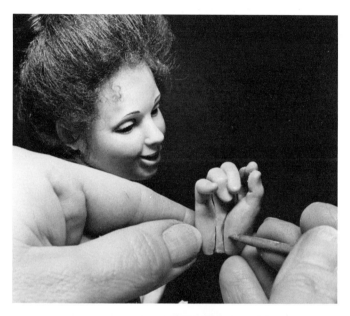

LEFT: *Five Toes* by Edna Nell Shaw. Detail of the child's face. *Photograph courtesy of Edna Nell Shaw.*

BELOW: Detail of the artist reconstructing the original wax sculpture of the hand of the mother in *Five Toes* for final finish molding. Note that the hand has to be cut to make three separate molds in order to achieve the final position. *Photograph courtesy of Edna Nell Shaw.*

BELOW: *Five Toes*, porcelain sculpture of a mother and child by Edna Nell Shaw. These are planned as a limited edition of 50. The figures have ball and insert jointings, set-in blown glass eyes and hair of sheep wool. The heads are incised: "Five Toes" and the year produced. *Photograph courtesy of Edna Nell Shaw.*

BELOW RIGHT: *Five Toes* by Edna Nell Shaw showing the detail of the sculpted and jointed porcelain figures. Notice the sculpted-in-one high top shoes and rolled stocking top. Each part of the anatomy has been carefully studied and engineered for perfectly smooth movement and posing. No detail has been overlooked. *Photograph courtesy of Edna Nell Shaw.*

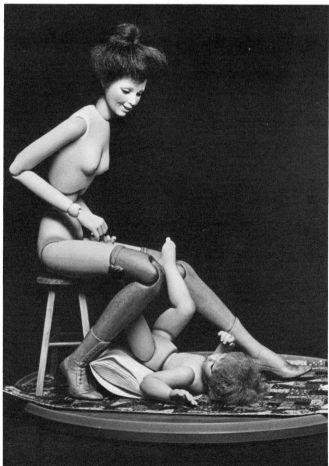

ABOVE: *Mary Contrary*, a nursery rhyme interpretation in porcelain by artist Edna Nell Shaw. *Mary*, one of an edition of 50, is 9½in (24.2cm) standing, all-porcelain bisque. *Photograph courtesy of Edna Nell Shaw.*

ABOVE RIGHT: Detail of Edna Nell Shaw's *Mary Contrary's* face and bonnet. *Photograph courtesy of Edna Nell Shaw.*

RIGHT: *Jack Horner* by Edna Nell Shaw. Limited edition of 50, one of a series of six. *Jack Horner* is 6½in (16.5cm) tall, all-porcelain bisque with flush-jointed hips and ball-jointed neck. The clothes are hand-stitched and the eyes are set-in blown glass. The head is incised: "Jack Horner" with copyright, signature, number of edition and year produced. *Photograph courtesy of Edna Nell Shaw.*

ellen turner

Ellen Turner's impressive and poetic figures are produced, she says, by "the winds that blow through my studio in the Blue Ridge Mountains" and truly, it is not possible to separate the stands of folk, of art, of craft and of the atmosphere of the North Carolina mountain life that twine through Ellen Turner's work.

As a doll artist, Ellen Turner has received unusually nice recognition for her work. The fact that we are becoming more aware of our origins, our past and the earlier, more simple ways of life in this country helps. Her figures represent life as it can be remembered and the remnants that can still be seen. Her figures have been requested for exhibit at the Renwick Gallery of the Smithsonian Institute in Washington, D.C., The Appalachian Folk Festival in Ohio and the biannual fairs of the Southern Highland Handicraft Guild (where as one reporter put it, "A cage of squealing leaping monkeys would not have attracted more attention than did Ellen Turner's doll display!) and at the Folk Art Center on the Blue Ridge Parkway as well as at various galleries throughout the country.

A long time resident of the Southern Mountains..."always in heart and mind though sometimes not always physically"...Ellen has been making dolls for over 30 years from a variety of materials. Largely self-taught in the matter of doll making, Ellen studied art at the Gibbs Art Museum in Charleston, West Virginia, and the High Museum of Art in Atlanta, Georgia. Also a pianist, she studied piano at the Grenzland Conservatory in Aachen, Germany. The Famous Artist School course and the other art studies contributed to her knowledge of anatomy, composition and some handling of the various media, but on her own she studied costume and taught herself how to handle papier-mâché, rubber and fabric, as well as how to model clay.

What makes Ellen's work special is her sensitivity to the mountain folk and her ability to recreate the social and cultural milieu of that area as it was 40 or more years ago. She says she began to become attuned to the atmosphere of the area as a youngster visiting her grandparents who lived in the Carolina hills. During the war, when gas was rationed, Ellen would walk to the store daily to get the mail. On these walks she became aware of an old woman who, with her dog, appeared almost daily at the roadside graveyard to put flowers on her husband's grave. Even as a child, she was so moved by this lady and her obvious loneliness that she would often recall the scene and try to sketch her memories and impressions of it in later years.

More impressions came from meeting people and becoming familiar with their ways of dress, speech patterns and ordinary, everyday activities...all of this has been translated into the personas she now creates with fabric, wire and paint.

Chronologically, Ellen began doll making (for no particular reason, she says) in 1942, when at a very tender age she made her first doll, a gingerbread boy, from a pair of her father's summer army trousers. She experimented with many materials until she settled on her current fabric on wire armature process. Not surprisingly, her first Appalachian character doll using this method was *Frady's Widow*, an impression of the lady who visited the graveyard from her childhood memories.

Ellen's dolls are and are not romanticized figures. They are certainly not cute dollie figures, but rather, a reflection of the stoic attitude, strength of character and dutiful acceptance of role and responsibilities in the mountain way of life. Ellen, herself, says she does not think of her dolls as dolls, but more properly as a type of sculpture.

They are romanticized in that Ellen lives near an abandoned roadbed and many of her figures are the result of her imaginings and fleeting impressions of the people who traveled the road, who they were, where they might be going and why, and what they might do when they arrived at their destinations.

Even the names she gives her figures are names sometimes of real people, sometimes fictional, but always exactly the type of names that were and are commonly used in the mountains.

Listen a minute...
There is *Emma* "My hat, my coat, my rectitude"
and...
Emma's Auntie Mae "Her thoughts come and go as the shadows in the forest"
and...
Addie Mull "My, the tales she liked to sprinkle over our heads"
and...
Ida Gaines "You're the runninist, getting-into-troublest girl around"
and...
Pearlie Case and me, "Well, we likes to stand by the fence and talk."

"My dolls," Ellen says, "serve to express deeply felt emotions which I have acquired and which have evolved over my life-time. My principal interest is in the portrayal of the physiognomy of the woman of Southern Appalachia.

"I am particularly interested in the character, personality and feeling of these women who are born in what might be termed a

randomly chosen geographical area and in an arbitrarily provided body. The body, soul and emotions of these people are shaped and influenced in a crucible where the struggling personality is forged by numerous unavoidable outside influences and customs. The possible incompatibility of body, character and environment makes these women something special. Over the years the body changes to encompass the frustrations, heartbreaks and other special emotions which initially are only felt internally.

"I have lived in the mountain area of North Carolina off and on all my life. I have observed the effects of the hard life on the people, their independence, frequent loneliness, stern visage and demeanor. Some handle their challenges with great strength and determination; others collapse under the strain."

Her choice of dolls as medium of expression was because of their flexibility and multi-dimensional qualities for expression.

All of her work involves quite a number of different techniques from start to finish. The construction begins with a wire frame or armature for the body which is developed from a sketch of the idea. The wire armature is attached to a wooden base and "sculpted" by bending and twisting until it reflects the body position and attitude needed to reflect the character in her mind. Then the armature, which stays attached to the base so she can get the right feeling all along, is wrapped with excelsior and cotton padding to provide the muscular delineation. The faces are a combination of stitched and painted features. First, a fabric head is cut and sewn together and given a bit of definition (corners of the mouth and eyes) by taking stitches through the head with a long needle. Then it is sized (made stiff) with a glue mixture, dried and smoothed to take the paint. Finally, very graphic features, often very poignant, are hand-painted in acrylic paints.

The construction of the hands is done over the wire and is done very carefully as they must also reflect the character. The costumes, which Ellen makes without patterns, are constructed from old clothing and fabrics cut and sewn for each character. These costumes are a far cry from the elegant...buttons are missing, elbows are worn, bonnet strings dangle and pockets have realistically torn corners. "If I get her all dressed up and she looks pretty nice," says Ellen, "I rough her up a bit!" The accessories, illustrative of life among the mountain folk, are fashioned from objects the artist finds in her walks through the nearby woods...dried flowers, reed baskets, twigs for walking sticks.

Each doll has its own wooden base and when finished, its own individual bit of verse written on a tag as a means of introducing or explaining it.

Ellen Turner and her work is so much a part of the Blue Ridge folk that we can easily imagine a future doll maker making a figure of her and writing a verse that might go something like...

Come into my place...baskets, wigs and twigs, books and brushes, friendly spirits pass my door to become dolls done and dolls begun.....

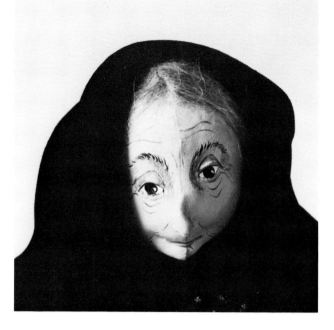

RIGHT: *Miss Callie Pace...*"Waiting to remember, it comes and then is gone." Figure by Ellen Turner. *Photograph by Ann Hawthorne, courtesy of Ellen Turner.*

BELOW: *The Songbird Young'uns...*"High, high on the hilltop, around and around they spin, the spinning, songbird young'uns -- Fern and Effie, Opie and Little May." Fabric figures with camel's hair and dressed in calicos, cottons, old lace and quilt tops by Ellen Turner. *Photograph by Ann Hawthorne, courtesy of Ellen Turner.*

BELOW RIGHT: *Minnie Moses...*"Down in the hollow she wonders at dawn." *Photograph by Ann Hawthorne, courtesy of Ellen Turner.*

ABOVE: *Sallie Bean.* Fabric on wire armature figure by Ellen Turner. *Photograph by Ann Hawthorne, courtesy of Ellen Turner.*

ABOVE RIGHT: *Sallie Bean...*"A little step to the right, a little skip to the left and here comes old Sallie Bean." A 26in (66cm) figure. Edition limited to ten by Ellen Turner. *Photograph by Ann Hawthorne, courtesy of Ellen Turner.*

RIGHT: *Granny Lee* and *Kittie Sue...*"He will come back to be with you." Edition of 25 by Ellen Turner. *Photograph by Ann Hawthorne, courtesy of Ellen Turner.*

FAR RIGHT: *Amos McCloud...*"Around the bend I came and right in the middle he stood, in the middle of the field." 31in (78.7cm) tall fabric figure dressed in cottons with felt hat and laurel walking stick by Ellen Turner. *Photograph by Ann Hawthorne, courtesy of Ellen Turner.*

LEFT: *Sarah Goings* and her children..."Between leaves threading over stones treading." One-of-a-kind group by Ellen Turner. *Photograph by Ann Hawthorne, courtesy of Ellen Turner.*

RIGHT: Close-up of *Sarah Goings'* child. *Photograph by Ann Hawthorne, courtesy of Ellen Turner.*

BELOW: Close-up of *Sarah Goings*. *Photograph by Ann Hawthorne, courtesy of Ellen Turner.*

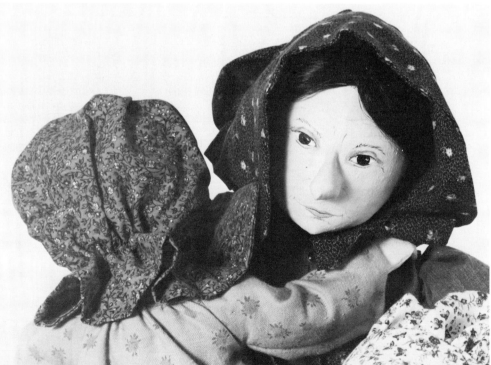

william arthur wiley

"I have always wanted to see fairy tale characters made the way I pictured them as a child, not just any doll with a costume."

William Arthur Wiley, fantasy doll maker, lives out his dreams and recreates his childhood impressions in clay. His dolls of porcelain and composition are personal expressions of favorite fairy tale figures and they stem from a long-lasting love of childhood things.

A collector of not only dolls, but all types of toys, he has amassed thousands of playthings from all over the world. One might say Wiley gets his inspiration from his environment; he lives above a toy shop. "I guess I'm living out all my childhood dreams," he says with a laugh.

A sculpture major at Philadelphia College of Art and Syracuse University, Mr. Wiley, who once worked for a woodcarver in Germany, began making dolls in 1983, and teaches sculpture for the doll artist, doll making and costume design when not developing an extensive line of fairy tale people.

Dolls are people to him. "They have to come to life before I am satisfied," he says. "I have seen too many dolls that are merely used as mannequins to display costumes. The people who have bought my dolls feel I've captured the way they have always pictured the fairy tale characters, not just by the costume, but by the faces of the dolls as well."

The dolls are a mixture of sweetness and caricature. Slightly exaggerated poses and proportions give liveliness to the characters and enhance the storybook illusion. Wiley dolls must tell a story and the artist is writing a book of his own fairy tales. Traditional tales now occupy his time. "I have plans for making 50 new storybook dolls over the next few years," he says, "ranging from 1 in (2.5cm) to 4ft (121.9cm)."

A full time doll maker with a new 5000 square foot studio in Vienna, Virginia, Wiley describes his procedures. "The first step in making a doll is coming up with an idea. The second step is collecting the fabric, wigs and accessories. Third, the head and body are sculpted from a non-fire clay. Then a mold is made. The doll is poured, fired, painted and fired again. Eyes are set in, wig is glued on, a pattern is made for the clothes, the clothes are sewn and fitted and then the doll is boxed. In making dolls everything takes twice as long as you think it will. If you realize that, you'll be O.K."

His dolls are generally handmade, but he does use some ready-made materials. "I use some prefabricated wigs, shoes and accessories, but I'm very discriminating. For some dolls I make my own wigs and shoes because they have special needs. For example, I needed a wig 24in (61cm) long for a *Rapunzel* doll that I'm working on, so I'm making the wig myself."

Sprinkled among the fairy tale characters and nursery rhyme people are a few portraits of real people. All are shaped with a personal vision. "I don't make a doll just to sell," he says. "I make them the way I want to see them." Many doll collectors like the way William Arthur Wiley sees his dreams.

Wiley dolls released in 1983 are:

Red Riding Hood; The Wolf; Mary, Mary; Goldilocks; Mary and the Lamb; Hansel; Gretel and *The Candy Witch.*

Dolls for 1984 are:

Rapunzel; Hector Protector; Little Boy Blue; Tom, Tom, the Piper's Son; Little Mermaid; Thumbelina; Puss in Boots; Emperor and the Nightingale; Viola Wiggly; Catherine; Santa; Mrs. Santa; The Three Bears; Humpty Dumpty; Elizabeth; Polly; Wee Willie Winkie and *Mother Goose.*

1985 dolls are sets of princes and princesses: *Cinderella and the Prince; Princess and the Swineherd; Frog Prince; Lisa and the Wild Swans* and *Snow Queen.*

Wiley dolls are marked with a carved-in number, above
© William Arthur Wiley,
which is painted on the doll. All Wiley dolls bear "Manhattan Sandcastle" wrist tags with short excerpts from their stories.

In a little over a year, William Arthur Wiley has gone a long way towards bringing to life his childhood dreams -- and those of many doll collectors.

The Candy Witch by William Arthur Wiley, 16in (40.6cm) tall. © 1983. Porcelain. Black hair. Blue glass eyes. Holds a broom in her hand. Striped dress of pink and black trimmed with candy. *Photograph courtesy of William Arthur Wiley.*

RIGHT: *Goldilocks* by William Arthur Wiley, 18in (45.7cm) tall. © 1983. Porcelain. Blonde hair. Glass eyes. Human hair eyelashes. She holds a small chair in her hand. Dressed in salmon and gold embroidered dress. *Photograph courtesy of William Arthur Wiley.*

BELOW: *Red Riding Hood and the Wolf* by William Arthur Wiley, 15in (38.1cm) and 19in (48.3cm) tall. © 1983. Porcelain and composition. *Red Riding Hood* has blonde hair, brown glass eyes and human hair eyelashes. Holds a basket of goodies in her hand. Red velvet dress and cream and red embroidered coat. *Wolf* has a porcelain head, gray fur body, glass eyes, holds a walking stick. Wears knickers, a wine waistcoat, a white shirt and a cravat. *Photograph courtesy of William Arthur Wiley.*

LEFT: *Mary, Mary Quite Contrary* by William Arthur Wiley, 18in (45.7cm) tall. Porcelain. Auburn hair. Blue glass eyes. Holds a pot of silk blue bells. Black velvet dress trimmed with gold and eyelet. *Photograph courtesy of William Arthur Wiley.*

BELOW: *Red Riding Hood* by William Arthur Wiley. © 1983. 15in (38.1cm) tall. Porcelain. Blonde hair. Brown glass eyes. Human hair eyelashes. Holds a basket of goodies. Red velvet dress. Cream and red embroidered coat. *Photograph courtesy of William Arthur Wiley.*

Hansel and *Gretel* by William Arthur Wiley, 15in (38.1cm) tall. © 1983. Porcelain. Blonde hair. Blue glass eyes. Human hair eyelashes. The dolls clutch cookies in their hands. Both are dressed in green. Dolls made in the first year (June 1983-June 1984) are signed in 14K gold. Dolls made in the second year are signed in silver. Dolls made after the second year will be signed in a different color for each year. Each doll wears a "Manhattan Sandcastle" wrist tag with its name and a short excerpt from its story. *Photograph courtesy of William Arthur Wiley.*

julia hills

Julia Hills has been making dolls since she was 13 and over the years has evolved to what might be called the "artist's artist." Her imaginative figures in porcelain have the ability to transcend any preconceived notions of "dollness" and be immediately recognized as works of art. She is one of the rare artists in our field that has the ability to tap into the universal imaginative consciousness of mankind. Her figures, while remarkably obvious as the product of her own hand, eye and point of view, are the clowns, fairies and creatures of the elements and fabrics of the earth that we can all experience. They do not demand that we recognize and name them; yet, we are able to identify and feel comfortable with them.

After leaving school at 17 Julia spent three years studying art at Croyden. At the end of those years, however, she says her inability to draw led her to several years of costuming and wardrobe work in the theater. Tedious and demanding work it was, too, but it provided an invaluable exposure to the fabrics, textures and sewing techniques used for both chromatic and symbolic effect...and this is most evident in the figures she creates.

While she spent time at home with a young son and working in various craft forms, she found that doll making would allow her the most scope in expressing the characters and costumes which formulated themselves in her imagination and daily life.

After experimenting with plastics and self-hardening clays, Julia learned to do ceramic and porcelain processes for sculpting the heads and hands that begin her characters. Here, her approach is non-traditional in that she sculpts directly into porcelain clay. Rather than making an original in clay or wax and pouring a porcelain slip into a mold made from the original, each one of her heads is one-of-a-kind work. No two are ever alike. She has also found that the placement of glass chips for eyes (which melt in firing) works better than purchased or painted eyes to achieve the effect she likes.

By 1978 Julia had generally worked out what is now her basic process for making dolls. She had decided that one-of-a-kind figures allowed her much more freedom to explore ideas and forms which she feels more important than being bound to the production schedules required by working in editions.

As pose and body positions are very important in her work, she had, by this time, melded her sewing skills and directions into the production of a tightly stuffed body which is sculpted into the attitude of the character and she found that she preferred to make costumes by applying fabrics directly to the bodies rather than by separate construction.

Even so, the form that she evolved continues to change as she, herself, discovers new concepts to explore. For instance, at the time of this writing she expected to be spending the next two years working on a series of seated figures and had already begun to experiment with the construction of a base which would be integrated with the figures, themselves. This inclusion of a base --which may be in the form of elaborate cushions or representations of earth forms in fabrics -- serves as a setting through which more information about the figure can be conveyed in much the same way as the background in a portrait painting. In all, Julia's work is very much directed to the creation of complete and unified pictures or images rather than "things" that dangle from purchased metal stands.

As you will have noted, some doll artists' work in a very analytical, step-by-step manner, drawing detailed sketches, templates and patterns for each part of the construction process. Others make few sketches and notations, letting the work and their eye for design and visualization guide them towards the end product. Julia's work is more of the latter type and what might be called more of the "inspirational" or "visionary" type. She says ideas may be mulled over for several months before she actually begins to sculpt as she says going from first concept straight into the work does not seem to produce as good a result.

When the head and hands are sculpted, she may or may not make a few sketches of the costume idea, but, if so, not more than a few lines. The bodies are begun by drawing the shapes she requires right onto the fabric -- an approach which can only be applied when one has a very good knowledge of the seaming necessary for complex contouring. Then the pieces are sewn, stuffed very tightly (so that they will hold their pose without a wire armature) and stitched into place.

Often Julia may not have more than a general idea of what the costume for the character will be and in these cases, she begins by stitching on a bit of fabric for a bodice and letting the rest develop with each successive piece dictating the next choice, and the next. Both new and used fabrics are used. If a color she wants is not available, she dyes fabric to suit. If there is not enough textural quality in the fabric, she embroiders over using yarns and piecing to heighten effect. The result supplies an ornamental feast of detail combining applique, embroidery and unique juxtapositions of color and texture.

Although, on occasion, costume parts like skirts or bodices may be assembled separately, all costumes become a permanent part of the figure and cannot be removed. With the exception of her figures from contemporary 20th century life (which are costumed in small reproductions of the real thing), she does not limit herself to a specific period or mode for each costume and often several fashion elements will occur simultaneously...whatever she feels best expresses the idea is what is used.

To those more accustomed to the "perfection" of finish in commercial and doll artist work, Julia's work might appear crude and unfinished. But to make a comparative judgement would be to miss the point of the design unity. Working directly into the porcelain, the finish is more rough, but her characters are *impressions* and they do not need to be "high-tech."

If one has decided to convey the idea of an "Old Man of the Hills" as Julia has, and if one has decided that the goal would be to convey the idea of the character as an outgrowth of the earth itself, then the finish of the work will necessarily have to reflect that very elemental idea. Julia's figure has hands that are knarled and knotted and as tough as old tree roots. His costume is of cottons and wools with applique and embroidery which carry out the impression of mossy undergrowth, grasses and leaves. The hunched shoulders and dangling arms indicate the solidity of a rock or, perhaps, the bend of an aged tree. A knowing smile and an appearance of a rheumy eye lend a sense of ancient wisdom lurking within. A polished, high-gloss piece would never have told this story...it could not have been successful done any other way. The materials, textures and imaginative stance in combination with the rugged appearance of the stoneware -- no one part predominating -- all work together to create the resulting visualization of great age.

As with many doll artists, all parts of Julia Hill's life, interests and activities merge in her art. Her recent interest in astrology led her to do figures representative of the planets. It also led her to the realization that there was a lack of the feminine presence in the zodiac which, in turn, led her to do a series of female goddesses representing female archetypes. In subject matter like the sun, moon, goddesses, clowns and mermaids, Julia presents figures that at once are interpretations of her personal experiences as well as universal symbols that anyone can relate to...her figures touch and match a part of any viewer's experience.

Corresponding to her interests in symbolism and her feeling for fabrics, Julia also does mandalas in silk for wall hangings. Using her costume construction techniques, she sews a line of colored pieced jackets for casual wear, too. Her daily life is a varied one and one that many artists would admire for it enables her to make her way doing those things which she enjoys most. She teaches astrology, doll making workshops, does vegetarian cooking, and helps run weekend retreats for contemplative prayer. Additionally, because her work is recognized as an art form, she has been able to receive grants from the Northern Arts and from the Crafts Council which have enabled her to live and purchase necessary equipment.

Julia feels dolls provide her with a vehicle for expressing those things that move her in her daily life. She feels "in tune" with clay, fascinated by people and curious about the "what and why" of the world. She does not care to reproduce figures of specific historical times; she feels her figures are hers and are uniquely of the present time whatever they may seem to be. They are a direct expression of the various sides of her own personality and have been for her an important means of both self-expression and of learning about herself as a person.

Currently, Julia spends the equivalent of three or four days a week working on dolls and finishes approximately twelve per year. These figures, which are often accompanied by verses that Julia composes, are seen at the exhibits of the British Doll Artist Association as well as in regular museum and gallery showings.

Peace, a mother and child in porcelain and fabric by Julia Hills. The mother is 18in (45.7cm) tall and has a goatskin wig. After much work on fantasy themes, Julia was inspired to do this pair by the desire to make a contemporary figure and a statement about peace. *Photograph courtesy of Julia Hills.*

Close-up of photograph above.

LEFT: *Fool with Mask* by Julia Hills. This figure with its incredibly ornate embroidery and applique costume is sculpted of earthenware. It has a fabric body and is 14in (35.6cm) seated. The *Fool* illustrates how the vulnerability of people is often hidden behind masks which deaden personality. *Photograph courtesy of Julia Hills.*

BELOW LEFT: *Aphrodite.* This 14in (35.6cm) porcelain and fabric figure by Julia Hills is the manifestation of the power in the underworld goddess...new life bursting from the old. *Photograph courtesy Julia Hills.*

BELOW: *Wood Anemone* was inspired by the beauty and simplicity of the wood flower. This was the first of several figures Julia Hills has done on nature themes. *Photograph courtesy of Julia Hills.*

RIGHT: *The Old Man of the Hills.* This 16in (40.6cm) stoneware and fabric sculpture is Julia Hills' attempt to portray in a figure the feeling of age and wisdom of the Welsh hills. *Photograph courtesy Julia Hills.*

BELOW: *Underworld Goddess.* A result of artist Julia Hills' own inner experiences, this 13in (33cm) porcelain and fabric figure presents a whole new interpretation of the idea of goddess. Notice how the idea of the underworld is subtly outlined in the construction of a hollowed out stone-like seat. *Photograph courtesy Julia Hills.*

BELOW RIGHT: *Oberon,* a commissioned figure 15in (38.1cm) seated, made by Julia Hills in porcelain and fabric. The elaborate costume was made separately by embroidering and appliquing silks and then stitching them directly and permanently onto the figure. *Oberon* is signed on the foot, as are all Julia's figures. *Photograph courtesy of Julia Hills.*

Rapunzel and the Witch by Julia Hills. Julia made this sharply contrasting pair of seated figures for an exhibition of work by the British Doll Artists Association at the Museum of Childhood in Edinburgh, Scotland. This 14in (35.6cm) porcelain and fabric setting is now part of the museum's permanent collection. *Photograph courtesy Julia Hills*

tuck dolls

Gary Henson and Margy Tuck

Tuck dolls have a charisma, a spiritual quality that sets them apart from the mundane. They seem in tune with a world just beyond the surface, an alternate reality in which savage fairies, nymphs and gods are earthily real. Perhaps this is because they are the spawn of dreams.

Gary Henson, the sculptor of the team, explains their source. "They come from sleeping dreams, awake dreams, thoughts. I tend to think in pictures, so I think the way I work. I'm full of pictures and the dolls just take those pictures and they give them a little body to live in."

If he speaks as if his creatures were real, it is because they are, to both Gary and his partner, Margy Tuck. Since 1979 they have collaborated, spiritually and artistically, developing their dream dolls.

"Of course, dolls are people," Margy says, "and they have lots to say."

"Dolls are just little non-moving people," Gary adds. "But, then again, when you're not looking at them, they feel like they're moving. Who's to say? Dolls have a life of their own, and it's THEIR life, and doll's life is not a pale imitation of a human life. And, though they do look like humans, they look like humans from another world. And, therefore, they're legitimate."

These other-worldly creatures are given physically perfect, multi-jointed bodies (with up to 23 separate parts, at times), sculpted from a special clay mixture Gary has developed.

A sculptor since the age of four, when he began to sell his work, Gary grew up in an artistic environment. His mother, Inez Running-Rabbit, was a well-known artist in the Southwest and encouraged his precocious multi-media talent. His passion is clay. He has invented special clays for every step of doll making, from modeling to casting. They are made from earth he digs up and transforms.

"I make three grades of plasteline (for modeling): hard, medium and soft. And the hard is stiff enough that when making a doll 15in (38.1cm), 17in (43.2cm) tall, it'll hold itself up. I don't require armatures. I'm the only one I know who makes his own plasteline, and makes different grades, who's alive."

He has a special empathy for clay and is attuned to its presence, a feeling which is almost spiritual, which seems to be translated into his sculpture as he works with the raw material.

"Once the image of the doll is set in my mind, the actual physical handling of the clay and giving a body to that image is very, very enjoyable.

"I enjoy the clay and the feeling and the manipulation of that clay.

"Wherever I go, I'm always aware of the earth underneath me. And I'm familiar enough with it because I've grown up with clay that I can smell it and I can feel it through my feet. When you're walking on clay the ground has a certain spring to it -- a liveliness to it that you can feel.

"So that, when I'm walking and I feel that feeling, then I'll always bend down, maybe dig a little bit, pull up some clay, smell it, maybe taste it, feel it, to know what it is. And I'll come back for it later if I like it. But just to know that it's there, know what it is, satisfies me."

Margy Tuck brings out the personalities of the sculptures through paint, fiber and design. Her studies of dance, costume, theatrics and art meld together to firm up the visions developed by the doll making team, whose work blends seamlessly.

"Gary and I have known each other and worked together for eight years now," she said in 1984. "His work and mine are close philosophically and spiritually, although our mediums and styles differ somewhat.

"We work together well because we're coming from the same place, the same scheme of things. And we both have tremendous respect for each other's work. We're always yaking about our inspirations and ideas and, now that we're a bigger business, we take the best ideas and decide at a meeting what doll we'll be doing next.

"The marvelous thing I feel about our collaboration is that our artwork and our dolls are more powerful and more beautiful when we work together than when we work separately."

Both partners feel that art verges on the spiritual and that their dolls are in tune with this force, which is found in its purest form in nature. The work they do that pleases them best is most closely allied with it.

The team intends its dolls to positively affect viewers; they expect the life force in them to extend to the humans in their sphere of influence.

Margy puts it this way.

"We expect a lot from our dolls. We expect them to be fine art. And I expect that from other artists' original dolls. Of course, art verges on the spiritual. And I want the person who has one of our dolls around him to become a better person in some way -- more aware of the music of life around him, aware of the temporal or magic that's always there."

She describes the way that magic gets translated into a doll.

"Right now I'm involved with a doll that is a woman, night, subconscious, dressed in black and real light china silk.

"I'm fascinated with cloth that's so see-through it seems to disappear. It's not there and yet it's there, like the fairies themselves -- or like the subconscious or god. It's there and not there.

"The message I seek to convey is walking up to mortality, or a state where this lifetime is so temporary and precious. God meant for us to make the most of every moment of existence and there's an immediacy in our lives. I feel this (doll) makes you want to do something about it. This is probably one of the secrets of our dolls and why they sell so well, too. And why collectors buy them with such passion."

Collectors also buy them because they are technically excellent. The sculpture is exquisite, the painting expert, the costuming and accessories meticulously rendered. And the jointing is unbelievable. Tuck dolls are sculpture, engineering and clothing combined to recreate dreams. But most important to Gary, they are toys. One can play with them.

"I want people to be able to play with my dolls," he says, "to move them around. There's a whole lot of expression in the movement of arms and legs, and we can virtually talk to each other to a great extent just through the movement of our bodies.

"My dolls do that also. That's one thing a doll should do."

He achieves this mobility through multi-piece, multi-jointed construction, conceived at the time the doll is sculpted in plasteline. He describes his method.

"To allow for shrinkage, the plasteline master is done a little bigger than the original in the first casting. After I get the plasteline ready, then I'll make a waste mold. Then I'll cast it in plaster. I'll carve and sand and file it in plaster until I've got it refined down and real smooth. Then I'll make a piece mold and a lot of times, in order to allow for undercuts and that sort of thing, I'll make what's called a wedge mold.

"So I'll have multiple piece molds. I think it's a terrible restriction that most doll artists have to try to keep everything to two-piece molds. So, I'll make any number I need to get what I want. And that takes me weeks -- to make that mold.

"Then I'll go out and dig my clay and work it up and pour the parts."

Gary sculpts many types of figures. The man and woman dolls, considered fashion dolls, are 17in (43.2cm) high, anatomically perfect, 13-piece dolls with ball joints. He has done children and fairies and, occasionally, portraits. But they, somehow, are almost too lifelike. There seems to be something in the clay that causes empathetic reactions between subject and object.

Gary describes one such situation.

"I was doing a portrait doll of a very beautiful friend of mine once and I was working on the nose. I decided to take it off and start over. So, I picked up my knife and cut off the nose and, as I did that I heard a small scream and the woman who was modeling for me was over there and she had her hand up covering her nose. Her eyes were wide with fright and she had felt, sympathetically, that her nose had been cut. The image of her face had had its nose cut, as well."

Gary and Margy make approximately 300 dolls a year, including some 20 to 50 new editions. Some are one-of-a-kind, some editions, such as *Pan*, are very small but most are of 25 dolls.

When a doll has reached Margy's standard of completion, it has acquired sufficient life force to affect the viewer in the special way the sculptural team intends. Each Tuck creation has, in its way, a gentle didactic purpose. Gary describes it.

"I would like our dolls to tender a sense of wonder and open the viewer to possibilities that the world is more alive than he would normally feel that it is. And, to extend that grace to a doll is a very human thing."

Whether they be citizens of a mundane or alternate reality, Gary and Margy's creations extend the parameters of dollmaking.

Leif and *Margo*, ballet dancers by Margy Tuck and Gary Henson, 17in (43.2cm) tall. Fully-posable, hand-painted, multi-jointed clay dolls. Margy, a ballet dancer and theatrical designer for many years, has a special affinity for this subject matter. *Photograph courtesy of Tuck Dolls.*

RIGHT: *Nymph* and *Pan* by Gary Henson and Margy Tuck. Multi-jointed, fully-posable clay dolls. Hand-painted. Costumed by Margy Tuck. *Photograph courtesy of Tuck Dolls.*

ABOVE LEFT: Fairies *Lea* (left) and *Lilith* (right) by Margy Tuck and Gary Henson, 17in (43.2cm) tall. Multi-jointed, fully-posable, hand-painted clay dolls. *Photograph courtesy of Tuck Dolls.*

ABOVE: Detail of fairy *Lea* by Margy Tuck and Gary Henson. *Photograph courtesy of Tuck Dolls.*

LEFT: *Luna, the Savage Fairy* by Gary Henson and Margy Tuck, 17in (43.2cm) tall. Multi-jointed clay body. Hand-painted features. All accoutrements fashioned specially by the artists for the doll. 1984. *Photograph courtesy of Tuck Dolls.*

RIGHT: *The Shoemaker's Elf.* Prototype doll by Margy Tuck. Polyform, fabric and shoe. 1985. *Waugh photograph.*

BELOW: *Dancing White Cloud* by Gary Henson and Margy Tuck, 17in (43.2cm) tall. Multi-jointed, fully-posable, hand-painted clay doll. *Photograph courtesy of Tuck Dolls.*

BELOW RIGHT: *Miss Tiggy Winkle* by Margy Tuck. Prototype doll in polyform. 1985. *Waugh photograph.*

robert keene mckinley

Author's note: Bob McKinley is, as he describes himself, "a children's clothing designer by day and a hopelessly insane doll maker nights and weekends." His creations -- the result of inherent talent, years of professional experience in design and graphics, and a particularly good eye for character and the human condition -- are done largely for his own amusement and artistic satisfaction. In addition to his everyday design and doll work, he has also built and performed with marionettes and created both sumptuous and controversial figures for the famous Tiffany store window displays in New York City.

Unlike many normally loquacious artists who become mum when asked to commit their artistic feelings and experiences on paper, Bob took our questions as an opportunity to explore his relationship to his work and supplied copious notes and fascinating points of view. Since his answers were so spontaneous and so very typical of the doll artist and his involvement with his work, we present his story pretty much as he told it.

Why do you make dolls?

Ha! That's easy...for the complete and total joy of it and the freedom of doing only what pleases me. I work from nine to five, but after five, it's my turn! If my work pleases me -- terrific! If not, tough! I do it for myself and it tickles me no end.

Any interesting experiences happen to you in relation to your dolls?

Oh boy, we don't have time or space for all the stuff that has happened since I began this. One sharp memory is of the time the incredibly sophisticated career woman broke into tears when she saw one of my old ladies (the one with the mask) -- it scared me to death! Another was being interviewed on camera in front of Tiffany's and being besieged by people wanting my autograph because they saw the camera and thought I was "somebody." I have the interview on tape and it's a hoot watching myself in a suit and tie (rarely wear 'em) trying to explain and remain with a shred of dignity (the giggles took over and I crumpled into a mass of jelly on the sidewalk!) My favorite thing is having met two wonderful people through my dolls. One is Gene Moore, Artistic Director for Tiffany, and the other is Helen Bullard, founder of the National Institute of American Doll Artists, whose books got me started in the first place. Have you noticed that for the most part doll artist people are all terrific? I have!

Are your dolls people?

They are not real. They are, however, based on reality for the most part. I do invent little biographies as I go along unless it is a portrait (which I don't like to do). The *Last Duchess*, for example,

was sculpted with no aim in mind -- just something to do at the beach on a rainy Sunday. (I can't stand being idle, even for a minute!) When the features were roughed in and the expression began to form, I saw the beginnings of a very strong willed, haughty woman of a "certain age"...a survivor, as it were. I thought, "Okay, here we have a woman who has been through a lot, but is undoubtedly an aristocrat, so let's give her a title, make her what? Russian! She has survived the Russian Revolution and must have lost her family, but, due to circumstances, retained her wealth. Now, that dictates a period piece in turn-of-the-century costume as she would still be in mourning after all these years. She would be bitter, perhaps suspicious, very well dressed, her head held in a certain way...a <u>duchess</u>! The title also dictated the stance -- exact, no nonsense, <u>regal</u> and she is <u>that</u>! All these shenanigans go through my head typically and make the creation more fun...and, <u>sometimes</u>, the pieces comes across as I intended.

Are your dolls "art" dolls or "play" dolls?

I have made a few play dolls for the fun of it, but the majority of my work is for display. What is art? One could argue about that until doomsday. Art, I think, exists on all levels. In the realm of dolls, excepting commercially produced dolls (I am a snob!), every one done is "art." Some of it good, some not so hot, some great, but "art" all the same. Someone defined art as the end result of the creative process that evokes an emotional response in the looker, be that response anger, tears, or laughter. He was speaking of painting, but the theory applies to dolls as well. I consider my work and the work of other doll artists to be sculpture. Simply because our figures are clothed does not make them any less sculpture than Duane Hansen's life-sized fiberglass castings or George Segal's plaster casts -- good grief, just as much work goes into dolls...maybe more!

How do you know if a doll is good?

I use a term picked up in the garment industry. If a figure "talks" to me, tells me at a glance what statement it is making before the details take over, then I have succeeded in making a good figure. If that statement is made strongly enough, I can overlook the ever present flaws in construction. Indeed, sometimes the flaws re-inforce the statement. If the hands are a trifle too big, I cringe unless the gesture they are making is important. *Stella's* eyes wouldn't focus when I painted them, but it gave her such a faraway, dreamy look that I left them that way.

What don't you like about dolls?

Bad proportion drives me nuts! There are rules to be followed

Titania and *Bottom* from "A Midsummer Night's Dream" by Robert Keene McKinley. This pair, again, were commissioned figures used in the Tiffany window display. *Photograph by and courtesy of Robert McKinley.*

Lady MacBeth commissioned by Tiffany and Co, New York. One-of-a-kind original sculpture in Super Sculpey by Robert Keene McKinley. This figure was never satisfactory to the artist and he says, "It went down the incinerator" when it was finished being on display! *Photograph by and courtesy of Robert McKinley.*

and even when those rules are bent to make a statement or to create a style, everything must remain relative. For example, if a figure is being made in a cartoonish style and the head is oversized for the body, then the hands and the feet must remain in proportion to the head or the whole will jar the senses. In my own pompous opinion (!), a good doll must be based on good anatomy. They (the dolls) are based on the human figure and while every muscle, tendon, hump and bulge does not have to be executed with precise accuracy, legs, arms, hands, etc., are shaped in a certain way. If one veers too far away from the correct form, one has a mess on one's hands.

What sort of a reaction do you want your dolls to produce?

I really don't care what sort of a reaction one has to my figures -- just PLEASE react one way or the other! If there is no reaction at all, then the work is a dismal failure and should go straight to the incinerator. I am constantly getting into controversy when my figures are displayed publicly, which is never my intent, but I must admit I like it a lot! I never explain or defend a particular piece -- I tried once and came off in the interview like an idiot! I am my own audience and find that when I do something to please someone else, the whole process is an unhappy one.

What part of the doll making process do you like best?

I get the most satisfaction out of the simple joy of just making them, that's all. It amounts to almost ecstasy to see in my mind a figure and to be able to bring it forth, to create it, to make it real! I am never happier than when I am up to my neck in Sculpey and dreams.

What medium do you use? What methods?

Sculpey for the most part -- actually Super Sculpey. Most figures are completely sculpted, bodies and all, in the stuff although some have cloth-over-wire armature bodies. I have also worked in latex composition, low-fire ceramic, plastic wood, papier-mâché, needlesculpture, celastic, and once porcelain! I make everything inherent to the doll -- jewelry, hats, shoes, etc.

How do you get the ideas? How do you go about making a doll?

I'll try to explain this...Well, nuts, they are all different. Let's say that I am going to do a Flora Dora girl from the turn of the century. I'll start out by finding out what they really looked like. Luckily, I am a book junkie and have just about everything ever published. I do find I have a book (with pictures, ta da!) historical theatrical costume and there is a picture of a Flora Dora girl. Mmm, my, what hefty ladies they were...wearing those corsets must have been like wearing a battleship! Okay, we are going to be doing a fat lady.

Next question: What do fat ladies look like? Aha! A book on comparative anatomy gives me photos of nude fat ladies and I make careful drawings in scale, front and side view, for the body. I measure the heads -- usually about 2in (5.1cm), and begin. I have a lady friend who is not skinny, but who will not pose nude for me (chicken!); although, she will be delighted to sit for a photo assuming the facial expression I want. The rough sculpture goes fast -- an hour or two at most, but then I might spend weeks working on the refinements until I am happy with it.

Then the body is sculpted, again, very fast...in an evening, perhaps. The hands take at least three days. They are hard to do and very important. I do all the parts separately and then everything is glued together in the end. Usually, they balance on their own without a stand. After all the components are done and glued together, I paint the head and body (best part, I love it!). I actually begin the costume before the figure is joined together. Hose go on the legs, then the shoes (usually made of real leather), then the heels (carved). Then join the legs to the torso and check the balance. Finally, costume the rest except for the sleeves. I join the arms and do the sleeves under magnification. Now, we have a glorious -- and bald! -- *Flora Dora*. At this point, I set it aside and go off dancing for a week because I hate to do hair. After a week of relaxation, I hold my nose and do the hair. She is finished.

"Here's Rosemary" offers Robert Keene McKinley's *Ophelia*. One-of-a-kind sculpture. *Photograph by and courtesy of Robert McKinley.*

Masks, a vision of aging by Robert Keene McKinley. One-of-a-kind. *Photograph by and courtesy of Robert McKinley.*

I never sketch costumes any further than the roughest indication of the idea. If I do more than that, I feel duty bound to make the doll like the sketch...and they never will come out satisfactorily alike.

Can you describe your studio?

It is a room in my two-bedroom New York apartment with a dynamite view of the Hudson River and glorious sunsets. The room, itself, is neat as a pin except for the worktable -- I am happiest when working in a big mess. Bookshelves line two walls and ordinarily I sculpt while lolling on the bed with one eye on the television.

How long have you been making dolls?

I guess about four or five years. I am getting the hang of it and if I ever become so arrogant as to believe I've mastered it or feel I am not growing, I'll stop. I learn something new on each doll...with the *Last Duchess*, I learned how to place ears correctly, then promptly covered them up with the hair!

Did you make dolls as a child?

No dolls. Puppets, yes. The only doll I remember is the *Terri Lee* doll that the little girls next door had -- I would have murdered for it then...finally got one for myself at age 36.

Could you list the dolls you have made?

No way! I don't do editions, rarely sell my work, hardly have the vaguest notion (come on now!) of what is coming up next except that tomorrow I am going to start a *Carmen Miranda*...did you know

she was only 4ft 11in (27.9cm) tall??

Well then, how many have you done?

I don't count them. I am not on any schedule. If I am going "full-tilt boogie," I will not let a day go by that I haven't accomplished something on whatever I am working on.

Has your work ever been produced commercially?

I did it once. The results were terrible. It was not the fault of the company who was really very kind. Again, I was trying to reach an audience other than myself and I was working in a medium that I didn't really understand (porcelain). The work that I do that satisfies me does not lend itself to commercial production. Artists who understand the public and how to design for it can succeed with a quality product without sacrificing any artistic merit. Faith Wick and Suzanne Gibson -- both marvelous artists -- have incredible track records in commercial production.

Done any portraits?

Gene Moore owns one of himself. Peggy Lee has two -- in case one gets sick. Angela Lansbury has a portrait of herself as "Mrs. Lovett" in "Sweeney Todd" as does Hal Prince, the director, and Franny Lee, costume designer for "Broadway" and "Saturday Nite Live," and, I think, that's all.

Did we forget to ask you anything?

Nothing except my shoe size which I have forgotten anyway!

RIGHT: *Miss Havisham*, 12in (30.5cm). Sculpey head and cloth body created by Robert Keene McKinley in 1979. *Miss Havisham*, "a bride to her dying day," wears a costume which Bob has aged for authenticity with a number of unusual substances...including cigarette ashes. The artist has recently completed a second interpretation of this character with changes in size, stance and costume. *Photograph by and courtesy of Robert McKinley.*

BELOW: *Juliet*, 24in (61cm) tall, created by artist Robert Keene McKinley for the Tiffany window displays. The figure is a one-of-a-kind sculpture with heads, arms, legs and chest plate of Super Sculpey and body of cloth-over-wire armature. *Photograph by and courtesy of Robert McKinley.*

Peddler, Super Sculpey and fabric by Robert Keene McKinley. This particular figure was later completed as a sewing lady complete with baskets full of bobbins and scissors hanging around her neck. *Photograph by and courtesy of Robert McKinley.*

The Flora Dora Girl by Robert Keene McKinley. One-of-a-kind sculpture which, most incredibly, has only a hard sculpted head. All the rest of the body is constructed of stuffed fabric over wire armature. The fabric is especially treated to make it stiff and seams are spackled with glue to give the effect of solid sculpture. The whole is a powerful testimony to McKinley's phenomenal ability to cut, seam and fill fabric...few have reached such a maximum usage of the potential in fabric sculpture. *Photograph by and courtesy of Robert McKinley.*

Fate. Not perhaps the most obvious choice of name but, after her completion, artist Robert Keene McKinley had the feeling that the character was laughing her head off at the whole human race. The head is sculpted of Super Sculpey and the body of treated fabric over wire armature. The colorful bodice of the figure's costume has been created by weaving colored ribbons. *Photograph by and courtesy of Robert McKinley.*

Flower Peddler, a whimsey with head of Super Sculpey and cloth body by Robert Keene McKinley. *Photograph by and courtesy of Robert McKinley.*

jean heighton

Jean Heighton's father was the commercial artist who invented the "Jolly Green Giant." She has certainly followed in his footsteps.

Inventor of more wonderful, "off the wall" fantasy creatures than just about any doll artist, Jean imbues her work with humor and whimsy. She is able to make the most improbable juxtapositions of characters and costume work, to make dreams reality.

Most Heighton dolls spring from books, and, when they don't, it is just because the book has yet to be written. *Sherlock Holmes, Alice,* the *Duchess* and *Pig* from *Alice in Wonderland, Tevye* from *Fiddler on the Roof, Mother Goose, Merlin* and such crossbreeds as *Red Riding Rat* and *Billy the Kid* (a cowboy goat doll) indicate the scope of her "literary" dolls.

Heighton animal dolls, however, do not need a "source" from which to derive existence. From 8 to 17in (20.3cm to 43.2cm) tall, made of porcelain, occasionally ceramic clay, with either clay or soft (wire armatured) bodies, they are flights of fantasy that reflect their maker's sense of humor. "I aim for the doll collector from 10 to 100," Jean says. "I want people to see my dolls and remember their childhood fantasies." But, she admonishes, "My dolls are not toys. I sew their clothes right to their bodies."

Born in Chicago, Illinois, in 1927, ("an important year for Lindbergh, Babe Ruth, T.V. and my folks"), Jean studied painting, figure drawing, illustration and sculpting for three years at the Art Institute of Chicago. Her art career includes work as a spot illustrator for a Chicago art studio and 18 years as a custom milliner, as well as two years of ceramics study at the College of San Mateo. Retirement from a teaching career gave Jean the chance to put everything together and make dolls full-time.

"I design eight to ten dolls or more a year, and make several hundred a year," she states. "Doll making is a full-time occupation for me. I spend six to eight hours a day with my doll business. (My husband says it keeps me off the streets and out of bars.) I make dolls because I love it. To me it's fun, creative, exciting and fulfilling. When it gets to be work, I'll quit."

One can see, from the expressions on her critters, that the artist is enjoying herself. "Dolls are people to me," she says. "While creating them, I live a fantasy life in them. They are much like my children. I want them to be loved by the people who buy them. I wouldn't want to know if one were destroyed. It would break my heart. It would seem like losing a part of me."

Whence come her ideas?

"Everything seems to inspire me," she states. "My head is full of ideas I'll never have the time for."

She describes how she brings her fantasies to life.

"I have a workroom for sewing, typing and playing the piano. My workroom is semi-mess. I have an outside work area where I do all the messy mold making, pouring and cleaning. I do a lot of that in the summer. My two kilns and storage area are on a covered deck outside my dining room. I am not what you could call a neat person. I work like crazy towards a deadline; then I clean up to start over.

"I have this fear that I'll never live long enough to get all the dolls I have inside me out.

"I start by sculpting head, hands and feet of Super Sculpey. I sculpt while watching T.V., often ending up with the face I'm seeing most.

"I make a plaster mold. If it's an animal, I try to keep the head a simple two-part mold. I can always add ears, nose, teeth, wrinkles and whatever later in the leather.

"If I make a wolf, I pour brown porcelain, add the ears made from scraps, add a black porcelain nose and white porcelain teeth and eyeballs. After cleaning his feet and hands, I wet the tips and put little dabs of white porcelain slip on each finger and toe. When dry, I clean all and paint high fire gloss on eyes, nose, teeth and nails and fire, then china paint.

"On people faces I china paint cheeks and such with the tips of my fingers. I always leave openings in the tops of heads so I can set in eyes if I like and stuff the heads so I can sew on hats and wigs.

"The other day I stuffed a head so tight it cracked in two. Now I'm more careful.

"I sew a body for people and attach the legs, insert a wire in one leg, all the way into the foot, up through the body, across the shoulders and back down into the other leg, stuff tightly, wire arms the same way, add head, dress, wig and hat."

Although Mrs. Heighton considers artist dolls fine art, she is not elitist. Dolls, for Jean, should be both art and fun. She explains her rationale.

"The doll artist is a part of the art world. The doll world is a part of the doll artist's world. The doll world belongs to collectors, kids and doll lovers."

And Jean Heighton's dolls belong to the child in all of us.

Polly Possum by Jean Heighton, 9½in (24.2cm) tall. Porcelain head, hands, feet and babies. Babies are hand-molded. She holds a girl and a boy in her arms and one or two on her long tail. An extra baby or so can be ordered. She and the kids are chocolate brown porcelain. She wears a cotton print dress, silk shawl and carries a basket shopping bag. Natural straw hat trimmed in flowers. Limited edition of 50. Signed on back of neck. *Photograph courtesy of Jean Heighton.*

Mother Goose by Jean Heighton, 16in (40.6cm) tall. Porcelain head, hands, feet and goose. Wired and stuffed body. Wears custom-stitched velvet hat trimmed with multi-colored silk flowers; velveteen cape matches hat. Either a striped or a printed overskirt and top (leg o'mutton sleeves), pleated eyelet underskirt. White eyelet apron and collar. Black high heel shoes and gold buckle. Trimmed with lace and silk ribbon. Wears granny glasses. Holds a walking stick and a goose. Limited edition of 75. Signed on inside of goose and back of neck. *Mother Goose* has a music box inside of her which plays a nursery rhyme. *Photograph courtesy of Jean Heighton.*

RIGHT: *Sherlock Holmes*, 16in (40.6cm) tall. Porcelain head, hands and pipe. Brown hair, eyes and lashes. Wire stuffed body. Composition black shoes with gray spats. Wears plaid deerstalker hat, checked cape, coat, slate gray wool pants. Holds a tobacco pouch. Designed at the request of the Baker Street Society members. Limited edition of 25. Signed on the back of the neck: "Jean Heighton --year -- ODACA." *Waugh photograph.*

BELOW: *Alice in Wonderland* by Jean Heighton, all-porcelain doll. Blue eyes, brown eyelashes, long blonde hair. She wears deep blue dress and matching hair bow, white pinafore apron with trim, white pantaloons, black shoes and a sweet smile. Limited edition of 25. *Photograph courtesy of Jean Heighton.*

BELOW RIGHT: *The Duchess and Pig Baby*, 11in (27.9cm) tall. Porcelain head, hands, feet and pig. Wired and stuffed body. Wig of brown curls. *The Duchess* wears high gold net 15th century escoffion with silk net veil; satin print dress with train, an off-white satin and lace coat with train, trimmed in mink. The baby, that turned into a pig, wears a christening gown. Limited edition of 25. Signed on back of head: "Jean Heighton -- year -- ODACA." *Photograph courtesy of Jean Heighton.*

LEFT: *French Basket Peddler* by Jean Heighton, 16in (40.6cm) tall. Porcelain head and hands. Composition shoes. Stuffed and wired body. Porcelain pipe. Carries about 15 baskets. He wears brown tweed knee pants, gold sweater, brown vest and brown felt hat. Limited edition of 50. Signed on back of neck: "Jean Heighton --year --ODACA." *Photograph courtesy of Jean Heighton.*

BELOW LEFT: Close-up of *Basket Peddler* by Jean Heighton. *Photograph courtesy of Jean Heighton.*

BELOW: *Precious Pig* by Jean Heighton, 12in (30.5cm) tall. Porcelain head, arms and legs. Body stuffed and wired. She has wreath of porcelain flowers on her head. Arms and legs move up and down so she can sit or stand. Wears white peasant blouse, white pantaloons, eyelet petticoat and cotton print jumper skirt. Limited edition of 100. Signed on back of neck. She has a brother called *Practical Pig* who wears a black velvet jacket, red vest with buttons, a satin collar and black and white checked knee pants. *Photograph courtesy of Jean Heighton.*

lisa lichtenfels

Want to catch your breath?

Want to become dizzy with awe?

Take a look at the superlative needlesculpture of Lisa Lichtenfels!

Tackling a media which almost defies neatness and ease in usage, Lisa has managed to portray exceptionally life-like character as well as the true detail of the human body.

While we are fairly well aware of the ability of needlesculpture to delineate broad-stroke caricature, we rarely see it used to achieve photographic depiction of character. Lisa, however, makes people live -- jowls quiver, veins throb and muscles ripple with unbelievable reality in her figures.

Where did all this begin? While pursuing a very traditional degree in art, she got ahold of the very revolutionary idea that a doll could be as expressive and as much a piece of art as a painting! She came to believe that a doll had a more intimate and immediate relationship with its audience...whereas a painting always seems a bit distant and aloof. Lisa viewed dolls (which, by the way, she capitalizes with a "Big D" in writing) as a form apart from their usual concept as playthings.

In viewing one of Lisa's real-life figures, one should be able to see a bit of oneself. This is sometimes a delicate situation for a good many people do not have the ability to see humanity realistically or themselves either, for that matter. Lisa's figures are not for those who must have sugar and sweetness or for those who do not want to see reality in a doll figure. They are for those who can look at all of humanity and love it for what it is. Fat and wrinkles are far more interesting to Lisa because those are characteristics which one sees in real people -- what makes them living personalities. And what makes them, in their own way, even more expressive of the beauty and the differences allowed in the human condition.

Reactions to her work, as might be expected, are interesting and varied. She tells of an experience when one of her figures -- a tiny baby -- was stolen from an exhibit. She went down to make a police report. "The police department was ominous," she says, "You had to have been there to really feel the atmosphere." The desk officer was behind 4in (10.2cm) of plate glass and all the policemen were wearing guns, stoney faces and very much "just the facts, Ma'am attitudes." After what seemed to be an unending session of questions, the officer asked her, through the microphone in his glass wall, if she had a picture of the stolen object. She passed a photograph through the grille and then heard a booming voice through the mike say, "Lord Almighty, this looks just like a real baby!" Then all the policeman were gathered around exclaiming, "Unreal, man!" and "Look at those itty, bitsy fingers!"...all those tough, business-like officers just went to jelly over a picture of Lisa's baby in needlesculpture!

As for the doll making itself, well some doll artists cannot wait to make the doll so that they can concentrate on the creation of fashionable and elegant wardrobes. A Lichtenfels' creation, however, is successful because of the total concentration of its maker on the perfection of the basic construction processes of the body. She describes the body making process as being like "making a Frankenstein."

First, she makes a full-scale drawing -- and it is a big one as her figures average about 30in (76.2cm) in height. Then she overlays the drawing with tracing paper and draws the skeleton on the tracing paper, like taking an x-ray of the doll, she says.

The skeleton is constructed of aluminum wire and is made to be as anatomically correct as possible. "Most people do not realize that everyone's skeleton is unique to them," Lisa observes.

Once a well-meaning person suggested that she should just do up a whole bunch of skeletons at one crack and build up the bodies as needed. She had to reject this idea because she knows that if the bones are not just right, the final doll will not be either.

She has worked to perfect her skeletons and now has them to the point where they can bend in all the right places. "The closer I get to nature, the better," she says. "They can stand on their own without support and, recently, I improved the structural technique so that the shoulderblades move freely, but I am still working on achieving a satisfactory jointing movement for small bones like those in the wrist."

The bones, all of wire except for the skull which is carved out of styrofoam, are assembled and wrapped in yarn. The basic "guts" and muscles are built up of traditional batting and cotton which is sewn to the bone yarn. Muscles are attached to the yarn covered bones by sewing just as they would be in a real body.

The figure is then "skinned" with nylon stocking material...this is a tricky business. "You want to hide the seams as much as possible," Lisa notes, "or at least seams that can't be hidden must be made as invisible as possible and that means very careful stitching." If you look closely at her work, you will see that those "necessarily shown" seams are very carefully integrated into the whole and positioned to the best advantage of the design.

"I am always going for that elusive invisible seam, but am beginning to wonder if it exists!"

Another problem with the skin is that the stocking material seems to have a mind of its own -- you want a bulge or a wrinkle in a certain place, but the fabric just won't oblige. On the other hand, luck strikes in the oddest ways and sometimes what it wants to do produces an even better result than the original plan!

The face, of course, is another big battle between what the artist wants and what the media will do and, overall, it has its own very special building processes. As noted, Lisa's early experiences and studies of animation techniques for film making have stood her in good stead. Soft sculpture is one thing, but as far as we know, Lisa is the only doll artist who can construct a mobile or animated facial movement in soft sculpture. She does this by means of an intricate wiring system built into the jaws and the lips and connected into a carved out box at the back of the head.

Stop to consider this a minute. We are all fairly familiar with the animation of the hinged mouth or rolling eyes of a marionette. Now, imagine this same sort of movement...only more of it built into layers of fabric and stuffing. Incredible!

Again, going under the surface, Lisa has achieved teeth! Now that may seem a bit funny to the non-artist, but, again, stop and think, teeth are usually only suggested at one remove in sculpture. For instance, a porcelain doll head is all porcelain -- both flesh and teeth are the same material. Lisa literally builds teeth out of polyform (Sculpey) and makes a set of dentures which are set into the jaw. Gums of fabric are constructed and sewn around the teeth to hold them in and lips are applied around them in the desired expression.

The eyes are made of marbles painted to be very realistic in appearance
Amazing!

Over the facial base, the nylon stocking is manipulated to form features -- wrinkle smile lines, dimples -- whatever is demanded to bring the full character out.

Half the making of a good face, Lisa feels is working the surface into the proper wrinkles and bulges and the other half, of course, is the proper build-up of the underlayment.

One can understand that with all the concentration on body structure and character development, Lisa would wish that all her dolls could remain naked -- and so many do. Her direction in character delineation is toward the body and the face and the clothing while absolutely correct for the character, never becomes an over-riding element in the total concept -- just enough to tell the viewer who the person is by dress. As Lisa observes, "I have the consolation of knowing that everything under the clothing that should be there is there."

What is a successful doll for Lisa?...one that is a very unique individual, one that when viewed at first glance appears to be alive. The closer they come to capturing something of the essence of the individual, the better...and, in the end, it is successful if it delights someone other than its creator.

Lisa's work falls into several categories. Naturally, there are the ones that she makes because of her own particular wish, fulfillment and interests and then there are the commissioned portraits including fantasies -- as in the case of the lady who wanted Lisa to do a portrait of her husband as a rabbit because she called him "Bunny." Lisa also does historical and notable figures and fantasy -- surely -- anything her mind or your can conjure up. And, last but not least, she does full scale dioramas which not only capture character of individuals who populate them, but also create an ambience or environment of place.

Basically, Lichtenfels' work can be seen and obtained at the Rosenfeld Gallery in Philadelphia, Pennsylvania, on an on-going basis; portrait commissions go directly through her studio in Indian Orchard, Massachusetts.

Nancy, Lisa Lichtenfels' portrait of First Lady Nancy Reagan at that time just after the President was shot when she looked so very vulnerable and doe-like. Mrs. Reagan is shown wearing a pink dress and her hair is of dyed roving (Clairol "smokey ash!"). *Photograph courtesy of Lisa Lichtenfels.*

Eleanor, a 36in (91.4cm) portrait commemorating Mrs. Roosevelt's 100th birthday. She has a purple dress with flowers on her shoulder, and hair of gray and brown roving...not to mention an uncannily life-like resemblance to the real first lady in her needlesculpted features. *Photograph courtesy of Lisa Lichtenfels.*

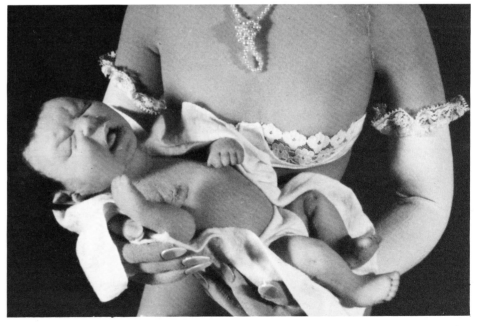

TOP: *Marlena,* a 32in (83.1cm) needlesculpture figure by Lisa Lichtenfels from her "Krazy Horse Saloon" diorama. *Marlene* is the main attraction...a dancer who trots out on the bar to perform for the customers. *Photograph courtesy of Lisa Lichtenfels.*

LEFT: *Oriental Dance Hall Girl,* another "Krazy Horse Saloon" employee. This figure is getting ready to perform. Her baby sitter did not show up and so she has had to bring the baby to work. *Photograph courtesy of Lisa Lichtenfels.*

ABOVE: *Baby.* The dancer's baby is shown doing just what babies do...cry and fuss. He has a blanket and diaper but also comes with a portable crib and bags for used and unused diapers, bottles, and so forth. *Photograph courtesy of Lisa Lichtenfels.*

ABOVE: *Octopussy*, a fantasy work in needlesculpture by Lisa Lichtenfels inspired by the James Bond film of the same name. Her color is blue-green (!) and the face is a combination of Negro and Oriental features. There are no clothes and no accessories on this 32in (83.1cm) figure. It is pure form. *Photographs courtesy of Lisa Lichtenfels.*

LEFT: *Drunkard.* Every saloon has a fellow who has obviously had one too many drinks and this fellow is the one who hangs out in the "Krazy Horse Saloon." *Photograph courtesy of Lisa Lichtenfels.*

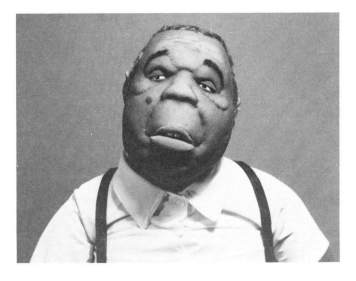

ABOVE: *New Orleans Man*, a "Krazy Horse Saloon" figure that Lisa often moves around the set. Sometimes he plays the saxophone and sometimes he is just a patron. *Photograph courtesy of Lisa Lichtenfels.*

LEFT: *Sad Vampire*, 34in (86.4cm), nylon stocking needlesculpture. This is a-turn-of-the-century American beauty who has been bitten by a vampire...what she might look like after 80 years of living, unaging, in the world of the undead! Lisa adds that it is somewhat of a comment of the plight of many women at the turn of the century ..their sad, restricted lives were not unlike the dead, restricted lives of vampires. *Photograph courtesy of Lisa Lichtenfels.*

BELOW: *Flower*, a doll Lisa says she often uses in the "Krazy Horse Saloon." She is an older woman who wants love affairs. In spite of the seeming impossibility of getting what she wants, she continues on, bolstered by a deep sense of dignity. *Photograph courtesy of Lisa Lichtenfels.*

beverly port

Beverly Port's dolls have long captured the public's fancy, perhaps because of the freshness of their vision. She prefers to work in a menu of media to keep her interest alive and, maybe, to keep her customers on their toes.

"I don't like to do traditional dolls," Bev says. "I'd rather do something offbeat, something that interests ME." Her interests are vast, ranging from sweet-faced hand-painted cloth dolls, a wax cowboy with swivel neck, a two-faced doll that combines two colors of porcelain, nostalgic international Father Christmases, to -- especially -- Teddy Bears.

Bears and dolls are interdependent, each borrowing techniques from the other. The dolls came first; she began making them at age 11 during a "hardship Christmas." Fashioned from pillowcases as gifts for her twin sisters, with crayoned faces and yarn hair, they were the only dolls received that Yule. "My sisters loved them to pieces," Bev says.

She studied art at Olympic College in Washington State, but nothing directly applicable to doll making. Art dolls, descended from the play dolls she designed for her children, entered her repertoire in 1969.

In 1974 she entered two dolls into competition at the IDMA convention in Reno, Nevada, and both won prizes. Representing the extremes of her artistic vocabulary, *Percy*, a porcelain black boy holding a teddy by the paw and *Jenny*, a nostalgic painted-face cloth doll, are milestones in her development. When *Jenny* won the blue ribbon, she set off a nonstop list of orders for dolls that seems to pyramidically expand. And *Percy's* dangling friend was her now-famous literary collaborator, *Theodore B. Bear*, making his maiden public appearance.

Theodore has become Bev's alter ego and spokesbear and has acted as the artist's passport into the world of ursine journalism. "He has taken on a life of his own, separate from me," she writes. "People write to him as well as to me. He wrote his own column in two magazines, *Doll Revue* and *Bambini*, from 1976 to 1982. He narrates two UFDC National slide Programs, and has written many freelance articles in the "Teddy Bear Cause," almost wearing out his paw. He now assists me with my column in *Teddy Bear and friends*™ magazine."

Actually, it was the other way around. Beverly worked eight years for a newspaper, before doll making days. A collector of dolls and Teddy Bears for over 25 years she has a wealth of knowledge on them, and eagerly shares it. Slide programs, demonstrations, lectures, articles and heart-to-heart talks are among the ways she disseminates information. Word has gotten out; when Bev makes appearances, she is usually mobbed.

People relate easily to her work; it seems to touch a warm fantasy-related part of them. Much of Bev's output revolves around fantasy in one way or another. She delights in creating magical animal dolls who seem to have larger than life presences. One of her most popular is *Puss in Boots*, who had the honor of gracing the cover of *Doll News*®, one of the few artist-created dolls to do so.

The artist has a special love for *Puss*, who was designed "from life," and made of porcelain which, apparently, is "trompe l'oeil" (a term used to denote still-life paintings which look so real one has to touch them to ascertain that they actually are made of paint and canvas or wood).

"People have asked," she relates, "if I used real fur on the head of *Puss-in-Boots*, seeing him at shows in artificial lighting. But each "hair" is carved in the porcelain and recarved for additional detailing after it comes from the mold. I did many sketches from life for him, observing even which direction the fine hairs of his face grew in as I watched my sleeping cats."

Other dolls combine human faces and animal bodies, such as *Bunny*, a winsome child-faced doll in a white bunny suit, or *Bearby*, a portrait of her niece in her Halloween Teddy Bear costume. *Bunny* is googly-eyed; it is easy to see that she is a doll. *Bearby* is another story.

"I was exhibiting *Bearby* in Eugene, Oregon, in 1978, and several people were so taken with her that they would come back time and again to look at her. One man finally said, 'That doll almost looks like you have a live child in a bear suit.'

"Later, I carried her out of the convention center in a blanket to protect her as it was raining hard and another man opened the door for me and asked if my 'baby' was a boy or girl. I said 'It's a doll,' and he said, 'It sure is.' He was surprised when I said, 'REALLY. IT IS A DOLL.' I think he was a bit embarrassed when he looked closely."

Both of the above dolls combine porcelain faces and fur bodies. This technique was carried over to the Port Teddy Bear dolls. *Cocoa* and *Mocha* (1976), fully-jointed 18in (45.7cm) teddies, are typical. They sport sculpted faces with inset glass eyes. Another example is *Happy, the Clown Teddy*. His face is porcelain, with jester designs carved into the porcelain and china painted. His body is two-toned; his music box plays, "Send in the Clowns." These designs combine doll making techniques with a real knowledge of and feeling for antique bears, and were the means by which Bev established a reputation as one of the first Teddy Bear artists in America.

Beverly, who may be the finest among her bear artist peers, began teddy experiments in an aesthetic vacuum. When she started, few bear artists had put out shingles; the term was as yet uncoined. She toted her art bears to shows where they became instant hits, paving the way for the current nationwide enthusiasm.

"The explosion of interest is phenomenal," Bev said. "I'm glad I had a part in its beginnings."

Most famous are the *Time Machine Teddies*, which were copyrighted and first exhibited in 1980. These nostalgic, gentle creatures from a dream world take the viewer on a memory journey to a time that was simpler, kinder, when a Teddy Bear hug made everything right. They displayed Port's silverish medallion, with Ted and text, "Won't You Be My Teddy Bear?"

Like her dolls, from the start the Teddies won prizes. Bev is particularly proud of the "Best of Show" awarded *Time Machine Teddy* in 1981 at the Teddy'n Friends event held in Minneapolis, Minnesota. From a roll call of 150 candidates, the Port entry exerted the most impact on the 17,000 viewers.

Each *Time Machine Teddy* offers a surprise. Sometimes a music box (key-wound or crank-driven), a growler (or both) establishes the internal makeup. The tunes they play complement the teds' personas.

Some bears explore literature, like *The Lavendar Bear King from Oz* (who is accompanied by *Ozma*, a porcelain doll), others fantasy, like *Beary Mab*, a diminutive furry fairy bear with translucent wings. All of them, however, have an intangible "something" that sets them apart, one from the other, and paws above the ordinary ted.

While her teddies usually can be hugged and dragged about, the dolls are more fragile. Bev insists, however, that they should be potentially playthings, as well as artwork.

"My dolls can be played with and moved. All are jointed or on wire armature bodies. The cloth ones are huggable. However, I consider them art, or mobile sculpture.

"Dolls are a representation of people, fantasy or animal figures, as my imagination interprets them and my hands bring them into three-dimensional form. They are sculpture and DEFINITELY art. Some could be played with, but in a limited manner, due to cost, they would not be a child's play toy."

Port dolls take many, many hours to construct. Porcelain and cloth are Bev's chief media. Wax and composition are also used. She seems to work in almost everything, and to invent new, wonderful ways of using art materials.

One of her dolls has been given a patent. The *Pinafore Pals* is a double doll, combining two colors of porcelain to produce a two-faced girl, black on one side, white on the other.

She has developed a special secret wax formula that enables her to make swivel-necked dolls such as *America's Cowboy*.

Her cloth dolls have sweet, nostalgic hand-painted faces that have to be done correctly the first time.

Perhaps her favorite "human" dolls are the *Santas* and *Father Christmases* she has done, in all sizes. Usually of porcelain, they meld many elements and materials to make their statements.

Her use and adventurous combinations of media have won her a fervent following and an endless waiting list. This creates problems for those wanting already-disseminated designs. As with any artist, Bev wants to move forward. "I enjoy coming up with new designs," she says. "It's always fun to see a new idea, something that just popped into your mind in a brief flash of imagination, come into being.

"My work area is messy. The creative process is NOT orderly with me, but something of an explosion. Working in so many different materials is always complicated. I need supplies for each type, from large to miniature -- everything from antique fabrics and lace to modern plush. I work everywhere in the house and lose things when I 'organize.' Every so often I straighten up things so I can again create artistic 'fusion confusion.'"

Beverly's designs may be so popular because she is in tune with what collectors desire, having been one for over 25 years.

"I work for myself," she explains. "I make what I enjoy, the best I can at time of completion. As I finish one, I see how I can improve the next. Each one I strive to make the best. I'm looking for 'timelessness'

Time Machine Teddy by Beverly Port, 15in (38.1cm) tall. © 1980. Fully-jointed original bear wears Beverly Port trademark neck medallion that says, "Won't You Be My Teddy Bear?"™ He won "Best of Show" in the "Create-a-Bear" competition held in Minneapolis, Minnesota, in September 1981. *Photograph by and courtesy of Beverly Port.*

-- something artistic in expression, but capable of evoking emotional response -- the unforgettable doll or bear. I'm trying to capture my imagination and bring it into three-dimensional reality. I'm 'painting' with fabric, sculpting a classic to be an heirloom of tomorrow today."

From time to time, Beverly considers having her ideas commercially produced because there is no way she can keep up with orders. People wait sometimes years for a Port creation. So far, this has not happened but the doll maker is not averse to commercialization of doll artistry. She explains.

"If an artist produces a model SPECIFICALLY to produce commercially and KNOWS the production changes it will go through, there is no compromise and his creation can go to children and many collectors at a price affordable to the general public. It can be enjoyed on a different level from those one-of-a-kinds or special orders that are more expensive and fewer can afford. An artist can do BOTH types if she is versatile and has a wide spectrum of designs. A highly fluid designing base can produce wonderful non-commercial creations as well as those for commercial production with no conflict. One must know and plan which direction each specific design will ultimately take."

Bev is always planning designs, working simultaneously on a half dozen projects. The common thread that unites them is the exploration of personality and character, whether the doll be a *Sherlock Holmes*, a bear like *Miss Emily* or an anthropomorphic creature like *Puss-in-Boots*. They are brought to life by a combination of vision, skill and love.

LEFT: *Bunny* by Beverly Port, approximately 20in (50.8cm) without her ears included in measurement. © 1978. A small girl dressed up in her rabbit suit for Halloween. Porcelain face. Googly antique glass eyes; shy smile. White fur fabric body with swivel neck. Jointed at shoulders and hips. Long ears; round fluffy tail. Holds an Easter basket with green grass and bouquet of colorful handmade felt flowers. A small cluster of the same flowers nestles at base of one ear. Green and blue ribbon around neck. She has a music box in her body that plays "Easter Parade." *Photograph by and courtesy of Beverly Port.*

BELOW LEFT: *Puss-in-Boots* by Beverly Port, approximately 18in (45.7cm) tall. © 1976. Sculpted porcelain head with inset glass eyes. Whiskers, tufts of fur in his ears and ruff around his neck. Long tail of fur. Wool cloth body with posable arms, swivel jointed legs. Velveteen outfit. Leather gloves and boots. One hand on sword; the other holds a brace of pheasants. Won first in "originals" at San Francisco United Federation of Doll Clubs National Convention, 1976. *Photograph by and courtesy of Beverly Port.*

BELOW: *America's Working Cowboy, P.J.* by Beverly Port, approximately 24in (61cm) tall. © 1976. Wax swivel head on separate wax shoulder plate. Wax hands. Secret formula wax that withstands temperature extremes very well. Fur wig hand-fashioned to fit head. Inset glass eyes with eyelashes. Cloth body with posable arms and swivel-jointed legs. Leather hat, vest, chaps and boots. Gunbelt with gun and bullets. Shirt, kerchief and Levis. Also available in porcelain, approximately 19in (48.3cm) tall. *Photograph by and courtesy of Beverly Port.*

192

LEFT: *Ozma of Oz* and *Teddy Bear King* by Beverly Port. © 1976. Doll versions of characters from *The Lost Princess of Oz* by Frank L. Baum. *Ozma*, the lost ruler of Oz, is found through the magic and efforts of the life-size Teddy Bear Sorcerer. *Ozma*, approximately 12in (30.5cm) tall, has wax shoulder head, hands and feet, long human hair wig, painted features and cloth body. Dressed in green and wears a crown. *Teddy Bear King* is approximately 14in (35.6cm) tall. Made of lavender fabric. Wears a crown; holds a wand and a small "magic" pink bear, *Pink Pinkerton*. Bears are fully-jointed. *Photograph by and courtesy of Beverly Port.*

BELOW: "Pinafore Pals," *Liza Jane* and *Lisa Ann*, approximately 14in (33cm) tall by Beverly Port. ©1975. Patented in 1977. First of a series of "Twosy Dolls," this two-face character child has a porcelain head, shoulders, double hands and feet combining two distinct colors of porcelain, not just white with overpainting. Swivel head and shoulders are "half and half," as is the cloth body. The porcelain hands and feet are double -- one pair hidden under the clothes depending on which side is being viewed. *Liza Jane* has black fur wig, *Lisa Ann* has human hair in braids. Both have glass eyes. The dress, bonnet and pinafore are double front. "Instead of having the black doll as only a 'second face', turning around on a white doll's body with hands, I had the thought of showing a more equal relationship, reflecting the changes in our times. Each side is 'No. 1.' when viewed." Patent No. 678, 173: "The Convertible Doll." *Photograph by and courtesy of Beverly Port.*

Percy and *Theodore B. Bear* by Beverly Port. © 1974. *Percy* has a porcelain head that swivels on separate shoulders, porcelain arms and legs. Brown glass eyes. Sawdust-stuffed body. Wool stockings and leather shoes. Real caracul fur cap. Dressed in all antique material. Faded denim overalls with many pockets -- for hanky, slingshot, pencil and other childhood treasures. Holds bag of marbles and his friend, *Theodore B. Bear. Theodore* is fully-jointed and has swivel neck. *Photograph courtesy of Beverly Port.*

St. Nicholas by Beverly Port, 17in (43.2cm) tall. © 1981. Porcelain head with fur wig, moustache and beard. Painted eyes. Carved teeth in open-closed mouth. Full-wire armature in body. Antiqued velvet robe trimmed with real fur holds green tree and staff plus leather strap of brass bells. Antique gold braid around waist. Leather boots. "Theme" doll for United Federation of Doll Collectors Region I Conference, 1982. *Photograph by and courtesy of Beverly Port.*

Jenny and Her Doll by Beverly Port. © 1970. *Jenny* is approximately 18in (45.7cm) tall. From a series of hand-painted cloth dolls with an "old-fashioned" look. Polka dot dresses and leather shoes on both dolls. Fur wig on small doll. *Jenny* was runner-up for the Gold Cup for Best of Show at International Doll Convention, Reno, Nevada, 1974. *Photograph by and courtesy of Beverly Port.*

194

blythe collins-kretschmer

"Oh, Mildred, look at these dolls...they are sooo unique." Now, there is a cry one could hear anytime, anywhere near an exhibit of dolls by Blythe Collins-Kretschmer.

Blythe, herself, says, "At doll shows people have certain expectations as to what they will see. I make dolls for people like myself and they always seem to catch people off guard. People either stop dead, really liking the work or walk on by quickly. Either way, they experience an emotional reaction."

Hard to say what Mildred truly thought because everyone reacts to a doll in a different way, but it is pretty clear that Blythe's work is all doll and all art. They are refreshing. They are elegant. They are comfortable and calm. They are everything one could want in a doll form.

Most all would agree that a universal idea of a doll can be described as sculpted head, hands, feet, with a soft body of fabric. Blythe's approach is to take this basic and traditional mode of doll making and inject it with her own highly individual point of view and specialized abilities such that the resulting phenomena is an extremely contemporary body of work.

Blythe has an impressive list of apprentice work and study in the field of ceramics...and it shows. Up to her elbows in clay, her studies began in an apprenticeship with the Unicorn Pottery in the summer of 1969, continued at The Great Barrington Pottery in Massachusetts and included private instruction from New York sculptress Faye Spahn. She has also taken seminars in china painting from Connie Walser Dereck and Neva Wade Garnett. During her eight years of being a production potter, she specialized in masks, animals, plants and flowers as well as satirical pieces and all of those elements have been turned to good use in her pieces.

What stopped "Mildred's friend," and a great many other viewers is the immediate and dynamic impact of the heads of Blythe's creations. Their execution and expression is exceptionally dramatic. In the "Gilded Lily" clown series, Blythe shows her years of solid experience as a porcelain craftsman. Each has an exquisite garland of delicately modeled ceramic roses, posies and leafy details directly applied and painted in springtime pastels. Each of the "Gilded Lily" faces is a unique individual in that eye treatment and direction of glance are changed to make each a distinct persona.

It is quite obvious that Blythe's forte is painting. She admits it. She loves to do it. She says that she could go on and on painting faces, always giving a new interpretation and never, never running out of ideas.

"I find it impossible to repeat myself...especially when it comes to the "Akimbos" and "Gilded Lily" styles. I change colors and moods and brush strokes for each group I produce. I could paint them forever and they would continue to evolve along with me. Even so, where I used to rely heavily on my painting ability, I now am spending more time on the sculptural stage and increasing my dimension there, too."

It is very difficult to achieve a rendered effect in painting a doll head. Most doll makers paint lines and fill them in with color... usually solid color. Blythe's work in rendering achieves the detail of graphic work pen drawing with all the subtleties and effects that go along with it. It is as if the eye meets and flows into the surrounding face. A butterfly motif painted on the face seems to appear and recede giving a worldly wise, perhaps even sinister and mysterious effect enhanced by the addition of beads, bells and ribbon streamers for an almost mystical oriental visionary effect.

Although there is no way to actually put one's finger on the reason, Blythe's clowns carry a strong feeling of the orient. Perhaps, it is the shape of the head and the suggestion of curvature in the nose and lips which seem somewhat reminiscent of the statues of Buddha or the costume masks of the Kabuki theater.

In the clowns, the impact as we have said is carried in the head and its relationship in color and texture to the body covering and secondarily in its relationship to costume and form; however, the doll idea is always present in Blythe's work. Her child figures have the same companionable feeling as some of the older composition dolls. They are quiet, utterly charming and easy to be with. Dolls are definitely toys to Blythe and she does not mean to make them as showpieces. Her dolls are meant to be held, touched, handled and to be a familiar part of the home environment.

Between the full fantastical of the clowns and the warmth of the children, Blythe's work takes a third dimension in the development of character figures. Still in cloth bodies, these are wired to assume a permanent pose and depict a character idea. The delightful *Humpty Dumpty* (especially commissioned by her three-year-old daughter, Emily) is well and truly the personification of "egginess" -- the quintessential ovoid with arms and legs -- just as literal an interpretation as a three-year-old would want. *Ambrose* at the time of this writing was the most recent forming, the first of a limited series of 35. *Mother Nature* is another character which Blythe laughingly called a self portrait of herself at age 85...an age she says she looks forward to being.

Why does Blythe make dolls? She says, "because it is rewarding to convert an image in your mind to something you can hold in your hands.

RIGHT: *Humpty-Dumpty*, a jointed, glazed porcelain figure measuring 9in (22.9cm) from head to foot. This famous egg personality can be made either with or without handmade flax wig. The tuxedo is made of wool and the clothing is not removable. *Photograph courtesy of Blythelin Dollworks.*

BELOW RIGHT: *Ambrose*, a 27in (68.6cm) porcelain character by Blythe Collins-Kretschmer, edition limited to 35 pieces. This character is one of Blythe's newer editions. Each member of the edition will have a one-of-a-kind costume of handwoven materials with velvet and feathers. *Photograph courtesy of Blythelin Dollworks.*

"I have always enjoyed sculpting, and I respond immediately to people, especially fairytale characters. Ideas? Lots of them come from fairytales and illustrations in children's books. I would like to think that imagination and sense of humor is reflected in everything I do. I also like the complication of doll making, the many intricate details, choices and decisions. It is a tremendous satisfaction to make something from beginning to end and to be able to do it as a family enterprise (daughter Emily suggests ideas and husband Scott is in charge of sewing on arms...often until 2 a.m. on the night before a show). It is a very satisfying and "holistic" way of life."

("Blythelin," her business name, is a combination the names of herself, of course, and her Aunt Thelma who has done quite a bit of costume sewing, and her sister, Linda, with whom she still plays dolls, although on a grown up basis these days.)

"There is no such thing as an eight hour day, especially when you work at home," comments Blythe. "It is a full-time occupation.

"If I am not actively making dolls, I am doing the business end of it. I produce between 80 and 100 finished dolls per year and one or two new design originals. I am always adding new dolls to the line and that leaves less time to make dolls in the older editions. Each edition is usually about 35 in limit.

"I am always trying for an organic wholeness...every part has to look like it belongs to that specific individual doll. I can tell," she says, "by the way people respond whether I have achieved those whole person looks.

"I don't use synthetic materials. I try not to overdo anything... just enough to bring out the character of the doll. Too much limits the privilege of the owner viewer to interpret and to relate. My dolls don't demand any rarified environment. I always feel they are going to cope very well in whatever circumstance they find themselves in."

196

ABOVE: *Mother Nature* by Blythe Collins-Kretschmer. *Mother* is a 15in (38.1cm) porcelain bisque edition limited to eight pieces. The hair is natural mohair or raw silk fiber. The eyes can be either glass or painted. The head is cast in a mold but the hands are modeled separately for each figure. Although the idea for this figure came from a book called *When the Root Children Wake Up*, Blythe often says this figure is a self-portrait of herself at age 85. *Photograph courtesy of Blythelin Dollworks.*

RIGHT: *Walter* and *Delpha* are 18in (45.7cm) porcelain bisque children which Blythe says are her twins from Europe. They have simple country clothes and hair of flax...very unassuming and very easy to be with. *Photograph courtesy of Blythelin Dollworks.*

ABOVE: *Gilded Lily* 27in (68.6cm) glazed porcelain clown series. No two are alike. Each doll has approximately 20 handmade porcelain flowers and leaves attached to its head from ear to ear, ending in a bunch of ribbons in coordinating colors. The ribbons pass through a hole in the head and are knotted on the inside. Each head is glazed in the cone 6 fire and then china painted and fired to cone 018 at least six times. The 14 carat gold skull cap is applied last and fired to cone 019. *Photograph courtesy Blythelin Dollworks.*

RIGHT: *Gilded Lily* and *Tiny Lily*, two variations on the theme with china painted eyes by artist Blythe Collins-Kretschmer. Because each face is different and because Blythe is always changing them, no final number has been put on the amount that will be made. *Photograph courtesy Blythelin Dollworks.*

nerissa

When Nerissa made her needlesculpture dolls, every Friday was Name Day.

"We named them individually," she says. "And that was a special time for us, giving the doll an appropriate name that would express its personality. We really kind of got into it and made a party of it. It was fun."

The act of naming the dolls seems significant because Nerissa's creations have strong personas. To her they are not people, as they are to some doll artists. But they come close.

"We don't do portraits," she explains. "We don't copy people. They aren't inspired by a particular person: they're more general. We strive for the humanness and try to build all the details that bring this out. And so they all have a strong personality. A lot of our customers view the dolls as people, though. And we refer to them by name for the most part."

Perhaps Nerissa's creations are not folk one would prefer to meet on the street. Born from a fine arts background, the early dolls were an extension of the artist's work in print making. They took on three dimensions and life, and are meant to make statements. Some of these are discomforting.

Begun in 1979, the needlesculpture dolls, done in an edition of 1000, represented, for the most part, elderly ladies. Nerissa terms them "happy dolls." She says that they are "prime time ladies," and had a positive purpose in creating the sculptures. Reactions, though, were mixed.

"We're happy about the dolls because they showed an elderly person, old and wrinkled. Some people don't like the age of the dolls, though. They're afraid of being old. They are into thinking old is ugly. But we didn't get that reaction from many people.

"Sometimes we could help people feel better about age and our dolls did that. The needlesculpture dolls represented the older people as altogether, happy, centered beings. They had earned their position in life. They were their own people, in total control. When we explained this to people, they understood and sometimes this helped them see the beauty and the strength that was in them."

Another series of needlework dolls was the transvestites, which are distinguishable from the ladies only in that they have no breasts, (sometimes a hairy chest, though) and are sexed.

The edition closed, Nerissa has prepared a kit for recreating her designs so they will continue to live. But she has progressed to other media.

Art for the Pennsylvania artist is always in a state of growth, of change. She discovers new ideas and materials and uses them to make new statements.

Currently (1985) she is working in porcelain.

"It's a medium I'm comfortable with," she explains. "I'm good at it, and it's a constant challenge, something I haven't done before. That leads to excitement and a sense of accomplishment when I achieve my goal. It's complicated.

"I did not one day say to myself, 'I am going to make dolls.' Even when I made my first one, I did not plan to do this as a career.

"I've worked in a lot of media and those media held my interest at that particular time. Dolls seem to be holding my interest now, but I don't know they always will."

The porcelain dolls were preceded by polyform ones, and are slip-cast. The first wee toddlers. Nerissa spent a good deal of time watching toddlers to capture their real attitudes, which she translated into small 2 to 5½in (5.1 to 14cm) porcelain head-and-limbed dolls. Like her other work, they are controversial.

"We studied toddlers; we captured the toddler look, the toddler expression, with the mouth open. People don't like to think of their children like that, of their children as anything but happy, with big smiles.

"Some people will say that they look like they're throwing temper tantrums because they don't have happy, big smiles.

"I think, though, there's a movement in the doll world not to idealize because many of the dolls that have been done have idealized, and the contemporary doll maker is in a genre phase that depicts people as they are."

Not all of Nerissa's people fit this category; they seem, rather, to be dream creatures, forged from fantasy. Her second line of slipcast dolls, the porcelain ladies, approximately 20in (50.8cm) tall, combines haunting imagery and rarified fabrics, building upon the physical types of her needlesculpture dolls. Somehow she manages to make the porcelain look soft, to capture the look of her earlier work.

Her series of clowns, which includes a wonderful anthropomorphic cat clown, seems gentle, almost introspective, self-satisfied and quizzical.

The all-encompassing characteristic of these beings is their life, a quality which Nerissa strives for.

"A doll has to have strength and life," she says. "And the sum of all the doll's parts has to be in harmony. The main thing is the life. I don't want it to ever look dead.

"It must have that essence. Artists talk about their pieces working or not working, and evoking responses or not evoking responses. A piece being alive or a piece being dead. They're alive in

RIGHT: *Lillian*, 20in (50.8cm) needlesculpture, edition of 1000 similars. Markings: "Lillian" on her right leg. "© 1980 Nerissa" on her left leg. *Photograph courtesy of Nerissa.*

BELOW RIGHT: *Louise*, 4½in (11.5cm) porcelain child designed by Nerissa. Removable dress and half slip. Wired fabric body. Markings: "L #16 © 1983 Nerissa." *Photograph courtesy of Nerissa.*

that sense; that they do have strength, they do have personality, but not in the sense of people.

"But they have life and energy as an art form. There is life other than people life. I don't like dead dolls; I don't like manikins or dolls that look like them. Manikins are dead."

The life in her dolls often calls out to purchasers, who contact the artist with news of their dolls' exploits. One couple bought a bottle of Scotch for their two Nerissa dolls, took a photograph of the dolls and the family on Christmas morning and sent the shot to Nerissa. She credits this to the personalities she tries to create in her work.

"They ARE dolls; they are different from people, but they have very strong personalities.

"Where, with real people, their personality is in flux, our dolls' personalities don't change. They will evoke responses from people because of capturing that little bit of human personality. They recognize this essence as something very precious, something to be guarded and taken care of, and, in that sense, they become art; they're not toys to that extent.

"A toy, according to the dictionary, is a demeaning object, a worthless thing. The dolls are art and sculpture."

Done in a studio-factory in Florida, Nerissa dolls are a full-time project for the artist and her helpers. She sells wholesale and retail all over the United States, and to several foreign countries. Her dolls are signed, dated and copyrighted, and the artist feels strongly that all artists should care enough to mark their work in this way.

At times, Nerissa and her partner, Roger, take the dolls to street fairs, especially one in Pittsburgh, Pennsylvania, where a regular population returns each year to buy from them.

"Selling the dolls in a street fair situation can be very, very difficult, yet there are great pleasures in doing it and one of the most pleasurable things for us is the kind of clientele that we pick up and people we see time and again. We have a lot of people in Pittsburgh who expect to see us every summer and want to buy a new doll by Nerissa.

"After five years some of them have quite a collection of my work. They become my friends. I can remember the names of the dolls I sold them five years ago, and I ask them how are *Jeffrey* and *Josephine*. I don't tell them that the latter dolls I don't remember the names of, but the first 100 I think I could list them all now and who owns them."

Nerissa's output these days is far higher than when she made the needlesculpture dolls. Although she still is careful to make every doll the best she has ever done, and she holds no favorites, claiming that they all are; they no longer have individual names.

Friday is no longer name day; there just is no time for christening parties. But her dolls continue to burst with life and with controversial personality.

LEFT: *Keiko,* 17in (43.2cm), porcelain, designed by Nerissa. Edition of 1000. Black silk hair, green eyes, leopard fabric body skin, black velvet skirt with tie in back, white cape with gold dots and black and gold bodice. Markings in porcelain shoulder plate: ''Keiko #12, © 1983 Nerissa.'' *Photograph courtesy of Nerissa.*

BELOW: *Carole,* 21in (53.3cm) needlesculpture by Nerissa. Edition of 1000 similars. Tussah silk hair, antique lace dress, full length fully-lined ''mink'' coat. Markings: ''Carole'' on right thigh, ''© 1980 Nerissa'' on her left thigh. *Photograph courtesy of Nerissa.*

Tickles, 19in (48.3cm). Porcelain bisque head and fabric body. Edition of 1000. Designer: Nerissa. Costume is black with white stripe. Accents and trim are primary colors. Signed, named, numbered and copyrighted on back of neck. Made February 1984. *Photograph courtesy of Nerissa.*

Ashley, 21in (53.3cm) by Nerissa. Porcelain head on soft body. White silk shirt, black body suit, black metallic cape, black and white checked shoes. Named, signed, numbered and copyright on back shoulder plate. Made November 1983. *Photograph courtesy of Nerissa.*

Myths of Motherhood. 22in (55.9cm) soft sculpture with polyform babies in skirt. Clothing is layered skirts, lace top and sleeves -- all in off-whites. Markings: "© 1983 Nerissa." *Photograph courtesy Nerissa.*

Marouse, 19in (48.3cm), designed by Nerissa. Porcelain head on fabric body. Features are china-painted and include a gold tear. This figure has orange silk hair, creme rayon velvet pants and jacket. Named, signed, numbered and copyrighted on back of neck. *Photograph courtesy of Nerissa.*

ʃuʃanna oroyan

One cannot be noncommittal about Susanna Oroyan's dolls. They reach out to the viewer and challenge his complacency, his ideas of what a doll should be and should do. To the orthodox and the unimaginative, they prove disconcerting.

This scarcely bothers the artist. Susie's dolls reflect her offbeat sense of humor and poke gentle fun at the foibles to which we are all prey. She sees subjects from a subtly skewed angle, interpreting even classic themes with unexpected twists that make the viewer reexamine his preconceptions.

Her *Mary Had a Little Lamb*, for instance, features a corpulent gray-haired lady, someone who might serve as *Old Mother Hubbard* in another's output. *Mother Goose*, on the other hand, is younger and sprightlier than usual, and is dressed in ruff collar, velvety bodice, calico skirt, apron and layers of crinoliny petticoats. She carries a huge basket of violets. Susie makes rules up as she goes along; they seem to work.

A dabbler in many media, the Oregon artist's mainstay is Sculpey, a low-fire synthetic clay from which she models one-of-a-kind wire-armatured dolls. Hardly playthings, these pieces are compositions in clay, wire, paint, fiber and space, meant to interact with their environment in specific ways, in predetermined poses to be viewed from various angles. Oroyan dolls are sculpture, using the universally understood doll form as ambassador for ideas.

An ideational approach has its drawbacks; not all collectors enjoy being challenged by dolls; Susie's visual, literary and cultural puns pass over many heads. She finds this sad.

When asked to describe her dolls in one word, she replied: " 'Weird!' No, 'fun' -- better choice. A lot of fun for me and I hope for those who see them. I really want the world to smile at the characters I make. 'Cute' or 'darling' in a doll is not what makes me happy.

"A lot of people say my dolls look like me. Good grief, I hope not! I hope when they say that what they really mean is that I am enjoying life and all its quirks and follies and foibles and it shows in the work. Of all the people in the world, I have no patience for and often plain feel sorry for it is the humorless realistic. If one can't enjoy and appreciate all the things -- good and bad, around him, he's going to be very unhappy with himself and the world and make others that way, too.

"The world is silly and does not organize itself into neat, pretty packages. My dolls are admittedly silly and don't reflect only the ideal. I like to poke fun or have fun or make fun of."

Susie's enjoyment in her doll making shows in the exuberant gestures, energetic poses, unexpected juxtapositions of fibers, colors and textures and the often satisfied expressions of her characters. These are dolls secure in their personas who reach out and try to involve the viewer for a moment in private worlds. Often they illustrate literature, sometimes slightly abstruse stuff. Susie's inspirations come from many sources, but lean on predecessors who were slightly off-the-wall.

"My all-time hero in the illustration department," she says, "is W. Heath Robinson, a man who invented the Rube Goldberg machine before Rube did, a man with a wonderful sense of the ridiculous. I have, from time to time, translated his drawings into 3-D figure form.

"Nursery rhymes are often fun and silly and fit character types and that is why I do so many on those lines."

Literary sources are just a springboard. Susie seldom sticks to her original concept; wonderful inspirations and combinations occur along the way.

"I make characters because of the absolute, total freedom they give me to do whatever I want to do. I can doodle around in the clay and, if something looks interesting, like a long nose or buck teeth, I can pursue it and play around with it and decide who or what it will be as it evolves.

"I HAVE made a few dolls where I absolutely stuck to an original concept all the way through. Most were not pleasing in the end. They were 'forced.' The only ones I had luck with were Sherlock and Watson and the only reason I can think of for that was that I was so very in tune with those characters. I already had a solid mental image of what they were.

"I often start out with a picture or illustration but mostly that serves as a starting point. Sometimes some really good faces just evolve. Rarely does one look like the idea that sparked it."

Dolls come slowly; in a decade only about 150 have passed standards and were allowed to migrate from what Susie terms her "working pig pen" of a studio. A good doll is one she would want to keep; anything less is relegated to the closet. Since she makes them up as she goes along, Susie is not shy about bending standard notions of doll making techniques to fit her concepts. But materials and physical limitations inhibit translation.

"I am frustrated continually because the super neat, crystal clear, detailed vision in my mind's picture tube cannot be made or exactly reproduced in reality. Sometimes this is because I am inept or am impatient. Sometimes because the materials I see are not available in the real world or, if they are, they will not scale correctly.

ABOVE: *Watch The Birdie,* one of a kind polyform sculpture commissioned by Delores Smith. Photo by W. Donald Smith.

RIGHT: Close-up view of the *Old Woman Who Lost Her Shoe. Photograph by W. Donald Smith.*

"I like the freedom of being able to costume and pose figures any way I feel I want. I'm not bound to do 'correct' historical costume. I can put a 16th century ruff on a character with a bustle (I haven't) if I am so minded. Generally, I pretty much 'go with it' all the way through, although attention to design coordination never gets neglected. I am always checking to see it has harmonious color, balance in movement and proportion, the best combination of textures, trims, scale of accessories, etc."

She seeks the same characteristics in the work of others.

"Primarily, a doll has to move the viewer and it has to move in space. Secondarily, it has to work with all the elements of design coming together harmoniously. I might add that the viewer I talk about is me.

"I prefer a doll that indicates life. It should be one that, if you were to catch a glimpse of it out of the corner of your eye, would seem in action or in stop-time.

"For this reason I tend to like what are more 'figures' than 'dolls.' However, even a well-done dollie-type doll has movement. Note the difference between a baby doll that serves no purpose other than to show of a ruffly dress and Martha Hand's children who crawl, recline, sit and do a number of 'real child' motions. Similarly, a beautiful lady is not a stiff fashion plate; she is motion and grace. That is part of the beauty."

Susie knows her views are not universal.

"I just hope the general viewer can appreciate what I have done whether or not he particularly likes it. I have a continual fight on my hands over making what I want as compared to what people want to collect.

"Life is not all ruffles and lace. People are not all pretty. Some of the most intereting people are dirty and ugly. But collectors would rather have something that does not disturb their environment. I really can't blame them; life is not all that pleasant. Who needs more unpleasantness? I would rather they thought life was made of

differences and that those differences can each be appreciated for what they are.

"Now, don't get me wrong. I like beauty and like to create it as much as anyone else. It is just that there is, and should be, room for all."

Susie delights in fabricating fancies; half of her means of self-expression is tied to them.

"Why do I make dolls?," she asks. "It is a compulsion, pure and simple. I do it because I absolutely must make things. I am driven to make things. If it wasn't dolls, it would be crocheted door stops or something. God knows, I might even take up creative cooking.

"It just so happens I am interested in the design in people's faces and lives that we call character and I think the best way to reproduce it is in doll form."

The left, or verbal, side of her brain constantly competes with the visual right.

"Presently I am schizoid in art and writing; they are two different brain functions. When I have writing on hand, I can't wait to sculpt, and when I am working on dolls, I itch for the typewriter.

"Still, of the two, I prefer the making to the writing. Why? Because if you put up two colors, the choice is obvious. A color is a color. Put two words together and you have 200 choices because of the semantic implications, grammatical necessities, etc. I'm probably too sensitive to all those niceties of language.

"Generally, my writing is a way of figuring out the whys and wherefores of life and art just the same as making dolls is a way of figuring out character and expressing all the possibilities and potentials of it."

Writing, art and a zany, upbeat life concept combine in Susanna's dolls. Not for the complacent, like their creator, they appeal to those who appreciate an intelligent, offbeat, wry point of view -- and a large dollop of fun.

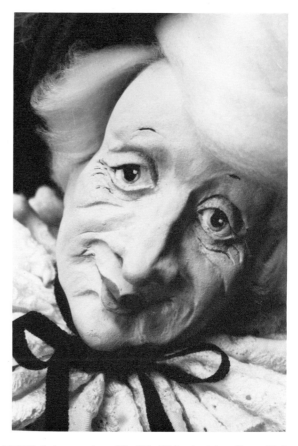

ABOVE: Susanna Oroyan admits she does not really feel comfortable working in small scale..."I seem to have several more fingers than is necessary for good work," she says. However, accepting the challenge of "seeing if she could," several small figures have been made. This little 7in (17.8cm) lady is a purely imaginative creation dressed in white chiffon with pink accents. *Oroyan photograph.*

BELOW: *Uncle Lubin* is a character in a children's storybook written and illustrated by W. Heath Robinson...Everything about *Uncle Lubin* is just a little larger and quite a bit sillier than life which greatly appeals to Susie Oroyan. He wears huge seven-league boots, has a large sombrero type hat festooned with flowers and patterned ribbons, oversized buttons and bows, but plays a rather small concertina. *Uncle Lubin* is a one-of-a-kind polyform figure and is 11in (27.9cm) in height seated. *Oroyan photograph.*

ABOVE: A close-up view of the 22in (55.9cm) polyform figure, *Mother Goose,* shows the detail of modeling and finish of Oroyan's polyform pieces. The finish is slightly textured by a special application of a spray lacquer which gives a matte finish. Note the strongly cut features. This type of sculpting does not easily lend itself to reproduction. *Oroyan photograph.*

BELOW: The figure, *Mary,* was created for the artist's own Christmas creche. She is dressed in a robin's egg blue gown of linen faille with a robe of royal blue lined with gold and rose brocade. *Oroyan photograph.*

RIGHT: *The Pied Piper* one-of-a-kind polyform sculpture. *Photograph by W. Donald Smith.*

BELOW: The inspiration for this 15in (38.1cm) polyform, one-of-a-kind figure was the nursery rhyme, "There was an old woman of Surrey who was morn, night and noon in a hurry, called her husband a fool, Drove her children to school, the Worrying Old Woman of Surrey." Poor dear looks at her pocket watch while the rest of her trappings of purse, basket, muffs, shawls and umbrella seem in danger of flying away. *Oroyan photograph.*

BELOW RIGHT: Close-up view of the *Old Woman of Surrey,* a one-of-a-kind polyform sculpture by Susanna Oroyan. *Oroyan photograph.*

RIGHT: Oroyan's fancy was tickled by the idea of an airbourne Uncle Sam as portrayed by Norman Rockwell in a 1930s advertisement. Our favorite uncle flies along serenely wearing the traditional costume with the rather unusual addition of flying cap and goggles and a harness with canvas covered bi-plane wings. *Oroyan photograph.*

BELOW: Artist Susanna Oroyan has made a number of fantasy world figures... especially fairies which have appeared in floating chiffons with flowers applied over the costume and gossamar gold and silver wings. *The Spring Blossom Fairy* shown here is a blonde dressed in white with the very palest of yellow blossoms. *Oroyan photograph.*

BELOW RIGHT: This figure was sculpted with no other idea than capturing a "pretty lady" expression, but the serendipity of finding a lovely rose patterned satin fabric soon set the artist's mind searching for a character named Rose. *Rose Maylie*, the kind daughter of a minister who helped the boy, Oliver Twist, in the Dickens' novel came to mind as the answer. *Rose*, a 17in (43.2cm) one-of-a-kind sculpture, has a costume of the 1840s with a moss green velvet bodice trimmed in ecru lace and, of course, the rose printed satin skirt. *Oroyan photograph.*

van craig

New York, August 1984. The Eclipse Gallery/Fine Arts Acquisitions presents "*The Sculpted Doll*," a dynamic exhibit of one-of-a-kind and collector dolls. A great day for artist originals and an especially great day for artist Van Craig whose work was featured on the announcement and in the show itself.

Just precisely what Van's work is not that easy to define in words because each has a highly charged individual aura. For the most part, they are crazy, satirical, intensely dramatic figures which satirize (like the toothy lady of "Customer Service") or fantasize the colorful atmosphere of the theater.

Van's direction with satire and caricature (not too long ago something people reacted to in extreme ways), has now turned out to be in the forefront of doll art. Now we have the Muppets and films like *Dark Crystal* and people are ready to accept the caricature face. People are reacting in very positive and enthusiastic ways. But those without fear and those with foresight recognized his ability right from the start. Artist Bob McKinley owns three or four of Van's pieces and crows with delight when he tells everyone he can about them.

Many of Craig's works, supposedly, might technically qualify as rod puppets. They have rods which protrude and allow manipulation. On the other hand, they are soft sculptured, too. As Craig says, "Terms make people think of set ideas...you have to see what I am doing to really understand it."

Most of Craig's figures have larger-than-life qualities. They are the result of his stage design experience. Things that are on stage have to carry across the footlights.

Many of the Craig figures <u>seem</u> to be portraits of recognizable people or celebrities. Well, they are to a certain extent. But Van prefers to call them "facsimiles." They are not meant to be faithful portraits as he would rather have the freedom to exercise creative options or interpretations that may occur along the way.

After looking at the whole cast, it is pretty easy to say that Craig's emphasis is on costume...and yet; although, he loves the use of the ornate, once in awhile he gives himself the challenge of <u>not</u> doing it. For instance, once he decided to give himself the challenge of doing a figure that had no beads, no bangles, no glitter or lace. He used different kinds of muslin, cheesecloths and went strictly for texture. The result is a stooped spidery female dressed in tattered robes...she is disturbingly real...As Van says, he is not sure what it is; sometimes it happens and sometimes it doesn't, but with that piece he knew even before the face was painted that it was going to have a life quality.

Another of Van's self challenges was the *Little Old Bo Peep*. On this one he went first for the idea of <u>really</u>, really old...at least 103. Then just to make a contrast, he also tried to incorporate as many kinds of laces as possible. The result is a hilarious juxtaposition of age and youth...a face that is a map of every wrinkle, sag and bag possible to acquire on top of a fully-fripperied costume imaginable.

Well, as hinted strongly, Van's background is in the theater. He drew and painted before he could write, he says, and then was a dancer for awhile before working with Disney and Henson Associates. He studied at California Institute of the Arts and on his own for a year in London. Returning to the New York scene, he became resident stage designer for Lam's Theater (more rod puppet experience) and since his costume designs have been seen in productions of *Funny Girl, The Apple Tree,* and *Puff the Magic Dragon* as well as in the famous Tiffany store window displays <u>and</u>, on Wayland Flower's puppet personality, "Madame." Van, himself, has performed in the Broadway cast of *Camelot* and on the road with Carole Channing in *Hello Dolly.* Currently, he spends part of his year back in his native California working as art director for Victory Films.

Although Van can find an inspiration from just about anything -- a face in the crowd, an old movie still or the challenge of a portrait commission -- he does generally tend to go about getting his ideas in a rather unusual way for even a doll artist.

Van haunts the secondhand and thrift shops looking for interesting materials. He says he can spot a piece of old beadwork or lace and know right away if it will work for him. Then, rather than deciding on a character, or even free-form sculpting a character first, he lets the material suggest what kind of a persona <u>it</u> needs.

Craig's figures are so intriguing that, of course, we had to ask what they were made of. Papier-mâché is the easy answer, but the actual material is Celluclay. "Wow," we said, as in our experience this is one of the world's messiest and hard-to-handle materials.

He works quickly. Most of the sculpture for a figure can be completed in a week, he says. Yet one should not make the mistake of thinking these figures are just whipped out. *Theda Bara* for Tiffany's window with the complete Cecile B. DeMille movie sets (throne, urns, fans and carved lions) took well over an eight-month period to complete.

Because of the Celluclay, the surface texture is perhaps not as fussily slick as a lot of collector doll pieces. But it doesn't have to be. It probably should not be. Van's point is made by the delineation of a character, caricature or just plainly, an idea about personality. That

is what needs to be conveyed. In the case of Van's work, the medium is definitely an integral part of the message. The surfaces are not especially colored. The background texture shows through... grayish looking which gives an even more theatrical, dramatic effect.

Most of the faces have very haunting, very arresting eyes. Everyone who sees the figures are especially taken with the expressions he achieves. Yet most of the eyes, themselves, are German glass...only a few figures have had painted eyes. The rest of the features? Oh yes, teeth. There are tiny, neat porcelain teeth which Van finds in a special garment district hideaway full of fashion mannequins from the twenties and thirties.

Van considers what he does an exercise in space, shape and capturing a moment. Asked what part he enjoys most, Van answers truthfully that he enjoys all the steps, but most of all when all the parts come together. He says, "I approach my pieces as any artist would approach any design project: Space usage, color, tension, movement, dramatic impact and, hopefully, to capture a moment in time."

There are a couple of words Van uses in talking about his work that the ordinary person would not usually associate with a doll artist. One of them is failure. He says quite frankly he fails all the time. That is, he continually takes risks, but that some of his greatest successes have come from his worst failures. Failure is an important part of the trial and error process that doll artists habitually use.

To put it another way: Many people think to make something one sits down, decides what he wants to do, figures out how it will go together and then follows a set pattern of steps from beginning to end. That is not how a doll artist works and it is not how Van Craig works.

The other word is success. Success for Van is when a doll comes from the heart and captures a little bit of life. If it is disturbingly real or has a life-like quality, then he can feel it is successful.

"My work continuously changes and grows. I want my audience to come back six months later and see that I have been able to take my work in a different direction...Change is the most important process of my work...and I think it is what keeps a collector interested."

Who is the audience? Anyone and everyone with a good sense of humor and a good feeling for character. Van feels, however, that out there for each figure there is one special person that it is meant for.

Fond as he is of his figures and much as he enjoys the making of them. Van is an artist who wants his figures to go out into the world. He makes them to sell them, not to keep in his back room.

Currently, and fortunately for the art world, Van's goal is getting more of his work out into the public. He is working with two galleries and already some of his figures have been used for poster and greeting card graphics.

Portraits? Not ordinarily, but unlike many artists, Van says enthusiastically, that he would not want to miss the opportunity to try. "I want to be open to any challenge and possibility."

"Why do I sculpt? Because I have to. My studio is right in the theater district and right in my own apartment. It's a wonderful thing to be able to hop out of bed at an early morning hour and jump right into doing work you love."

"Dramatis Personae," a group of artist Van Craig's original sculpture in papier-mâché ranging from 14 to 30in (35.6 to 76.2cm) in height. *Photograph by M. J. Magri, courtesy of Van Craig.*

Movie Star (three guesses who it is!) is a 28in (71.1cm) one-of-a-kind piece by Van Craig which now graces a private collection. Her costume is a steel blue satin opera coat with purple lining with a jet beaded skull cap trimmed with bird of paradise feathers. *Photograph by M. J. Magri, courtesy of Van Craig.*

No. 3 in Van Craig's Flapper series, this leggy creature wears a beaded and sequined cape of black against purple, opera hose and bronze-colored shoes. *Photograph by M. J. Magri, courtesy of Van Craig.*

The Debutante, a one-of-a-kind rod puppet costumed in white satin and net with silver and turquoise rhinestones. *Photograph by M. J. Magri, courtesy of Van Craig.*

Madame Dubet is unquestionably a "grande dame." She is a one-of-a-kind figure, 23in (58.4cm) tall with papier-mâché head and hands on soft muslin body. She wears a gown of antique jet beads and sequins with rhinestone and pearl jewelry. *Photograph by M. J. Magri, courtesy of Van Craig.*

RIGHT: *Mata Hari*, a 25in (63.5cm) papier-mâché character sculpture by Van Craig. The costume is composed of many varied beaded and rhinestone fabrics from the 1920s. It took four months to create this figure from start to finish. *Photograph by M. J. Magri, courtesy of Van Craig.*

BELOW: *Redhead* (left) with *Fay Templeton*, two of Van Craig's one-of-a-kind comic figures of papier-mâché. They have been costumed with antique jet and beaded work with antique feathers and pearls. *Photograph by M. J. Magri, courtesy of Van Craig.*

BELOW RIGHT: *The Laughing Flapper*, a 24in (61cm) papier-mâché sculpture, one of a series of fabulous females from the "Flapper Era" by Van Craig. The costume consists of a black opera cape with white feathers, a black skull cap with rhinestones and purple ostrich feather plumes. *Photograph by M. J. Magri, courtesy of Van Craig.*

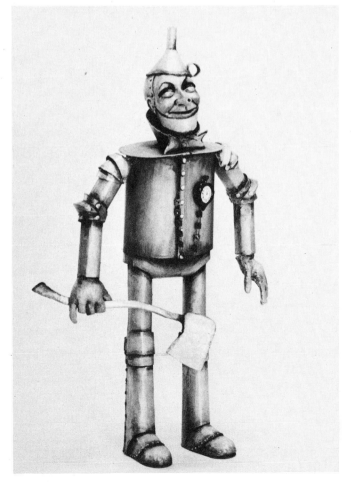

LEFT: Van Craig's papier-mâché impression of *Dorothy* and her little dog *Toto*. *Dorothy* is 28in (71.1cm) tall and dressed in blue and white check with the famous ruby red sequin slipper. *Photograph by M. J. Magri, courtesy of Van Craig.*

BELOW LEFT: *"The Tin Woodman of Oz*, a one-of-a-kind 28in (71.1cm) papier-mâché sculpture by Van Craig. *Photograph by M. J. Magri, courtesy of Van Craig.*

BELOW: *Natalia Makarova*, 28in (71.1cm) tall. This one-of-a-kind papier-mâché dancer by Van Craig is costumed in various shades of lavender and purple satin. *Photograph by M. J. Magri, courtesy of Van Craig.*

beginnings — the prototype

Ideas are dangerous and seductive things for artists. They cannot resist them. An idea once popped up must be pursued until the artist completes it to his satisfaction or sees where it must be improved to be satisfactory.

Ideas quite often arrive when one least needs, wants or expects them.

Typically, Carol-Lynn "got an idea" right in the midst of working on this book.

Typically, she immediately charged into the process of bringing the visualization into being.

The following pages, exerpted from her journal, detail the process of working out an idea and catch a bit of the everyday life of a doll artist at work. As you will see, the process of pursuing an idea is very non-glamorous. It has its occasional moments of joy when the visualized "something" works out. It is frustrating. It is messy. It is tiring and, many times, the end result is disappointing. One often has to start over again...and again, but with each experience, successful or not, more bits are tested, learned, rejected or accepted. The artist gains, the work improves, and, in the end, the doll world benefits...and in this case, one day, many children may gain two delightful new companions from the development of this particular design prototype.

designing a prototype doll

(or, Recommendations on How Never to Make a Doll)

When Susie and I contacted the artists in this book, we sent them an interminable super-elicitory questionnaire designed to evoke candid information on doll making procedures and preferences on all matter of arcane subjects.

As work proceeded, I realized that I had asked everybody, including Susie, about their penchants and predilections, but I never complied.

So, Christmas week, 1984, with the book sort of scheduled for completion on New Year's (we didn't make it), I set out to find out just how I make a doll. It had been so long since I had last made one, I wasn't sure.

My procedures and materials are probably atypical. I do not do editions of dolls for collectors anymore. Neither time nor temperament will afford me that luxury; once a doll works, I need to go on to something else. So my current dolls are prototypes for production, samples to be offered to commercial firms to be done in materials like vinyl or porcelain.

The models are done in latex composition, a liquid material that is usually sold in gallon jugs as "composition slip," for making bodies for reproductions of porcelain-headed antique dolls. I do not know why more doll makers don't use this stuff. It is wonderful. When the doll is done, it bounces. Children can play with it. Eric-Jon regularly absconds with my latex bears and gives them rides in his trucks and cars, sends them down slides and drops them on the floor, with no damage done.

As I have said before, I firmly believe dolls should be playthings, artist dolls included.

Latex composition does not have to be fired, can replicate a plaster mold in as fine a detail as porcelain, and, if the right mixture of it is obtained, is almost as easily cleaned and polished as ceramic greenware, without the health problems (and they are very serious -- I know from ten years' experience) of porcelain.

There are drawbacks to using compo slip (as it's called; it is also known as flexible slip). The quality of the product varies enormously. Some is s resistant to trimming as a rubber ball; there is no chance to fix your sculpture after a mold is made from it if you use rubbery slip. Some is brittle. It can harden in your mold, refuse to exit and ruin it. This happened with some of the latex I brought home from New York at Christmas time, 1984.

The reason I had to lug slip home is the biggest pain involved with compo slip -- it freezes. If it is shipped North (I get mine usually from Texas) in the winter, it separates into a rubber ball surrounded by smelly liquid and will not come out of the jug. At $24.00 a gallon,

plus shipping, I learned this lesson quickly and, as I live in central Maine, from late October until May I do not dare send for supplies.

I imagine that, if anyone else in the State used this substance, it might be stocked at the local ceramic shop, but, according to my personal census, about four people in the world probably use compo slip for original dolls, and one for original bears (that is me).

The final drawback about latex is the odor. Its fumes are powerful, especially if you harden your dolls in the oven. After the doll making episode herein described, I resigned myself to removing the latex from my oven. The vapors had baked onto everything, and I feared gastronomic reprises if anything potentially edible were placed therein. This was the maximum sacrifice; in six years of oven ownership, it was the first time I had ever cleaned it.

Tom Oroyan, elsewhere in this book, has drawn a sketch of Susie's workroom, which is probably typical of doll makers' studios. Although it is sort of like my entire house, I have no studio or workroom at all. I sculpt on the big red chair in the livingroom, watching old movies until six in the morning. I make my molds in the kitchen and the living room. A 100 pound bag of casting plaster sits on the front porch, wrapped in a heavy-duty garbage bag. I cast my molds in the kitchen, harden the castings in the oven, which precludes baked goods for the duration, paint and string the dolls on the dining room table, design the clothing on the same place and sew at the machine an arm's length away. It works, and I have taught the family to endure a fine film of plaster dust over everything at erratic intervals. Doll making, for me, is no longer a primary career so they do not complain too vigorously.

Most of my work is done upstairs in the bedroom where the word processor, easel and the desk on which I do all my photography are located. This room abounds with artist bears and dolls, with a heavy emphasis on ursine inhabitants. As I have often stated, I consider animal dolls, including teddies, to be full-blooded dolls. At least mine are. I make bear dolls, usually, sculpted Teddy Bears that are articulated and produced just like people dolls. They wear clothes.

Bears surround the word processor, fall off radiators and generally liven the atmosphere as I work. And, as I sculpt, I often will grab a bear or ten, drag them downstairs to the red chair and use them for insbearation.

In order to do this chapter fairly I decided to design a prototype human doll, something I have not done in quite some time. The doll would be large and combine many doll making techniques. It would be 18in (45.7cm) tall, have a latex swivel head and hands and a cloth body, which could stand and sit, but which would be very play worthy -- something Eric-Jon could drag around with him, something a commercial firm could make successfully as a toy. I firmly believe, as I have stated earlier, that dolls should be, first and foremost, toys.

As I now specialize in making smallish bear dolls, this project involved an enormous lot of retooling and took much longer than I imagined it would. I can make a Teddy Bear doll in a little over a week. This includes the sculpting, mold-making, casting, painting and clothing, if I work eighteen-hour days, which I inevitably do. The little teddy that the doll holds I made simultaneously with the doll, and it took maybe six days at most. After the doll was done, I designed a prototype Teddy Bear doll, 9in (22.9cm) tall, jointed at the limbs, which I call *My Friend Bear* (after the book of the same name). I did the sculpting, made multi-piece molds, cast two of them (a boy and a girl) in ceramic clay (no latex in February in Maine), fired, painted, strung them, and designed a twelve-piece bear wardrobe in eight days. Bears come easily, probably because I am tuned into them. People dolls are hard.

The child doll, *Eric-Jon*, took a month, almost exactly, to complete. It was a frustrating month of eighteen-hour days. Everything that could go wrong seemed to do so. Probably the fact that I only had a gallon of latex slip to work with, and no hope for any more, had a lot to do with it.

Artists and writers are frequently asked whence come their ideas. I have a writer friend who says his come in a plain wrapper from Schenectady, New York. Mine come from things that surround me, and usually occur in any of three situations: in the bath tub, walking home from the post office (in the block between the Congregational Church and the library) and in dreams. The idea for the *My Friend Bear* doll came in a dream. The realization that he was MFB came on the way home from the post office. The idea for the *Eric-Jon* doll came from Eric-Jon himself, and from the photograph of him and *Jimmy* bear, which stared out from the refrigerator door for a year and a half.

As I was designing and making the doll, to better understand exactly how and when I went about my art, I kept a record in my omnipresent journal. The following sequence of events is extracted from those notes.

Sometime in September 1984

Took a series of photographs of Eric-Jon: profile, full face, at angles and printed them in 5in by 7in (12.7cm by 17.8cm) and 8in by 10in (20.3cm by 25.4cm) formats, using whatever paper I had on hand. Will use these as guides for sculpting.

Early December 1984

Have decided to do the doll as both a girl and a boy. I noticed the remarkable similarity between the photos I took of Eric-Jon at six and those of Jenny-Lynn at the same age. The doll could then be done as twins.

Later on in December 1984

Noticed the photo of Eric-Jon and *Jimmy* on the refrigerator. Of course. This is how the doll should be dressed and he should have a bear with him. Everything I do needs a companion bear and this one can be old-fashioned; *Jimmy* is the oldest bear I own. He has a nice cinnamon hue. I will draw up initial sketches of the doll.

December 20, 1984

I started sculpting doll head in Sculpey. I have a pound of it; it is not enough, but will serve to start the doll. I made a base for the sculpture out of crumpled aluminum foil, with a fat dowel-like wooden block at neck level to serve as a handle. I decided the doll should be 18in (45.7cm) tall and began measuring the photo and the son, using calipers and measuring tape, recording measurements on a chart, making adjustments on the sculpture. An 18in (45.7cm)-tall doll needs a head that is just half-life-size, so it simplifies measurements considerably. I am badly out of practice. Bears are so much easier.

December 24, 1984

The sculpture is not done, and I pack it in a box, along with my tools and photos, and clay, and bring it down on the plane to New York for Christmas.

December 25, 1984 -- Christmas Night

I start work on the doll head in earnest, trying to replicate the photos in the dim light of my parents' living room. I wish Eric-Jon were with me so I could check on the measurements. Something is wrong that I cannot quite catch from the photos. Without him around, I just can't capture what I want. it is very, very frustrating. I am running out of clay.

December 26, 1984

I drive to Brooklyn to pick out human hair wigs and Teddy Bear plush to match, using photos of E-J's hair color as a guide. I think they are a bit dark, but it will work. Sculpting continues at night. There is something about the eyes that just looks wrong.

December 28, 1984

I make the trek into Manhattan and purchase eight pounds of Sculpey, a bunch of colored pencils and a pad of drawing paper. I work on the head all night, until 6 a.m.

December 29, 1984

Awake at noon, work on the sculpting all afternoon, and bring it across the street to Aunt Elvira's house for a fresh point of view. Something is still wrong with it, but sculpting while talking seems to help, and Aunt Elvira's always interested in dolls. We talk about Sasha dolls and about the deep-seated love that everybody female in the family has always had for dolls. Her house is full of them. It helps.

I return across the street, finish the sculpture and cook it in the oven. All night, until 6 a.m., I draw designs for doll clothing, and come up with eight outfits for twins.

December 30, 1984 -- Sunday

In the daylight I refine the sculpture, add to it, re-cook it in the oven and put it away in its box. The rest of the day I spend on a formal doll proposal. I miss the word processor.

December 31, 1984 -- New Year's Eve

I travel into Manhattan, find a color Xerox in Rockefeller Center and xerox my drawings, then purchase a quart of latex of unknown vintage, which requires a filler and is expensive ($20.00). A gallon of compo slip may not be enough. This stuff looks strange though. I return to Staten Island, catch the evening flight from Newark back to Maine.

January 1, 1985 -- New Year's Day

Worked on bear head and doll hands. They are too big. Jenny-Lynn thinks the bear should be plush. Maybe it could have a latex head and plush body. What an awful idea.

January 2, 1985

Worked on doll hands. Still too big. I will have to do two or more molds to shrink them.

January 3, 1985

The bear will be old-fashioned, definitely. Sent away for doll trunk for bear I will do later on, and socks for doll. Bought fabric for doll clothing. Did body and arms for bear, until 6 a.m.

January 4, 1985

The doll's hands are much too big -- way out of proportion. I am working much too slowly and am depressed. I am getting very little sleep. Finished sculpting bear 8 a.m.

January 5, 1985. I am 38 today.

The bear's legs are not quite in line with body but I don't want to redo them. I work so slowly. I need plaster for the molds and can only find a scroungey old bag of it in the coat closet. Went to the local doll shop and talked, something I should do more often; I feel so isolated working here. I treated myself to two *Ginny* dolls as a birthday present. Came home and made a clay bed for the two hand molds and the bear body mold. Activated the latex (stirred activator into half of the latex). It has to rest half a day before I can use it. Stirred some red latex paint into latex because the color, which is fleshy, is awfully dead, methinks. Slept from 5 to 9 a.m.

January 6, 1985

Sherlock Holmes' birthday. I worked on molds. Ran out of plaster. Finished three-piece molds for hands and head but the head mold does not release around ears. I should have made it with the separation entirely in front of the ears. So I had to mess up the mold to get the head out. Even so, the nose came off of the original sculpture of the doll's head and I had to glue it on with Elmer's. Poured the doll head in latex and cooked it overnight but tried to remove the casting too soon and it collapsed. The color of the head is too dark. I'll have to lighten it up in the next batch of latex slip; adding white paint should do the trick. Drat. To bed 6 a.m.

January 7, 1985. Dad's birthday.

Up at 7 a.m. Nothing works. Back to bed. Up at 2 p.m. Cast two heads and discovered the head needs more cranium. I couldn't tell that from the white Sculpey. This means I have to resculpt the whole thing and do the head mold all over again. Added cranium. This doll looks better with gray matter on top. To bed at 5 a.m.

January 8, 1985

Up at 7 a.m. To bed at 8. Up again at 3 p.m. Susie called in the evening. Did a rotten mold of the hands, second generation. This just won't work. The hands, even if I make a million molds, are just icky. I will have to re-sculpt them. Made half a bear mold, fixed the head and made a three-piece head mold. To bed at 10 a.m. It is 4 degrees outside this morning.

January 9, 1985

Up at 1 p.m. Poured three heads. The mold is the best I have ever done, on the inside. There are almost no seam lines. I coated the sculpture lightly with vaseline. The hands are no good though. I definitely have to redo them. To bed at 5 a.m.

January 10, 1985

Up at 7 a.m. Spent the day at the dentist. Sculpted one new hand. It is much better. Painted two heads. To bed at 5 a.m.

January 11, 1985

Finished second hand. Made hand molds. Felt ill and slept until 3 p.m. Tired.

January 12, 1985

Finished bear molds; poured five sets of hands. Hands look good. I am glad to get the plaster done. It makes me depressed. I hate to make molds and work too slowly. Activated second batch of compo slip. Added too much white paint to latex to make the color a bit lighter. The dolls look albino-yellow. The castings of the heads look absolutely sick.

January 13, 1985

Stirred and poured latex from New York into bear molds. It is too brittle. The casts came out rotten. The head cast is full of pits. I worked on body pattern, using knitted fabric. The body is blimpy, the proportion is off and incredibly fat. Continued to pour latex heads.

January 14, 1985

Poured the last head; hardly any latex is left. The heads have too many pits and the faces, for some reason, come out yellow. I use bleach to lighten color, dabbing it on with cloth. It surely is odoriferous, but sort of works. The dolls look pockmarked and jaundiced. I don't need this. But the bears -- bears are so much nicer. Who cares what color a bear is? The first cast from the mold using the compo slip is neato.

January 15, 1985

I should be done by now with the doll but I am not. Ran out of latex, but finished pouring three bears in all. I should be writing and I am going too slowly; I want this doll done. Jenny-Lynn says the bear's arms are too long. Eric-Jon says they are just right. I look at the doll and think, "this is the best I've done in a long time. I've done stuff I haven't done before, but it's not good enough." Can I ever get the body right?

January 16, 1985

Latex from New York spoiled bear molds. Salvaged them by gently picking off every darn hunk of hardened crust from the interiors. They must be redone though. Drat. Latex is gone. Did abortive doll body in the evenings.

January 17, 1985

Redid body pattern and sewed a good body, 18in (45.7cm) tall. The head swivels. Wire armatures in arms. Pretty good proportions; I think I have it now. The first prototype of the doll is done at 4 a.m.

January 18, 1985

Designed and cut out clothes for *Eric-Jon* doll.

January 19, 1985

Made all clothes for *Eric-Jon*, including sneakers. Repainted face. The doll is done. Asked, "Am I finished yet?" Eric-Jon picked him up, carried him into the living room and watched television with him. The nice thing about the doll is that he cannot break it. It looks rather nice as it is carried away under a little arm.

January 21, 1985

Got up 4:45 a.m. Finished, painted, sealed and strung bear for doll by 9 a.m. Ribbon at neck. I like him. He stands alone, has a nice pleased expression, a humped back and over long arms. He is golden with brown nose, mouth and claws, darker paws. Painted second bear cinnamon, strung it. E-J immediately played "bear car" with the two bears. Success!

Eric-Jon Rössel Waugh and *Jimmy* in their railroad outfits. October 1983. *Jimmy* dates from the 1930s, is cinnamon-colored and is of Japanese extraction. He was found in a barn in Maine, but no longer smells of goats and is one of my favorite bears. He has a large wardrobe, consisting chiefly of knitted Cabbage Patch doll clothes. This photograph was the inspiration for the *Eric-Jon* doll and his clothing.

Drawings done in December 1984, for *Eric-Jon* and *Jenny-Lynn* dolls with bears. At this time the bears were to be dressed like the dolls. A set of twins was planned.

Photographs taken September 1984, of Eric-Jon Rössel Waugh for sculpting. Full-face, profile, three-quarter view and full-length shots were done and printed in the bathroom. It is necessary to have good clear photos to work from, especially if the model is not at hand. The 5in by 7in (12.7cm by 17.8cm) head shots turned out to be exactly the size the head needed to be, and could be measured for accuracy.

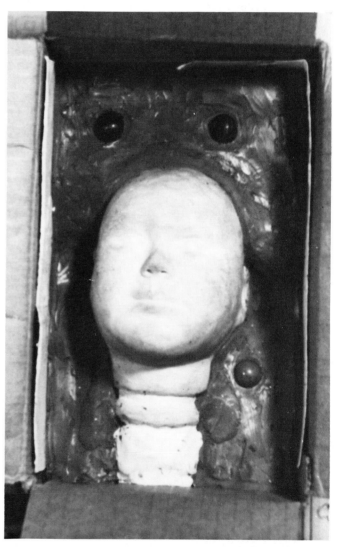

The photos and the sculpture after it was corrected. The lighter area at top was added when more cranium was needed. Never an exact likeness, the doll is an approximation of the subject. But he doesn't care; he likes it anyway. He is the only boy in his first grade class with a doll of himself. The head is sculpted in Sculpey, a synthetic clay that can be hardened in a kitchen oven, then re-sculpted and added to if necessary. It provides a hard model from which a mold can be made without distortion. The clay can be polished smoothly, and/or sanded, so a mold of good fidelity can be obtained from it the first time around, if one is lucky.

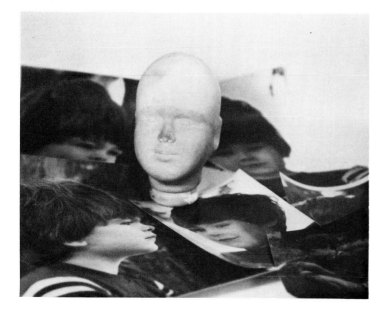

The original head in "molding box." In this case the molding box was an ordinary cardboard carton. I often use a "molding box" constructed of a board bottom with strips of molding around it which can accommodate various sizes of wood and can be pieced together to form a disassemblable box. But I had mislaid it at the time I did the doll and resorted to cardboard boxes and milk cartons which, remarkably, make nice molding boxes because they are waxed and are designed to hold liquid which is hardly the case with cardboard cartons.

A bed of clay is built up under the doll's head and marble "keys" are inserted into it, forming little circular depressions, which will eventually fit into little bumps on the other side of the mold and enable the pieces to correctly fit together. A collar of Sculpey is built up at the neck for a pouring spout.

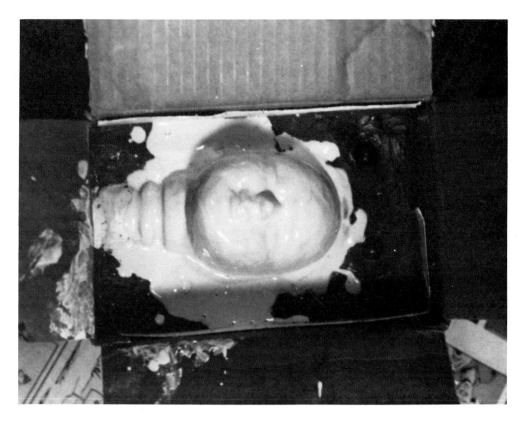

Before the mold is poured in plaster, the face is VERY LIGHTLY covered with a skin of Vaseline. This serves as a separator so the plaster does not stick to the sculpture. CASTING PLASTER (I buy it by the 100 pound bagful) is mixed up in the kitchen sink. I pour water into a large plastic margarine tub, about half full, then drizzle handfuls of plaster into it until the water has absorbed it; a smallish mountain of plaster builds up in the bowl. Then I stir it with my hands and wait until it becomes about the thickness of cream. At this point I smooth on, with my fingertips, a thin coating of plaster, making sure that no flaws, bubbles or lumps of plaster adhere to the sculpture. It this is not done, there is a good chance there will be flaws in the mold at just the place you do not want them to be.

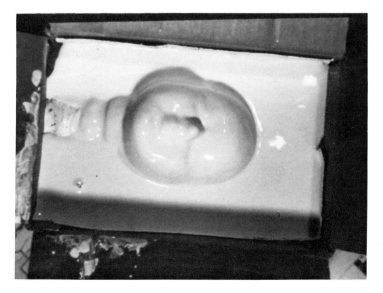

I then wait a bit until the plaster gets a bit thicker, not quite the consistency of Cool Whip, and finish pouring the plaster over the sculpture, filling the box entirely with plaster. When the plaster is a bit thicker, it is less likely to leak through the seams of the box. Once you have worked with plaster, you will be amazed at its ability to slither through cracks you never knew existed and mess everything up. So, it is good to wait.

The first part of the mold is done. When this photograph was taken the plaster was still wet. It is necessary to wait for the plaster to "set up," and this varies with the thickness of the plaster. If you mess with the mold too early, it can fracture at the most inconvenient places. I usually wait maybe a half hour to make sure.

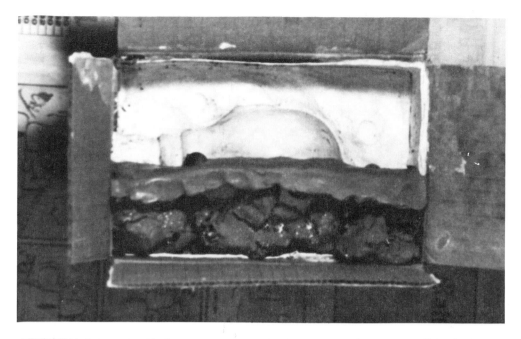

When the first half of the mold is done, I open up the back of the box and remove the clay bed, then remove the head and check the inside of the mold. If it has no flaws in it, I then clean off the head which has plastelina sticking to it. (Plastelina is a non-hardening sculptor's clay, usually grayish-green, which many doll makers use for their sculpting. I used to, too. But as I said, it does not harden so you have to be gentle with your sculpture, and that is a pair.) I use the darker plastelina for a clay bed because it is a good contrast to the Sculpey. It is oily and plaster does not stick to it. Also, it is cheaper than Sculpey.

The whole perimeter of the mold, excluding the face area and the head, receive a coat of Vaseline. Then I replace the head in the mold-front, build a dike of clay at the halfway mark on the head, stick greased marbles in it for "keys," and have prepared the second part of the three-part mold.

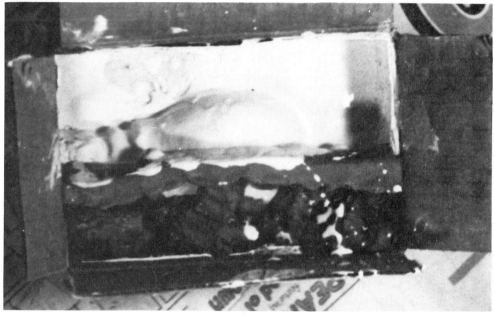

Plaster is mixed up and, again, a thin skim of plaster is smoothed onto the sculpture. The little depressions made by the marbles (which have been removed) will fill up with the plaster to form little bumps so the mold can be put together properly. The plastelina is only smooth where it needs to be -- on the inner face of the mold. There is no point in making work when you do not need it.

The shiny surface of the plaster in the photograph indicates that it has been just poured. This section has to harden; then the third part of the mold is made. The head is molded in three parts to be certain that it will come out of the mold. Sculptures often have what are called "undercuts," which are areas that hang out over others, like ears, cheeks, funny shaped noses, and so forth. Hands often have lots of undercuts. If a mold is made of these sculptures in, say, two pieces, the undercuts will become trapped in the plaster and snag the mold shut. No way will it be removable; the sculpture will remain embedded like a bug in amber eternally. So, just to make the odds easier, I make at least three-piece molds of almost everything, even when I do not have to; it is not that much work and it sure saves on the blood pressure.

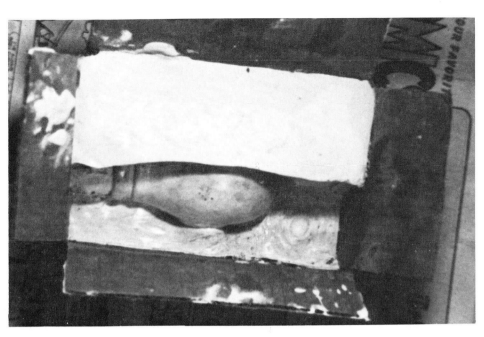

Here the clay has been cleared out, the head has been removed, cleaned and covered again with Vaseline, as have all the exposed sides of the mold, including the top of it and the walls and the area underneath the second section. Sometimes plaster will trickle underneath the sections of molds and lock them together if they are not coated.

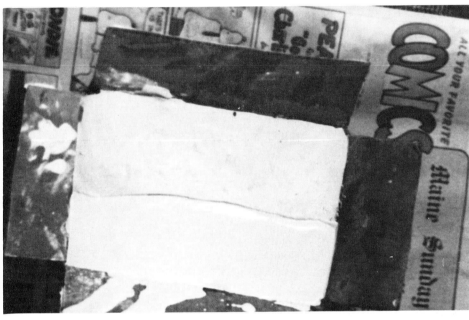

It is easy to see which side of the mold has just been poured; it is shiny and smooth. My molds never look too great on the outside; they tend to be lumpy but this can be cured by a chisel, one of my favorite tools -- that and a rubber mallet. It does not really matter what the mold looks like on the outside; the inside is important. As long as you can stand the mold up on end and pour into it, you are set.

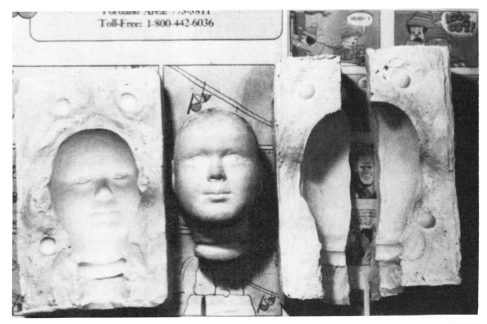

The moment of truth comes when the mold is hardened and you take it out of the box. The big question I always have to confront is, ''Will the darn thing open?'' Often plaster has a way of sneaking into cracks and sealing the fool mold shut. At these times a hot panic creeps up my spine and I feel like screaming. However, I use my trusty duo, the chisel and the mallet and, most times they open the mold. First I stick the chisel into the seam line. It has a wedge like blade about 1in (2.5cm) wide. Then I carefully work my way down the seam line, trying to force the mold open. Sometimes this works. When it doesn't, I get out the rubber mallet. I no longer use a hammer after completely destroying a mold with one one day. I place the mold on newspaper (Did I mention that all these steps should be done on newspaper? Consider it mentioned.) and wham it along the seam lines with my rubber mallet, in the hope that the mold will open. This and a few prayers to the mold god usually works. The mold will sometimes open at the halfway point and then you will have to redo the mallet act on the remaining portion. It depends on the way the mold wants to open, if it wants to open at all. This one did and you can see how the pieces fit together, with the little notches formed by the marbles. The pouring collar is at top and has been removed from the sculpture. The inside of the mold is remarkably good; the parts fit snugly together with very little seam area. The face area has virtually no pitting. It is too bad I had to redo the whole thing because the sculpture had to be redone. I open the mold and stick it in the oven overnight at 100 degrees F.

221

The mold looks grungey, but its inside is pure. It is banded together with rubber bands, courtesy of the Winthrop, Maine, post office. Every day's mail is festooned with heavy-duty rubber bands, just right for mold-holding. The gallon jug beside the mold holds composition slip which is poured into the mold. When it comes into contact with the surface of the plaster, the water in it begins to evaporate and the latex in the "slip" starts building up a thin scum around the interior of the mold. As it does, the level of "slip" decreases in the mold collar and has to be replenished. If there were no mold collar, the neck edge of the mold would be weak because it would receive an irregular flow of latex, and the head might not be usable.

After the scum has built up about the thickness of a nickel, it is time to decant it into the jug. The head has to be hollow or it will weigh too much, and the slip is far too expensive to leave extras hanging around in a doll's brains. It can be used again -- the portion that drips back into the jug -- but this stuff has a short half-life once it has been "activated." About a day before using it a chemical is stirred into the slip to make it set-up, I suppose. I never asked. After it is added, the slip has to be used in a very limited time frame. So sometimes it is good to pour half of the slip and half of the chemical into a jar, and just use that amount. I did that with the dolls just to be sure. I am not sure it helped. The casting has to harden. I stick it into the oven overnight, right in the mold, at 100 degrees F. You are not supposed to do that but it works. Then I take it out next morning.

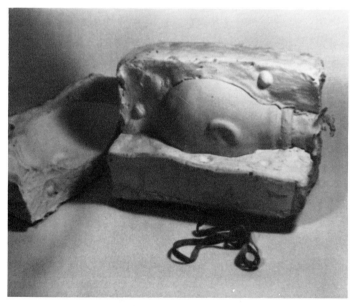

When the mold comes out of the oven, I open it, back first, and hope the casting does not collapse. Here you can see how the mold separates around the casting, the little round 'keys,' and how they fit together, and the collar on the neck. I wait until the mold has cooled. (Remember, unlike everyone else in the world, I stick my dolls in the oven, which makes for strange looks from visitors at suppertime. Most people don't have roast doll for dinner.)

I am very cautious, having had too many castings collapse. I always leave the head attached to the mold as long as possible. Here I have removed the front of the mold and half of the back, but the last section of the back is still attached. You can see why it is good to have a collar on the mold. The area where the slip is poured in is not particularly aesthetically pleasing.

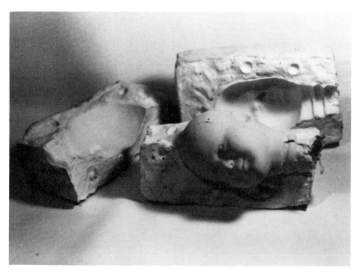

RIGHT: This is another view of the head still in the mold. You can see the remains of the cardboard box on the outside of the mold, and how the plaster has conformed to the shape of the doll head. It is held in place because it fits the sides of the plaster. When it is heated in the oven, the latex shrinks slightly, but just enough to make it easier to get the head out. It is not necessarily EASY, mind you. Often the casting will collapse.

MIDDLE RIGHT: This illustrates the cast head, removed from mold, and resting on it, with collar still attached to it. I let it sit for a while before doing anything with it.

BELOW RIGHT: After a while I trim the neck and throw away the pour spout. I then put the head, or whatever part I have cast, onto a cookie tin covered with aluminum foil, set the oven at about 100 degrees F., and cook it overnight. This seems to be a good, useful-for-everything temperature. Sometimes the oven will have an assortment of things cooking; mold parts, cast-latex and removed latex, all happily simmering together. It is about this time that the family wants the house fumigated. Working with latex, for this reason, ought to be done when ventilation is possible. I worked in January, with the outside temperature averaging 4 degrees F. Not many kitchen windows opened during the process, and everyone avoided the kitchen, except to sneak into the fridge and make a rapid exit.

BELOW: Latex shrinks, as can be seen in this shot of the original sculpture and the casting. Seam lines at the top center of the casting and at ear level can be seen.

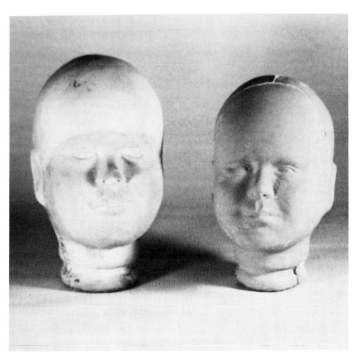

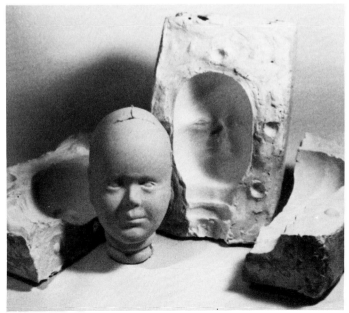

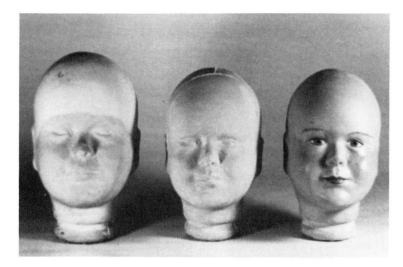

The original sculpture in Sculpey is at left, the untrimmed, "fired" casting at center, and the painted head at right.

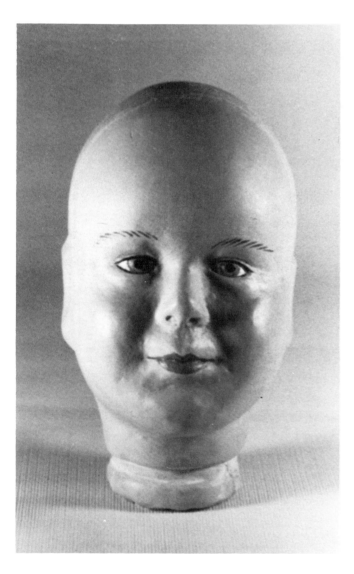

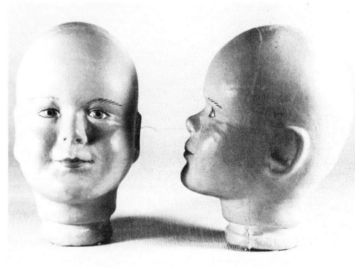

Front and profile views of the head after painting. I did two: a boy and a girl, painted slightly differently. I did not like the colors I obtained and wished I had had the time to repaint them in a more delicate manner.

The two heads with "girl" and "boy" wigs in auburn French human hair, and hats. The dolls are coming to life. The ridges at the bottom of the neck will enable the heads to swivel when placed into the cloth body and attached, at neck level, with wires.

The surface of the latex is not as smooth as porcelain. It could be, I suppose, but I did not have a lot of latex to play with to obtain perfect castings. It sort of has the look of composition, which is probably why it is called latex composition, so I am not pretending it is porcelain. I paint it with latex paints straight from the local crafts store and seal them with acrylic spray. The inside of the head I seal with lacquer, also sprayed on, so the head is protected. This is the first painting I did of the head. After the doll was done, I repainted it.

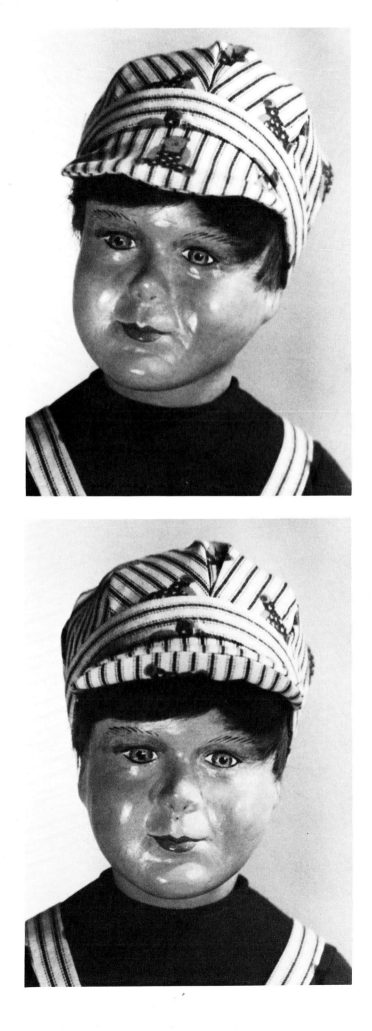

The head, after repainting. The colors are softer. I discovered that I could use watercolors on latex and affix them to it with acrylic spray.

ABOVE: Two-thirds view of *Eric-Jon* and *Jimmy*. The arms have wires in them so he can bend. I am still working on that. The railroad pants have bears wearing overalls on them; I may change that, too. They are blue, with cinnamon-colored bears wearing blue pants. The shirt is cranberry knit. All the clothes close with velcro.

LEFT: A full-face view of the doll. It is not an exact likeness but it will do. The railroad cap is a pretty good approximation of Eric-Jon's. Because the head can turn, it can assume a lot of human-like poses.

225

Profile view of *Eric-Jon* and *Jimmy*. The doll has a nice bottom and can sit; it has sewn-in knees on a cloth body. Everything but the head and hands is broadcloth and it is stuffed with polyester fiberfill. The doll is lightweight and virtually unbreakable. I suppose a vigorous child could pull off the head or hands or wig.

Full-length shot of *Eric-Jon* and *Jimmy*. *Eric-Jon* is 18in (45.7cm) high, wears railroad overalls, knit shirt, railroad cap, white socks and sneakers. Finished January 21, 1985. The two dolls took just about a month to make.

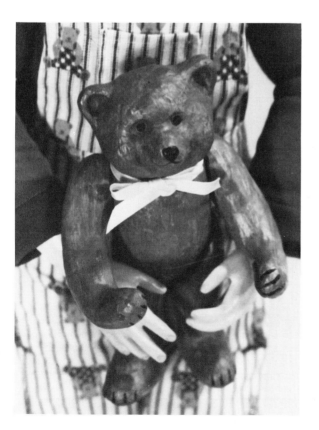

All photographs in this chapter by Carol-Lynn Rössel Waugh.

Close-up of *Jimmy*. He is 5in (12.7cm) tall, jointed at the legs and arms, and can stand and sit on his own. He has a humped back, over-long arms and pointed snout like antique bears. He has not quite become civilized yet and still looks a bit like he might bite. The ribbon helps. He is a rich cinnamon color with darker cinnamon pads.

a collector's guide

"...mimesis, that is to say, a speaking picture; with this end, to teach and delight"
An Apology For Poetry, Sir Philip Sidney, 1595.
In conclusion....
Artists at work, collectors considering purchases, judges deciding awards...all activities in the doll art world are essentially directed toward the discovery of good work. Arguments, discussions, questions and attempts to define will, by the very nature of the humans participating, differ and forever change as they reflect contemporary taste, design interpretation and emotional reaction. At the end we have only ourselves and one or the other of Sidney's two purposes with which to make our decision.

Look back then at the work we have shown you. If it stimulated new thought, illustrated a phenomenon or taught you to consider a different aspect about the world and the things that people are and can be, then it educated. If a piece filled you with wonder at the demonstrated ability to conceive and execute ideas, a wonder at the skill involved in the technical processes, or an appreciation of the harmonious use of design, then it delighted.

...and the very best would have done both in such a way as to make you catch your breath in awe or to make you feel a warm, rosy glow of enjoyment.

The Thrill of the Chase - Finding the Dolls

"Where Are They?" One-of-a-kind vignette in polyform by Virginia B. Taylor. *Photograph by W. Donald Smith.*

How do you buy doll artist work? Not as easily as other dolls, certainly! Many doll artists just do not make enough dolls to make it worthwhile to advertise or to go to many shows so, often, it is just plain hard to find out where to find original doll art.

As a rule, you will find original work through advertisements in the doll collector publications, at doll shows, and through the printed lists available from the doll artist organizations. You could get a good start by investigating the magazines and artists listed at the back of this book.

The best way, of course, is to go to a doll show or an exhibit and actually see the dolls and meet the artists personally. But, because of the distance and expense involved for the artists, dolls you might see at shows are just the tip of the iceberg, so to speak.

Doll show dates are listed in most of the major doll collector publications. The notice might not say that there will be original dolls offered for sale, but almost every doll show or sale has a few tables of original work. Shows are usually listed in the classified sections of the local newspapers. Keep an eye on the listings for "collectible and antique" if there is no special classification for dolls and toys.

Doll art is most regularly seen at conferences of the doll artist organizations or the regional and national conferences of the United Federation of Doll Clubs. Artist organization conferences are usually announced within the collector publications; however, the conferences of the United Federation of Doll Clubs are only announced in its own publication, *Doll News®*. These conferences are ordinarily open to the public for specified hours with payment of a special admission fee and, depending on the conference set-up, open to registration from the general public.

If you do go to a United Federation of Doll Clubs Conference, you should be aware of the way in which original dolls are shown there. On the one hand, there are doll artists who may have regular sales tables in the commercial room -- and they must, themselves, be members of UFDC in order to qualify as a dealer. There you may buy dolls just as would anything else offered in the room. if you wish to take a doll home with you, be prepared to pay in full on the spot because all dealers, not just the artists, are asked not to take deposits in the sales room. If orders are taken, layaway money should not be taken. The artist will usually put the buyer on an option list which means that the buyer will be contacted by the artist when the doll is made and ready to be sold. This procedure is to protect both the buyer and the seller.

Also at UFDC functions, if time and space allows, artist groups may have "open house" hours. These are part of the program and a

sort of "show 'n tell." In most instances, during open house exhibits, artists do not sell dolls or take cash layaways for two very good reasons: They are given the space for display as opposed to having to pay rent for space in the commercial room and because no arrangements will have been made for local taxes and licensing. On occasion, artists groups may be able to make special arrangements which allow them sales during an open house exhibit. If you are not sure, ask. The nice thing is that at a show or conference the collector has the opportunity to meet the artists, to see and examine the quality of work firsthand, and, if desired, to make future orders and layaway arrangements.

The alternative to attending doll shows and sales is, of course, shopping by mail. If you do not mind taking a little time to write short notes, a whole world of dolls can be available.

There are a few things to be aware of when working from ads, however. In many cases the photographs in an advertisement may be of a doll no longer available because in the lag time between printing deadlines and publication, the edition may have sold out. Do not be disappointed; be ready to see what else interesting and new the artist has on hand.

A growing number of artists are making arrangements with shops and galleries to handle special editions or, in some cases, all of their work exclusively. They do this in order to free themselves of business tasks and the price of dolls sold in this way are set by agreement between the artist and the shop. If the doll you are interested in is advertised by a retailer, do your correspondence with him and not the artist. Chances are the artist will have already completed and delivered the dolls in question to the shop. Neither will a discounted price be available by dealing directly with the artist.

Take a chance on the classified ads. Just because there is no photograph, it does not mean the work might not be good. Something very tasty may be lurking about! Think of it as a mystery! Sometimes the budget conscious artist or one doing a very small amount will advertise by means of the small classified notices. A couple of stamps and some small change might find a real prize.

You may note that an advertisement includes the letters SASE. This means "Self-Addressed, Stamped Envelope." The advertiser is asking for you to send an SASE when you write your inquiry. Generally speaking, an SASE gets a faster answer because the artist does not have to wait for a post office trip and it also means that the artist is sure of having an address as well as a correct address!...you would be surprised at the number of notes that come in without a return address on either envelope or inside note. When you enclose an SASE, do make it a long, business sized envelope. It takes an origami expert to fold an ordinary brochure into a small notecard envelope!

The advertisement may ask for a small amount of money to cover the cost of a brochure in addition to or instead of the request for and SASE. For those artists who do large enough editions, it is feasible to have a printed brochure. This involves taking a great many black and white photographs, plus costs for screening, laying up and printing. Again, these costs get figured back into the total cost of the doll unless the artist can otherwise balance the expense. Other artists who do only small amounts or one-of-a-kind dolls will send photographs of the individual dolls available. This again requires a considerable investment in film, processing and copying prints. These artists often request that the photographs be returned and enclose an SASE of their own for this purpose. Do return them and do not be embarrassed if you decide not to buy. It will not hurt the artist's feelings one little bit. They do not want you to feel forced to buy, but they will very much appreciate the return of the photographs.

After you have written, you may get a reply by return mail or you may have to wait a few weeks. This will depend on what the artist has on hand. Many times the artist might be in the process of finishing a group, working furiously to get things ready to photograph, or, perhaps, just be waiting for his photos to be developed.

Is That All?

Fini, one-of-a-kind polyform sculpture by Virginia B. Taylor. *Photograph by W. Donald Smith.*

As of 1985, in the United States and Great Britain there are probably about 300 artists producing work worth the collector's attention. Of the artists covered in this book, the average production per year per artist is about 12 finished pieces. When you stop to think about it, that is a very limited amount of doll art "merchandise" available on the market in any given year...roughly, 3600 pieces --very rare and, understandably, very hard to come by. And, of course, many doll artists do not produce as much as the average. So if you have bought one or two pieces in a year, you have done fairly well.

Why so few? Quite bluntly because it takes time to do good work. As we noted, the artist works to satisfy himself, to improve himself and to satisfy his own curiosity. All have set very high standards for themselves. Additionally, there are the more mundane problems with materials and techniques. Some types of ceramic work is best done in dry weather, some types of paint will not dry when it is excessively humid. Supplies and materials are hard to find and often a vital component or material will be back ordered for months (even though artists are notorious stockpilers of supplies for "just in case"). It might take visits to six or eight shops -- a whole day or more out -- to find just the exact type of fabric or trim required by the design. Then, very basic to the artistic nature is the element of "mood." Most artists will agree that there are days when no matter how hard you want to, no matter how hard you try, everything goes wrong. It is also difficult to fill an order for a baby doll when you are in the mood to do a character and it is difficult to costume well when you are in the mood to sculpt. Almost every artist will say that work attempted when the mood is not right will not be successful. Most artists, however, are very keyed into their work habits and will not force the issue, but rather work with what is going smoothly at the moment so as not to lose valuable time. These are not excuses for nonproduction; they are just the facts of life for doll artists. Doll artists are organized and are very conscientious, and do operate on schedules, but the pattern may not resemble anything like the straight-forward "make it" and "sell it" of the larger commercial world.

Should You Buy It?

When you have received your photographs, brochure, price list or seen the dolls at a show, the next question is to buy or not to buy...and, if to buy, which to get. Several factors have to be considered...type, prices, investment possibility, and, above all, whether you like the work.

It is very difficult for one person to tell another specifically what is good or not good about a particular doll because, as we noted, the element of taste always enters in. We can tell you some of the things that we would look for and that an art critic or appraiser would look for.

First of all is the general impression. Does the doll "say" something to you? Does it tell a story? Does it illustrate a character? Does it project some sort of action? Does it appeal to an emotion or an experience of your own? If it is merely a figure standing there in clothes, it has not proved anything more than someone put together materials and a form. Is there some sort of special individual touch -- something that makes that particular artist's work unique amongst his colleagues? For instance, it might be a trick of painting or a style of sculpture...a "signature" of some sort which would be identifiably present.

Next, does the whole thing tie together? Is it well designed as a whole? For all originals, overall design is of great importance. Foremost is the quality of the sculpture...the line, proportion, balance, harmony and modeling. The hands should be of the same material as the face and so should the feet/legs if the figure is built on "dollie" principles. The doll should be well-proportioned and should show good use of materials and scale. A beautifully sculpted and finished head should have an equally well-executed body and costume. Costumes should always fit neatly and look as if the doll was actually wearing clothes made for it. The figure should show some evidence of color scheme. That is, chosen colors should not clash with each other and should enhance the overall appearance rather than distract from it. Also important is the treatment of small details. The wrong type of lace or trimming poorly applied can ruin an otherwise finely done doll.

Some people are exacting about the movement capabilities of a doll. Doll artist work is about 50-50 jointed or armatured; there is really no saying that one or the other method is better. It depends on the statement or direction the artist is taking. Both are equally valid in the history of the doll figure from the beginning of time.

The value of the object is essentially carried in the ability that the artist has shown in imagination and in combining all the small elements in a way so that one good impression is conveyed. A doll that is obviously meant to be a light and delicate fairy fails if it has clunky feet, no matter how well they may have been finished technically. Nor would it be a success if it was dressed in heavier weight fabrics, even if perfectly stitched.

Another factor in making a selection is all too often fragility. Let's face it...all dolls can break. Not a one that we can think of could not be damaged in some way. Ceramic will break, fabric will fade, wax will melt. On the other hand, as we have mentioned, modern waxes are amongst the hardest and most durable materials known. We have fabric dolls and wax dolls well over 100 years old and in good condition. Any serious collector makes a good effort to protect his pieces from extremes of heat and cold and from damage due to moisture as well as accident and injury. In the long run, about the only materials the investing collector would want to be wary of are dried fruit materials and rubber types which, through no fault of owner or maker, can deteriorate under certain conditions.

Last but not least is the question of rarity. Important for your choice here might be the number made. Editions of ten will always be more valuable than editions of fifty.

Also, in considering the artist's original, one must look carefully at the actual technical level of achievement. This means that to some extent one has to become familiar with the media used in order to see if it has been used as well as possible. For instance, a cleverly dressed original in porcelian should show good ceramic craftsmanship. There should be no mold lines showing, no pitting, no mildew, and it should show good, rich application of color. An original in fabric should show neatness in sewing and be well stuffed. Although we all strive for the best combination of technique and design, not all artists can achieve it in every doll. Each artist is an individual and the work will show it. A top-notch sculptor may not be the best seamstress and a very good painter may paint very ordinary faces. The best artists, however, will show a consistent high level of achievement on all areas of design and technical method.

For some collectors investment quality is a factor to consider. At this point doll art is appreciating; although, perhaps not as fast as the antique dolls. Still, even though it may be a bit of a cliché, those who made the antique dolls of today were artists and those who make originals today are making the antique dolls of tomorrow...and it looks like tomorrow may soon be upon us. Notice that when Victorian dolls became extremely desirable with escalating prices, the collector turned to modern dolls. These, in turn, have appreciated enormously and have become, themselves, rare because of the demand. It seems likely that the collector will turn to the artist doll in greater numbers, again, increasing demand and price in this field.

"Tomorrow's antique," one-of-a-kind vignette in polyform by Virginia B. Taylor. *Photograph by W. Donald Smith.*

230

REAL MONEY - How Much is It?

Price, price! That question so crucial and close to the hearts of both collector and maker!

We have been gently tiptoeing around the question of price for some pages now. We have outlined some of the ways in which price is arrived at by the artist and some of the ways the collector can know if a piece is worth or will be worth the price. Truth is, actual dollar amounts per figure per artist are best left to the collators of serial price guides and auction reports. The best we can say is they vary! They vary upwards and downwards, like any other art object, according to demand, artist reputation, artist emotions, time involved, what can be asked and what will be given.

However, in order to help the collector understand the current market, we did take a look at the price ranges offered by the artists we covered in this book...and they represent a very good cross section of type and range. These were prices asked in 1984 for the most expensive item and the least expensive item on the artist's lists.

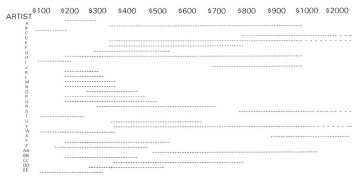

Average prices for original dolls, 1984.

As a rule, the highest prices are generally asked for those figures that are one-of-a-kind, very small editions (five or so), very special in costuming or structural treatment (jointing), and totally made by the artist's own hand. The lower ranges occasionally, but not always, include prices for figures that the artist has "done for fun" or that he has been able to produce inexpensively. If you take a look at the graph, you will notice that the high price range extends off the margin and you should be aware that there are very limited special editions by artists whose work is in great demand in the art market and or artists who are no longer producing which range close to $6000 dollars per figure as of 1984.

There are dolls that are available for less than the amounts listed here, but, again we would like to point out "caveat emptor" or buyer beware. You get what you pay for. Once in a while you will also find a doll that is over priced. Not for long, usually, as the dealer or artist soon learns that no one will pay an over-inflated price. If you are serious about establishing a good collection, then be as serious about planning your purchases. Too many people have a number of dolls on their shelves (or in boxes!) that they wish they had not bought...and that would not realize the purchase price if resold.

Should I Pay the Price?

If you have considered the "art" value of the doll as well as its true and basic appeal to you personally, there still remains the question of cost to you. Looking at the doll and knowing what is in your pocketbook, the price tag may seem out of sight, but is it? Let us look at the numbers involved.

The individual artist making one-of-a-kind or edition pieces spends at the very least one full month to make a doll. That is one month of ten hour days and six day weeks if all goes smoothly and the artist is a fairly rapid worker. We know at least a half a dozen artists making editions who spend close to 400 hours bringing a figure from first conception through research, modeling, mold making, pouring and firing. This is nearly three months of work with several more months necessary to finish pouring, firing, painting and costuming the rest of the edition.

Even if we figure a one month average, that is about 160 hours of time at a minimum. Multiply 160 hours times the minimum wage being paid currently and you arrive at a base figure for worth -- the least amount not counting any aesthetic consideration. It should be worth a great deal more than that as a finished piece of art. Looking back at the graphs of prices asked, you will note that those averages are still below a minimum wage for time involved. Allowing for aesthetics and design, business expenses and materials, you can see that most dolls are essentially sold at a loss. All things considered, artist dolls are a bargain for the collector.

Coming to Terms

Figured into the price of the doll is the collector's budget. You may feel that the doll is worth the asking price, but you may not have the money to make a purchase outright in cash. Many artists will take deposits or layaway. Do feel free to ask about terms. Some will require a layaway to have a certain percentage down to "hold," with payment in full to be made within a specified time. Some will take monthly payments. Some will even take a charge card! Artists doing editions will sometimes not take a deposit, but will notify you when the doll you want is ready for purchase. This allows several months in which to prepare to make payment in full. In this case, you should be ready to respond quickly when notified. If you have changed your mind, notify the artist without delay so that he can go on to contact the next person on his list. Most artists will understand if you have to cancel your option, but they do also need to have the doll back on the market as soon as possible. If you are making time payments, be prompt just as you would with your other obligations. Most artists are very, very understanding and flexible. Some we know have probably been too kind and have received poor treatment from collectors in return for their kindness. If you are unable to make the agreed date, correspond immediately with the artist to make new arrangements. An agreement to buy a doll is just as binding as any other kind and, as it is a highly personalized relationship, honesty and courtesy on both sides are extremely important.

In turn, the artist should notify the collector in case he or she is unable to meet the time of delivery specified. If a doll artist belonging to an artist organization should fail to give your correct treatment, you could contact the organization's president for help in working things out.

Lastly, you should remember that many doll artists have orders to fill for a year or more ahead. Most will tell you a specific waiting period -- if so and, if they do, be patient. Do remember that the artist is primarily a creative person (as well as a family person) and will be working on new ideas as well as filling orders.

In the past there have been some understandable complaints from collectors who had waited as many as three or four years for a doll they had on option only to be notified that the price had tripled in the meantime. It was a very difficult situation for both artist and collector. The artist, naturally, was glad to take an option as it meant he would have work to do and income to look forward to; however, but if prices on his other work had gone up according to demand and quality, he did not want to let equivalent work go below its current value. It is very difficult to take $100 for a doll ordered on paper three years back when one has a table full of dolls that took just as long to make and maybe are even better work selling at $400 a piece. On the other hand, the collector is miffed because he waited with good faith and intention (and without happy companionship of the doll of his dreams!) only to find out it was out of his grasp again! The happy end to this story (You noticed we started by saying "in the past.") is that both artists and collectors have learned how to handle ordering better. Most artists we know will not take an order or an option for a doll that cannot be delivered within a year or, if they do (because sometimes a collector can be insistent), they will tell the collector that the price is not guaranteed. More and more artists are making large efforts only to show editions that they have in process or completed. This means that they are making smaller editions and thereby having more time to go on to new ideas. It also means that if a collector sees something he likes, he ought to order, layaway or purchase on the spot. In the long run, a serious collector who is definitely interested in the work of a particular artist would be well advised to make sure to keep in contact with the artist, to get on the artist's mailing list so he can be advised of a new piece's availability as soon as it is ready.

Special Orders

Some artists enjoy the challenge of special requests or portrait work and their advertising will state this. Other artists do not like to work under restrictions and, unless the artist specifically indicates great enthusiasm for your idea, it would be better to find another. If you do want a special type or portrait, it is important to choose an artist who works in a style you like and whose ideas are similar to the way you would like to see your ideas portrayed. These are the ones to contact for special needs. In all cases, do always bear in mind that a special order is a unique item. If you are unsatisfied or refuse the order, the artist will have a large investment of materials and time lost. A special order may cost a bit more because of this, and because the artist is undertaking the extra stress of working to suit someone else, he or she may request a non-refundable deposit.

Overseas Purchase

Many collectors hesitate to follow up on a nice doll they have seen just because they fear the complications of overseas correspondence and exchange. It does take a little more effort, but, in the long run, it is well worth it in order to add something special to your collection. It often turns out that the most difficult part is just finding out the foreign artist's mailing address!

After you have ascertained where to write, initiate your correspondence to find out what the artist has on hand and price just as you would with someone in the next town. If you have decided to make the purchase, call your bank and check the rate of exchange. They will be able to tell you as of the day. It is polite to send payment in the currency of the country where you make the purchase, i.e. if you are buying a doll from an English artist, pay in British pounds. If you send the artist a personal check written in dollars, he will have to pay an enormous charge to have it changed and, futhermore, banks in other countries are just as cautious about taking "non-local" personal checks as yours are.

In your correspondence (which should always be done airmail -- it is not that much more) ask if the purchase price includes a foreign exchange allowance (most probably, it does not) and how he will ship (air or sea mail).

The customs question: This will depend on each country where dolls are being sent as the receiver has to pay. The artist/ shipper will have to declare an amount on the package and, if the receiver wishes it to be insured for the whole value, he will have to declare the purchase price. Buyer and seller should come to an agreement before items are sent as to the matters of insurance and valuation.

The next step is going to the bank to purchase a draft in the currency desired. This is essentially a cashier's check made to the seller's name, but because it is a check that you have purchased from a bank, the foreign bank will not be as concerned as they would about a personal check. You also have the option of purchasing a draft on a bank in the country where the seller lives which will make it even easier to clear the funds. For instance, an American buyer can buy a draft on Nat West, Lloyd's or any of a number of British banking firms or a British buyer can purchase a draft on Bank of America, First National or any other nationwide banking firm. You might wish to ask the seller which bank he prefers. Whichever you chose, do not send cash!

Be prepared to pay a tidy sum in the purchase of a draft. Banks in all countries are organized for a profit. It is an expense for them to handle foreign exchange and they will charge extra for making this service available.

After that, make a photocopy of your correspondence and the check for your records -- things do get lost in the mail. Then, send to the seller. If the doll ordered does not show up in a reasonable amount of time -- six weeks for sea mail, seven to ten days airmail -- write airmail to inquire if there has been a delay or to find out when you should expect the package.

Most artists will notify you by separate note when your doll is being mailed so that you can expect it. Many will ask you to let them know when you receive it and in what condition it was when it arrived...a postcard may be included in the box for this. If a shipment does not arrive within a reasonable time or does not arrive in satisfactory condition, please let the artist know because it is the artist who will have to initiate a postal or freight trace or insurance claim.

Some dolls might require special set-up instructions. These will either be packed in the box or mailed separately along with an invoice statement and any other pertinent materials such as certification or receipt. Please heed care and handling instructions with respect. Most artists have had pretty good experience with shippers, but should a doll arrive damaged, report it to the artist by phone, if possible. Also report any problems within a maximum of ten days. If all is well, drop the artist a note saying so...once the doll is shipped, the artist is in a state of suspense wondering if it will be all right and if you will like it.

Record Keeping

Let's make a portfolio!

Sounds a bit like a holiday craft project, doesn't it? But seriously, in the art world the history of a piece -- where it came from and where it has been is called "provenance" and it is extremely important for the collector to maintain the provenance for each of the dolls in his collection. Works of art are always a bit more valuable and a bit more appealing to the potential buyer if they have a good provenance.

Certainly, if you have a tidy amount of expenditure in building your collection, you owe it to yourself, to the dolls and to your family to keep records for each one. How many times have you seen a tag on a doll that says "handmade, maker unknown?" Poor things! With artist and origin unknown, they are the unvalued orphans of the doll world.

The purpose of the portfolio is to keep a nice record for yourself of what you have, how you got it and all the little details about the doll that should be remembered. Did it win a ribbon? When? Was it a member of an edition? How many brothers or sisters did it have in the edition? Wasn't there a little dog that went with it? How long have I had it? All these questions might come up and it is difficult to keep all these fine points in one's head.

The purpose of the portfolio is also to keep a record for insurance valuation. Practically no insurance company we know of will reimburse you for loss at true value if you have no verification records...most preferably a sales receipt or an appraisal and an actual photograph.

Another purpose for making the portfolio is to provide for the dolls in case you are removed from the scene. If something happens to you, do not think the family will "just know" they are valuable pieces or who you intended to have them. Your portfolio should give anyone who needs to know current value and all the information necessary to get the best value in case of sale. Your portfolio is also a will and testament for the dolls, themselves. It will provide for them, their treatment and disposition. If you have promised someone that they can have one or that they could buy it, then write it down because unsettled wishes can be devastating amongst the survivors. If you want your dolls to be sold as a collection by a certain dealer or if you want them to go intact to a specific museum, state that in your portfolio and be sure to include an address for making contact.

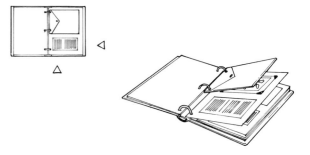

In making up a portfolio, there are any number of possible formats. We suggest the easiest might be to copy the sheet in this book on heavy cardstock or index weight paper as many times as you need and gather the sheets in a loose-leaf binder. Also provide a 5 by 7in (12.7 by 17.8cm) manila clasp envelope punched to fit in the binder for every doll's sheet...this will be handy for holding all the miscellaneous items that might make up the provenance.

RECORD SHEET

NAME OF DOLL _____ COLLECTION NUMBER _____

ARTIST / DESIGNER _____

ARTIST ADDRESS _____

NUMBER IF EDITION _____ ONE OF A KIND _____ DESIGNED _____

PURCHASE PRICE _____

MARKINGS ON BODY _____

MARKINGS ON CLOTHING _____

HANG TAGS _____

DETACHABLE ACCESSORIES _____

DESCRIPTION _____

_____

_____

color photo

PLACES EXHIBITED / AWARDS WON _____

_____

_____

INVESTMENT INFORMATION _____

_____

_____

_____

Filling Out the Record Sheet

1. *Name of Doll* Fill in the name that is on the hang tag or that the artist has called the piece. Be sure to note if the doll is actually two or more figures in a group or vignette setting.

2. *Collection Number* This refers to the collector's numbering of the dolls he or she has. Usually, collector's will number items in order of purchase.

3. *Artist/Designer* Write out the full name of the maker of the piece. Be sure to note organizational affiliation, if any. Also note if the artist uses a business name, e.g. "Susan Johnson, DGA, Peerless Poppet People," or the like.

4. *Artist Address* Write artist's current address or name of agent. Try to keep addresses current, if possible.

5. *Edition* If the piece is a member of an edition, note the number of the doll and total number of edition. This is usually written: 6/23 meaning that the piece is number six of an edition that was closed when 23 pieces were made. If a doll is a one-of-a-kind, just check the box.

6. *Purchase Price* This is simply the amount you paid for the piece and date of purchase, but it is very important to have on the record.

7. *Markings on Body* Note all markings as they appear on the body. If you do not see any, ask the artist if there are any. Sometimes the costume will cover signatures or markings made on the back of the shoulders and neck. A typical body marking might be: The artist's initials or name and/or logo, plus copyright mark, year made/designed, and sometimes the name of the piece as *Bobby* or the like.

8. *Markings on Clothing* Often an artist will insert a cloth label or ribbon pocket tag between the body and the costume. Note if one is on the piece and what it says as these can often be lost.

9. *Hang Tags* Hang tags are probably the first thing that can get lost. Do be sure to describe the tags, if any. You may want to remove the tag and keep it in the manila envelope for safe keeping.

10. *Detachable Accessories* Accessories such as purses, hats, Teddy Bears or anything loose enough to fall off in transit should be noted. Accessories can also include furniture and/or specifically built settings. You want to be sure that all items that make up the complete work of art are included in your inventory. Lost items will detract from value.

11. *Description* Here you will want to write out a brief description including such facts as height, items of particular interest, if portrait, if a special order for you, general description of costumes, character -- whatever extra things that are important for the "story" of the doll.

12. *Places Exhibited/Awards Won* If you have loaned your doll to a special exhibit at the Smithsonian or a local museum, note that here. If you have entered the doll in a competitive exhibit and it took a ribbon, make a note of where, when, and what...all these things make the doll a bit more interesting, a bit more valuable, and certainly should be kept for the next owner in case of resale.

13. *Investment Record* List or make notes of any changes in price you happen to see in advertisements or auction reports, or at sales. If, for instance, another member of the edition sells at auction, or if after a few years, the piece becomes in demand, note the prices that are being paid for similar works in the edition. Most collectors keep their eyes open at sales and in reading ads and price guides and, from time to time, should keep track of changing prices in their records. Also note if the doll artist becomes inactive or deceased.

14. *Color Photograph* Take a nice, clear photo of the doll, full length, front view for the record. It does not have to be an "art shot" -- just enough for a good identification, if need be, by an appraiser or insurance evaluator.

15. *The Envelope, Please!* Any miscellaneous award ribbons, photographs, certificates, receipts, correspondence and the like are easily kept together in the manila clasp envelope, hole punched to fit your notebook portfolio.

16. *Safekeeping* Keep portfolio or copy in your freezer. It is the best home safe!

Insurance

If you have a collection of any size, you should carry insurance for mishaps at home or out on exhibit. Insurance for collections can be obtained through the agent who carries your home insurance; however, you will be expected to provide a list of items and valuations for him because usually his company will have to underwrite a special rider to your policy. Insurance may also be obtained through companies which underwrite policies for collections. Insurance of any kind will require you to undertake special considerations in packing, care, travel and record keeping in order for a claim to be paid. Always read your policy carefully and ask questions if you are not clear.

The Owner and the Copyright

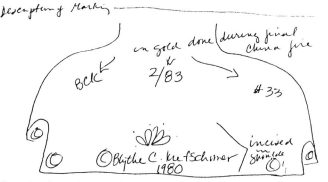

Example of artist's copyright marking. *Sketch courtesy of Blythe Collins-Kretschmer.*

Whether visibly marked or not, all original doll art should be considered copyrighted by the artist. The only possible exceptions might be in the cases where the artist has made a prototype for commercial production or has made a piece while under the employ of another and has sold or assigned the copyright.

For the collector this means that buying the doll in no way means that the copyright comes with it. The doll may leave but the copyright stays with the artist. There are three areas where this can particularly affect the owner:

1. The work cannot be reproduced by anyone other than the artist or by persons the artist has given permission in writing. Often collectors buy older dolls and make molds from them and produce copies or reproductions of them. Sometimes these reproductions are for the collector's personal fun and sometimes they are sold as completed dolls. NO artist original should ever be reproduced either for home or commercial purpose without the written consent of the artist copyright holder. In case of artists deceased or no longer producing, permission must be obtained from the heirs or authorized agents of the artist. Do not assume that copyright has expired. Under the new copyright laws, the period of rights is considerably longer and, in many cases, the copyright may have been renewed.

2. Under the new copyright law, artists have a great deal of control over the use of copyrighted items even after they have been sold. For example, let us say a doll is sold to a collector and then the collector, in turn, sells it to a person who owns a chain of toy stores or fast food restaurants. If the new owner decides to use the doll as part of his promotional advertising and the artist does not feel that the doll is being shown correctly or is being used in poor association with product, the artist may require that any picture, drawings or verbal mention of the work be deleted from the advertising...and depending on the situation, may take legal action.

3. The same rights pertain in reference to photographs taken by the owner/collector. Any photos of the doll, except those taken for home use only, may not be used for print without the artist's permission. For instance, you may wish to take photographs of the dolls for your own records, but if you wish to show the work in a book you or someone else is writing, you must get the artist's permission or signature on a model release. Most artists freely give this permission; although, there will be cases when permission is granted for one-time use only or cases when a royalty may be requested.

4. Do not borrow the artist's idea. Imagination and invention are what makes the artist a unique individual. If you take his idea, you take part of him personally. No artist likes to see a costume idea, or a face or a special effect he has come up with on someone else's doll...in fact you can just about be guaranteed that he will be mad

enough to spit nails if he sees it! Certainly, there are types of doll themes that can only be interpreted within narrow boundaries --Little Red Riding Hood is a little girl in a red cape with a hood, as we all know, but the artist's touch is in that ability to see the accepted and the ordinary and be able to give it a new interpretation. Variety is the spice of this business; don't copy. Think up your own, new artistic and imaginative treatment.

Display

Just the minute collectors acquire more dolls than will fit on the top of the television set, the piano and the coffee tables, they are brought face to face with the problem of display!

Usually we do the obvious. We get shelves -- anything from do-it-yourself components to made-to-order cabinetry. Sometimes we go looking for and make large investments in antique cabinets. But still problems arise. Some dolls do not fit the shelves; some dolls are too small and get lost in the crowd; some cases have door trims and shelving that actually obscure the view -- frustrating, yes indeed!

Instead of coming at the problem from a "group solution" standpoint, let us look at the doll itself. Each doll is made by the artist to be seen and appreciated and enjoyed as a single unit. When the artist makes the figure, he rarely considers any other possible way of looking at it...at that time it is the only piece on his worktable. Furthermore, a work of art is a unique individual and it should be given its own "space." But how to do this in the ordinary household situation?

Consider what a museum or gallery does in mounting a doll display...or any other kind of art display. Much time is spent "designing" to achieve the best possible setting and viewing for each piece. Those displays that are most effective have a limited number of figures, carefully chosen for type and size per case or setting. In a gallery paintings are hung so that there is plenty of space between them and so that one does not distract from the view of another. Lighting is crucial and carefully placed. Those museums that least impress us are the "messy" ones where dolls are "cold decked" in solid ranks and rows. We go away from these places with the impression of a blurred haze of "things" and we wonder if we really have seen any one piece at all. As a collector or artist, you might wish to consider some of the following possibilities for display which will give you the fullest enjoyment of your dolls and allow your visitors to appreciate your treasures as much as you do.

Before making the investment in furniture or building materials, take inventory of the collection with regards to size and shape. Arrange your dolls on a table or some place where they can all be stood up at one time. Sort for size and make rows for each height. This will give you an idea of how many shelves you will want and how much space should go between them. Then arrange each row with 3 to 6in (7.6 to 15.2cm) between each doll or setting -- no skirts overlapping, no hands in another's face -- each one in its own "space." This arrangement will give you an idea of how much space you will need in running feet. You will find that, on average, each doll takes up at least one square foot, maybe more.

Oops! Now, you say, "Ooh, I'm not going to have space enough to put all the dolls out if I used the whole house! Don't worry. Remember, you are going to proceed on "museum" principals, right? At this point, you need to give some thought to establishing a core group for a permanent display and, perhaps, some "revolving" displays.

Pick out dolls by groups for specialized display. Depending on the types you have, it may be possible to create special Christmas groupings, groupings of babies or groupings of fashion, and the like. You might wish to make a display of the month featuring ladies for February and Valentine's Day, fairies and elves for March and April, and, maybe, brides for June. Arrange your permanent display, arrange one "revolving" display and carefully pack up the rest for a while. Every month or so change the display. That way you can show off the individuals to their best advantage; your visitors can really see what you have and why you collect, and all the dolls will get their turn to be special. Additionally, each time you change the display, you will have a chance to renew your excitement about the dolls you have -- a rediscovery of the fun of it all!

Not long ago a doll artist came to my house, looked around and said, "My, how well you have integrated your dolls with your living." She meant this in a complimentary manner but I immediately realized that things were, in truth, just a bit "overly integrated." There were dolls on the mantle, dolls on the hearth, dolls on the piano, dolls on the sofa, a whole case fairly stuffed with them and some more had spilled over into the dining room. Some of the more durable types can be worked into the "decor" but, of course, you do run the risk of having the cat choosing one for his favorite pillow (they always do!), company spilling coffee on them or any number of damaging possibilities. I decided to do the "gallery" thing and chose one for a feature -- the "piano doll of the month" so to speak. In a true museum or gallery setting, dolls and sculptures are often shown on an individual pedestal so that they can be seen from all angles. In the home situation, a special feature doll case could be acquired or a pedestal case built. With a little feature lighting, special pieces can be quite dramatically highlighted.

Some fortunate collectors have the ability or facility to make their own "museum" in a spare room or by adding a room to the house. Before clearing out the back bedroom and lining it with shelving, think a minute about what could be done to make a striking display for about the same amount of investment.

First, no distractions and pleasant atmosphere are wanted. Paint the walls (do not paper) in a soft neutral color; add a carpet in a coordinating solid color, if you can. Then, carefully design a case system that will show off the dolls in a way so that they are easily seen. Glass or plexiglass -- and as much as possible -- will be best.

Another consideration is placement so that a viewer does not have to bend or squat down or crane his neck up to see the pieces... remember not all the dolls have to be out at once. The idea is to appreciate the art work and not to impress with sheer numbers.

The illustration shows the "optimum" display. With some easy variations to fit your space and budget, something similar might be possible for your collection. When you are all done, add good lighting -- either by installing track lights or small lights within the cases and provide a nice chair or two. Sit down and relax with your lovelies!

Terrors! Every once in awhile there comes a need to pack up a doll and put it into the hands of the postal gorillas. Artists and collectors shake and tremble with vision of what they DO to packages of dolls in transit! We are sure that OUR package will be the very one selected for the employees lunch time soccer game. We live in dread of the possibility that OUR package will be first under a van load of encyclopedias and barbells. We listen to baggage trucking into airline cargo bays and know that the big trunk mashed right into our suitcase full of dolls.

All in all, in ten years of traveling and shipping, we have had little damage and find that most of what has happened could have been prevented by better packing and planning on our part.

One of the biggest problems in shipping any doll is the eventuality of damage coming to the doll from the doll itself. Sound crazy? Not really. Arms and legs can strike against each other, stands can mash and over tight packing materials can crush.

First, take the doll off the stand or base. Wrap base separately and make sure it is well padded. Now, cut foam rubber squares or rectangles at least 1in (2.5cm) thick and place them top and bottom of each hand and leg...make a sandwich around each one of these delicate parts and tape together. If foam rubber is not handy, use bubble wrap or cut strips of disposable baby diapers. If the figure has a hat or any lose accessories, take them off and wrap them separately. You will want to box a hat to keep it from getting squashed. If you think that foam rubber in contact with the dolls' hair might damage the styling, cover the head first with a soft silk fabric, then wrap with foam rubber or bubble wrap. (By the way, foam rubber scraps can be purchased at upholster's shops; bubble wrap can be ordered through stationery suppliers.) Then, wrap the whole figure with bubble wrap or disposable diapers. If a skirt should not be crushed, put a layer of wadded tissue between the body and the skirt. When wrapping or padding parts, at NO TIME exert pressure...pressure at this point is the most likely cause of damage, particularly with more fragile pieces.

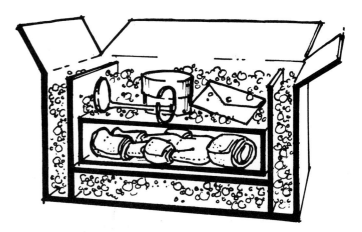

In traveling with dolls, taking them to exhibits and conferences yourself, the first thing to do is use hard sided luggage. Never, never pack dolls in soft sided suitcases...that is asking for it! If you are not taking many or they are small enough, pack them carefully in boxes or cases that can be taken along with you in the passenger section.

When your figure is all carefully wrapped, place it in a box that is about 2in (5.1cm) larger than the doll all around. Or, if a box the right size is hard to come by, build your own from cardboard. Only the doll, no accessories or stand, goes in this box.

Pressure and the avoidance of is the key thing throughout

packing. If you are packing for travel in suitcases, check placement and close lid carefully to make sure that pressure of the lid will not crush the packed items. Never force the lid down, not even gently.

If you are packing for mailing, you will want to double box. Cardboard boxes are tough. Most are marked "made to withstand 150 pounds of pressure," but you can add a bit more safety for your own peace of mind by adding support materials between the inside and outside boxes. These can be pieces of styrofoam "cookie" or "peanut" shapes or even wadded newspapers. The idea is that the material between the boxes will take the pressure and keep it from being directly exerted on the inner box and its doll. Before closing the box, place all extra packed materials such as stands, accessories, paperwork and the recipient's address inside on top where it can be easily seen on opening. If there are specific directions for unpacking and set-up, be sure to enclose them, too.

Always insure doll for full amount of value. If you do not, the shipper will only pay off in cents per pound in case of loss -- can you imagine a reimbursement of $5.00 for a doll worth $500. Do it!

Photography
Susie:

Taking pictures -- and getting good results -- is probably one of the biggest adjunct bugaboos in the doll making and collecting world.

Have you always thought you could not take pictures well? Does three fourths of your doll coming out looking as if it was shot in the fog or in a closet? Well, here is good news...It probably was not your fault!

Commercial film processing is done through a machine -- you can see this kind of a machine in operation at the "one-hour" film developing shops. These machines are set according to the type of film being processed. If the film is a color print type, ASA 100, the process will be marked on the box and on the film as "C-41." The machine is set for C-41 and the whole roll goes through the same speed. No matter how carefully you set up the lighting, tried to get special effects, or played with exposures to do something out of the ordinary, the film will be processed "all as ordinary." You will be lucky if two out of twenty shots are decent. Once in a while you will run across a processor who will reprocess your negatives at a lighter or darker speed and, in which case, you might pick up a couple more usable shots, but usually they will not reprocess more than once for free.

One solution, if you are pretty sure you have not done anything wrong is to find a specialty developer or amateur who has a darkroom who can handle each negative separately. Or you can learn to do the developing yourself. Both courses are expensive and time consuming, but probably worth it if you have a need to get professional-looking photos of dolls.

Another thing to know is that professional photographers do not get good results because they are experts. They hedge their bets by taking several shots of the subject with different camera settings each time. This is called <u>bracketing</u> and the idea is that one of, say, three will be the <u>right</u> one.

Bracketing hedges your bets.

In all cases, we would recommend using a 35mm camera for doll photography. Buy, beg, borrow or whatever to get one. Perfection would be a bellows camera with a portrait lens, but the investment would be more than one would ordinarily want to make. Pocket camera or "point and shoot" cameras are not adjustable for exposure and shutter speed, or depth of field focus at distances of less than 4ft (122cm). They are set up to take a uniform picture in the most common circumstances involving people and landscape... not dolls. Additionally, a pocket camera flash set-up will almost always wash out any subject taken at a distance of less than seven feet.

In the process of our "transcontinental authorship," I wrote the paragraphs immediately above as part of a rough compilation of things about photography I had learned by hard experience. I sent a copy off to Carol-Lynn with a plea for "rewrite" or "add-to as necessary." Carol-Lynn "caught the ball" and started out by making notes in the margin, then on the back of the sheet, and, finally...well, just read on. It is invaluable advice for any artist or collector.

The following checkpoints for photography will also be of help.
1. Use a plain background for all doll shots. A plain non-textured, non-patterned, UNWRINKLED piece of fabric (single-knitted LIGHT blue polyester works well) or paper that goes behind and continues under the subject is the best. Consider using a window shade. A nice, off-white window shade comes complete with its own dowel onto which it can be rerolled and stored for future use, or you can mount it on an actual window and put your photographic setup on a table under it, so the shade comes down over the table.

Gift wrap paper (on rolls) is nice, too, but make sure to get non-glossy paper; you do not want to have unsightly reflections in your photos. If your work is small enough or if you have access to large-sized sheets of poster board, this makes a fine background. You should be aware, though, that poster board absorbs the light, and that the color of the board will not necessarily be the same in real life and in your photographs.

Victoria Marie by Marcia Sibol, · 1984. Original artist bear, fully-jointed. Dressed in beautiful hand-beaded white dress and undergarments. Holds a flower as a prop. This photograph was taken against a white background. The bear is lost. *Waugh photograph.*

I mention color in background because it is very important in showing off your work. The background must contrast with your subject. If you shoot a bride against a white background, vital costuming details are bound to be lost. I once took a chance and shot a wonderfully garbed Victorian Teddy Bear in a flowing ecru tea gown and parasol. First, I shot her against a blue background. No good. She blended in. Then white, just to see. Horrible, All I saw was her head and paws. (She wore an enormous bonnet with flowers and veils.) Then I dragged out 2yd (183cm) of pitch black double knit, tacked it onto the bedroom wall (I do all my photography in the bedroom, the developing in the bathroom), and shot *Victoria*. Absolute Eureka. It turned out to be one of the most outstanding shots I had taken in quite some time.

Victoria Marie by Marcia Sibol, © 1984. The same bear, but what a difference! The angle I posed her at has something to do with it. The prop, her parasol, adds emphasis and drama, but the black background gives the shot "pow." *Waugh photograph.*

A word about "settings." Unless you are writing a book about dolls or Teddy Bears, taking publicity photos to convince a manufacturer to buy your product, or doing slide programs where you intend to knock the socks off your audience (the alternative to including sleep), do not photograph your dolls in settings.

In the first place, they are hard and time-consuming to do. I speak from experience, having shot over 2000 photographs of dolls and Teddy Bears in the last year. A convincing setting takes a lot of ingenuity, insight, design, props and luck. To make dolls or bears "come alive" takes patience and a real ability to see all four corners of the lens of the camera simultaneously, in order to envision the product-to-come. Focusing is difficult when there are lots of little picky things to worry about, and a macro lens is almost a necessity.

I could go on, but, if you have to do a setting, do not put a bunch of dolls or bears in it. (I keep talking about bears because I photograph them more often than dolls, and they are MUCH, MUCH HARDER TO DO. There is the matter of fur that comes in black and brown, which photographs horridly against light backgrounds, and the matter of eyes that cannot be seen, and of noses that stick out too far when you focus on the eyes. In this case, focus on the nose. Bears, anyway, to me, are dolls.)

A simple set-up with two antique dolls, one antique bear, all in undies and some old *Delineators*. The bear, *Hannah*, belongs to Marcia Sibol. The dolls are two of my old dolls. They are placed against gray seamless background paper. I was careful to set them all on the same focal plane so all would be "in focus." Note how the subject fills the frame. Here a horizontal treatment is best. *Waugh photograph.*

Crowd scenes of toys are distracting. In or out of "scenes," keep things simple. When I was finding people for the book, I talked to one of the artists at New York's Toy Fair and asked about photographs. She had lovely 8in by 10in (20.3cm by 25.4cm) shots of six of her dolls, standing side-by-side, professionally done. I told her they were nice but could not be used in the book. You could not clearly see the individual dolls; they looked like dolls standing waiting for the subway. She replied she wished I had never said that; each time she looked at the photo from then on, she would think of waiting for subways. You want your dolls to stand out as individuals.

Maybe I should emphasize this with a few other stories. I did a book several years ago called *Petite Portraits*. It deals with artist-made dolls that are miniatures 9in [22.9cm] and under). Taking photographs of dolls that are 1in (2.5cm) high is a challenge, one that many people just cannot meet. One artist who wanted very badly to be in the book sent me photographs, the regular 3½in by 5in (8.9cm by 12.7cm) size, of her miniature dolls. The shots had been taken with an instamatic camera, were slightly out of focus and looked like they were done during a strong March wind. The image size of the doll was about 3/4in (2cm) high. She said, in her accompanying letter: "I hope you can use these photos in your book. If you can't see the dolls too well, please use a magnifying glass."

Then, there were those who sent shots of interior décor-cum-dolls. I once attended a doll convention at which a rather prominent doll lady gave a speech with slides (the only way to give a presentation at a large doll convention) of her dolls. Most of them were taken with the dolls on top of her television set in the living room. We wanted to see the zenith of dolls; we saw Zenith instead.

If you are taking photos of dolls, fill YOUR WHOLE VIEWFINDER WITH DOLL. I cannot emphasize this enough. For some reason, people are afraid to fill up the viewfinder. They will maybe put the doll in the middle all right, but they will leave acres of breathing space around dolly so when you see the photograph, you have all this extra nothing surrounding the doll, when you could have lots of doll -- or bear. If you are using an adjustable camera, there is no excuse, except for bad habit, not to get right in there and face your subject nose-to-nose. Unlike people, who get queasy, sometimes, when you photograph them from 6in (15.2cm) away, your dolls will not peep if you get intimate.

My Friend Bear, © 1985, by Carol-Lynn Rössel Waugh. These two bears were shot against an oil painting backdrop with a sheet of poster board under them. To fill up the frame, the shot was done horizontally. Small bears by Alice Jones and Elaine Gamble. *Waugh photograph.*

Back to backgrounds and scenes. If you have no seamless anything for your backgrounds, find an expanse of painted wall (no wallpaper, please) and shoot against that. Posters of country scenes, waterfalls, the woods, paintings of similar things, or posters of gardens, of interiors of churches, and so forth, can be used to simulate environments for a desired effect. I recently shot a couple of rolls of my Teddy Bear doll in outdoor scenes. I propped an oil painting, which is sort of Impressionistic, against the wall and set a piece of green poster board against the frame at the bottom. What I came out with was a garden environment in which the bears could play and have tea parties. These shots, however, were done with a definite purpose: I write books, do commercial stuff. I knew what I was doing. At the same time, I shot a wad of photos of the same bears against a seamless white background (a roll of gift-wrap paper). The had a more formal effect.

If you intend to use your shots to sell your dolls in any way, take your shots VERTICALLY, especially if they are meant for publication. Vertical shots have more power, are stronger visually, and they fit into columns of printed text better without cropping. Crop with your camera, taking out unneeded blank areas. Usually you will find if you shoot horizontally, that there is a lot of space on either side of the doll that is just wasted. Most dolls, except for obviously horizontally-designed ones, like sleeping babies and scenes of some types, benefit from vertical shots. Again, focus on the subject's eyes. This is another reason for keeping things simple. It is hard to arrange three dolls with their eyes all on the same focal plane.

2. Use a tripod or place the camera on a sturdy rest when taking photos. You will be photographing in the luxury of your domicile. The dolls are not running anywhere. This is not a doll show where

My Friend bear, © 1985, by Carol-Lynn Rössel Waugh. The same two bears as in the previous illustration taken against a white seamless background vetical format. The effect is more formal. Small bears by Elaine Gamble and April Whitcomb. *Waugh photograph.*

chances for decent photos are negligible. (A whole other set of rules goes for that kind of shooting, outside the sphere of this discussion. Ask me sometime if you are interested. I will probably tell you don't bother; who likes crowd scenes of higgledy-pigglety crammed in dollies?)

Use a plunger-type of shutter release. Avoid all movement when taking a photograph. Hold your breath. At slow speed, under 1/2=30 of a second, even the pressure of the finger on the shutter release can cause a blur.

3. AVOID FLASH. It is great at parties and where you cannot find decent lighting, but flash causes harsh, ugly black shadows behind the subject. If you have to use a flash, use one that can be detached from the camera and hand held to aim the light so that it will not hit the subject directly. The aim is to bathe the whole area in light and to adjust any shadows, either to eliminate them or to make them fall in an enhancing way. This is best done by using three 200 watt bulbs in reflector pans placed around your subject.

Artificial lighting does not have to be expensive. I have taken hundreds, more like thousands of photographs of bears and dolls, and my total lighting investment is around $15., not counting the cost of light bulbs. I have three clamp-on screw-based light socket things for bulbs, with cords, into which the reflector pans and the bulbs can be inserted. I put two of them roughly at 45 degree angles at the front of the subject and one above and/or behind it, adjusting the light quality as the subject dictates.

The bad thing about flash is that it wipes out, flattens the area directly in its path. It also makes eyes red but dolls do not have to worry about that. The closer you get to a flash, the worse the situation is. And you want to get close to your dolls.

The most dramatic lighting for dolls comes from the side. It shows off texture and grain and profiles nicely. You will have to play around with lights to see what works best for you. But remember, those lights get HOT. This lighting setup is inexpensive, but it has served me for three books, dozens of articles and countless slide programs. It works well if you remember to be careful.

Of course, the best lighting of all is daylight. It has, at its best, a magical aura that can surround the dolls or bears and visually separate them from the mundane world. With medium-source daylight, the kind that comes through the windows onto an object which is strategically placed in its expected path, shadows are softened or almost entirely eliminated. The objects seem to glow with an almost other-worldly light, one that is very appropriate for doll photography.

I am not talking about photographing dolls outdoors in the direct sunlight. This usually is a disastrous undertaking because the direct sun washes out everything and causes harsh, unbecoming shadows everywhere. If you insist on outdoor photography, pick an overcast day, or go out right after the rain (the latter is not great for dolls though, unless you are doing a program on dolly in the mud). Early morning light is often beautiful. But sunlight, unless it is controlled, can be a real problem, as are "natural settings."

Recently I was photographing bears in my friend's backyard in Delaware for a slide program I was doing for a Teddy Bear convention. The day was perfect for photography. It had rained the night before. The sky was overcast. Because I could not transport her beautifully dressed bears to Maine, I had to attempt some sort of studio setup in the backyard.

While she got out yards of maroon wool and draped it over a chair for a seamless backdrop, I set up bears in the backyard, which was very much like the woods. I used a 100mm portrait lens to isolate the bears and cropped the shots very tightly in the camera, rendering the backgrounds into indistinct greenness that just suggested the bears were in the great outdoors. The overcast sky offered little or no shadows. Things were going along well.

When the wool was set up, I moved over to the "formal pose" area, and faced the bears towards the lighting source, crawling and bending all over the ground to get to the correct level to shoot the "fashion shots." I set up the final bear, *Queen Gwenibear*, a lovely Medieval beauty, when disaster struck. The cloud cover broke, the sun came out. Instead of cool and inclement, the day ended up gloriously sunny. The ugliest shadows danced all over *Gwenibear*. Fortunately, just before I left to catch the train to New York, the sun went under a cloud and I caught a shadowless shot.

Working with natural light, as you can see, is problematical. You have little control over it and have to work when it is available, which is why it is termed "available light." I often work late at night (some may think of it as early in the morning). Also, usable sunlight is often scarce in Maine in the winter. So, until recently, I have relied on artificial light. But, given my druthers, I would take shots in natural light. The results are often lovely.

4. Be very careful to know your camera's depth of field limitations. If you can imagine a slice in the air between 4in (10.2cm) and less than 1/4in (.065cm) thick running through your doll, this will be depth of field. Some parts of the doll may "stick out" behind or in front of the depth of field. It is possible to have the eye in focus and the end of the nose out of focus if you get too close for your lens' depth of field. The nearer you get to the subject, the narrower the depth of field. To increase the depth of field, you have to decrease the f/stop on your camera, letting less light in. This makes it more difficult to focus and necessitates a tripod. But you are using one, anyway.

With a Macro lens you will have 1/8 to 1/4in (0.31 to 0.65cm) of the whole doll's depth in focus at 3ft (91.4cm). This means it is very important to focus not only on the face, but, particularly on the eyes.

Just as in photographs of people, ALWAYS focus on the doll's eyes. If they are in focus and other parts of the shot are not, you may be forgiven. If not, the shot is lost.

5. Film.

I cannot think of any reason in the world to take color snapshots of dolls for professional purposes. I only use black and white print film and slide film. Prints can always be made from slides in a pinch. Actually, I use a film that permits both slides and prints to be made simultaneously, if one desires. It is manufactured by Kodak and is the ends of 35mm movie film. The nice thing about it is that it can be shot either daylight or tungsten (a whole roll has to be shot in the same lighting conditions), and then processed to compensate for what you have done. It can be "pushed" to four times its speed, and the slides are virtually grainless because the film is manufactured to be blown up on a movie screen. It goes by the numbers 5247 (ASA 100) or 5294 (ASA 400). Unfortunately, this film has to be sent away, usually to California labs that specialize in it. And reprints are not available from the negatives (you get back negatives and slides) at your local photo shop. The color balance on these negatives is different. So, instant delivery is out of the question. But the film is cheap and versatile and you can request both slides and prints in the same order.

Occasionally, I will have prints done up of a roll, but for every 50 rolls, this maybe happens twice.

If you are using the lighting setup I describe, you have to use film designated for shooting under TUNGSTEN lighting. That is incandescent lighting, the yellow kind found in light bulbs, as opposed to fluorescent bulbs which have a bluish hue. Most color film is marked "daylight," and can only be used outdoors, with a flash or with fluorescent lights. Be careful.

If you use daylight film with incandescent lights, everything will have a warm, golden glow, which can be nice if you plan for it. It is a pain if you do not. A blue filter on the camera lens can compensate for this.

A good rule for film is that the lower the ASA number (the ASA number tells the speed of the film), the finer the grain on the film. The finer the grain (caused by particles of silver in the film), the better the picture, especially in enlargements. This is critical in black and white pictures as opposed to some color photographs which are done by a dye process.

However, the lower the ASA, the slower the film, the less light it allows in, the greater your need for good lighting and a tripod. A compromise is in order.

Professional photographers often use black and white film of very slow speeds and come up with incredible shots. Amateurs using these films come up with incredible shots, too, but of different sorts. A popular black and white film is Kodak's Tri-X, with a speed of 400. This is great for action shots and the like, but it has large grain and lets in more light than you need if you are using 200-watt bulbs. The good medium is around 100 or 125 ASA.

When I studied photography, my teacher had constants. He shot everything at f/8 or f/11, used Pentax cameras and black and white film at 125 ASA. He swore by all of these and I understand why. It is difficult to go wrong with them. I now have two Pentaxes with macro lenses, buy ASA 125 film in bulk rolls and roll my own film, but I do not stick with f/8 or f/11. I still do not trust myself for that.

You should not either. This same teacher told me that for a professional photographer, film is his cheapest commodity. Be free with your use of film and bracket your shots. This means you should use the light meter in your camera, or a hand-held meter. Shoot the shot at the exposure indicated for it, then do another of the same pose at one step above and one step below the designated setting. Play with your lights. Move them around. Look in your view finder. Learn to see your subject with all four corners of the view finder in view at the same time. See through the lens -- really look at what is there, not with your ideas, but with the camera's eye, which is far different from yours.

My teacher also said that people who photograph children professionally consider themselves lucky if they get one good shot out of a roll of 36. These dolls are your children, are they not? And you are not professional -- not yet. So relax. TAKE YOUR TIME. It does take a long time to do a good job. But when your shots come back and they are just what you wanted, you can say, "I did it myself; it's darn good." And you probably saved yourself a bundle -- that bundle you never had to give the photographer downtown.

learning more

- Useful Books Relating to Doll Art

Both artists and collectors are "continuing education specialists." They read for breakfast, lunch and dinner and find that they are almost as dedicated to the pursuit of a good doll book as they are to a good doll. They have to be. In the doll world it is just not humanly possible to get to all the places necessary to see dolls...and the very rarity of the artists' work often means that a doll is made and sold before it is publicly displayed. Furthermore, there are very few places to go to study doll making. Artists learn on their own by trial and error...and books!

Good books in the field of doll art are rare and treasured. The greater commercial publishing world has not realized the demand for doll artist books. Those few published are often very limited editions with a very short bookshop shelf-life. Below we list those books which we have on our shelves that we have found especially useful in our studies of doll art and doll making. Most of these books can be ordered through Hobby House Press, Inc. A few are only available from the authors by mail order and those we have noted with addresses.

Bradfield, Nancy. *Costume in Detail: 1730-1930*. London: Harrap, 1982.

Brooks, Patricia Ryan. *Babes in Wood: An Introduction to Doll Carving*. SASE for price and ordering information to: 3840 East Wynngate Drive, Martinez, Georgia 30907.

Bullard, Helen. *The American Doll Artist*, Volume I. Falls Church, Virginia: The Summit Press Ltd, 1965.

_____. *The American Doll Artist*, Volume II. North Kansas City, Missouri: Athena, 1975.

_____. *Dorothy Heizer: The Artist and Her Dolls*. Monograph.

_____. *My People in Wood*. Cumberland, Maryland: Hobby House Press, Inc., 1984.

Carlton, Carol. *Modern Wax Dolls*. SASE for price and ordering information to: Post Office Box 95221. 159, Altaville, California 95221.

Cochran, Dewees. *As If They Might Speak*. Santa Cruz, California: Paperweight Press; Dallas, Texas: Taylor Publishing, 1979.

Craven, Winifred. *Costume Dolls and How to Make Them*. London: Pittman, 1962.

Grubbs, Daisy. *Modeling a Likeness in Clay: Step-by-Step Techniques for Capturing a Likeness in Clay*. New York: Watson-Guptill, 1982.

Hamm, Jack. *Cartooning the Head and Figure*. New York: Grosset & Dunlap, 1963.

_____. *Drawing the Head and Figure*. New York: Grosset & Dunlap, 1967.

Hand, David. *Martha Armstrong Hand's Living Dolls*. Cumberland, Maryland: Hobby House Press, Inc., 1983.

Lasky, Kathryn. *Dollmaker: The Eyelight and the Shadow*. New York: Scribner's, 1982, (Work of artist Carole Bowling).

Laury, Jean Ray. *Dollmaking: A Creative Approach*. New York: Von Nostrand Reinhold, 1970.

Luccesi, Bruno. *Modeling the Head in Clay*. New York: Watson-Guptill, 1979.

McFadden, Sybil. *Fawn Zeller's Porcelain Dollmaking Techniques*. Cumberland, Maryland: Hobby House Press, Inc., 1984.

Miller, Richard McDermott. *Figure Sculpture in Wax and Plaster*. New York: Watson-Guptill, 1971.

Nunn, Joan. *Fashion in Costume, 1200-1980*. London: Herbert, 1984.

Oroyan, Susanna. *Dollmaker's Notebook: Working with Sculpey*. Fabricat, 1983. SASE for price and ordering information to 1880 Parliament Street, Eugene, Oregon 97405.

Pompilio, Loretta. *Soft People: The Art of Dollcrafting*. New York: Crossing Press, 1979.

Portrait Figures in Miniature: The Carol Churchill Pierson Collection, Sloan Museum, Flint, Michigan, (survey of the work of artists Halle Blakely and Muriel Bruyere).

Ross, Joan. *Artist and Original Dolls: A Compendium of the Members of the Original Doll Artist Council of America*. New York, 1983. SASE for price and ordering information to 345 East 86th, 9D, New York 10028.

Spinning Wheel's Complete Book of Dolls. A. Christian Revi, Editor. New York: Galahad, 1975.

Tokyo Doll School, *The World of Japanese Dolls*. Charles Tuttle. Rutland, Vermont.

Walters-Van Bemmel, Niesje. *Dollmaking in Six Easy Lessons*. Hemel, Hempstead, Herts, England: Popular Crafts, Wolsey House.

Waugh, Carol-Lynn Rössel. *Petite Portraits: Miniature Dolls by Contemporary American Artists*. Cumberland, Maryland: Hobby House Press, Inc., 1982.

_____. *Teddy Bear Artists: The Romance of Making and Collecting Bears*. Cumberland, Maryland: Hobby House Press, Inc., 1984.

Witzig, H. and Kuhn, G.E. *Making Dolls*. Sterling, New York, 1969.

Yoneyama, Kyoko, *The Collection of Stuffed Dolls*. Ondorisha, Tokyo, 1976.

Note to the beginning artist: Doll making books will not tell all there is to being a maker...following directions in a one-two-three way will just not do it for you. In addition to practicing with your hand, you need to educate your eye. Familiarize yourself with the great works of the world. Learn all there is to know about design and illustration as well as the technical processes and methods. (The majority of the books on our shelves are on art and illustration.) You cannot know too much! The more you read and see, the more you will be able to remodel, incorporate and innovate in your own doll work.

sources and supplies

To get started in either the collecting or making of dolls, you need to tap into the doll world "communications network." It takes only a few stamps and envelopes. Once you have subscribed to a magazine, joined an organization or ordered from a catalog, you will find more information arriving in your mailbox daily.

BOOKS:

United States: Hobby House Press, Inc., 900 Frederick Street, Cumberland, Maryland 21502. Specialized catalogs of doll, toy, miniature, doll making and Teddy Bear books available on request. Ask to be put on the mailing list.

Great Britain: Images Books, Mr. Peter Stockham, 16 Cecil Court, London, WC 1, England. Dealer in books and printed materials relating to all aspects of the doll and toy world. Catalog available on request. Overseas correspondents should enclose two international reply coupons to cover postage.

MAGAZINES

Doll Reader®. Hobby House Press, Inc., 900 Frederick Street, Cumberland, Maryland 21502. Printed eight times a year, articles on all major areas of the doll world. Available by subscription, through bookshops and at doll shows and conferences.

Dolls. Collector Communications, 170 Fifth Avenue, New York, New York 10010. Printed bi-monthly columns and short articles on doll collecting subjects. Available by subscription and at news stands.

Doll Castle News/The Dollmaker. Castle Press Publications, Post Office Box 247, Washington, New Jersey 07882. Articles of interest to doll makers and collectors.

Dollmaking: Plans and Projects. Collector Communications, 170 Fifth Avenue, New York, New York 10010. Printed quarterly. Patterns, projects, articles on dollmaking in many media. Available by subscription and at news stands.

National Doll World. House of White Birches, Post Office Box 337, Seabrook, New Hampshire 03874. Published bi-monthly; often available on local news stands.

ORGANIZATIONS

The National Institute of American Doll Artists (NIADA).
General Information: Betty Motsinger, 213 Maple Court, Addison, Illinois 60101.

The Original Doll Artist Council of America (ODACA).
General Information: Betsy Baker, Rural Route 2, Box 87, Cold Spring, New York 10516.

The International Dollmaker's Association (IDMA).
General Information: Robert Archer, 1621 Heights Boulevard #15, Houston, Texas 77008.

The British Doll Artists Association (BDA).
General Information: Ann Parker, 67 Victoria Drive, Bognor Regis, Sussex, England. (Enclose two $1.00 bills for illustrated brochure.)

The United Federation of Doll Clubs (UFDC).
General Information: UFDC, Post Office Box 14146, Parkville, Missouri 64152.

*Note: With the exception of the United Federation of Doll Clubs, the above addresses are those of organizational office holders and are subject to change.

SUPPLIES

Dollspart Supply Company, 5-15 49th Avenue, Long Island City, New York 11101.

The Standard Doll Company, 23-83 31st Street, Long Island City, New York 11105.

International Marketing and Sales (IMSCO), 950 North Main Street, Orange, California 92667.

M. Wanke, Robert Bossch Strasse 6 D-6250 Limburg/Lahn, West Germany.

Importoys, Inc., (Cernit) Post Office Box 34488, Los Angeles, California 90034.

Polyform Products, (Sculpey/polyform) Post Office Box 119, Schiller Park, Illinois 60176.

Eberhard Faber (Fimo), Accent Import Export, 460 Summit Road, Walnut Creek, California 94598.

Commonwealth Felt Company, 819 Santee Street, Los Angeles, California 90014.

Sax Arts and/Crafts (art supplies-all media), Post Office Box 2002, Milwaukee, Wisconsin 53021.

Peak Doll Directory, (where to find it guide), Post Office Box 38411, Colorado Springs, Colorado 80937.

directory of artists

Some of the artists may be contacted at their home studios. These addresses were correct at the time this book went to press, but are subject to change. In all correspondence with artists, please enclose a stamped, self-addressed envelope. For overseas correspondence, enclose international reply coupons which may be purchased from your local post office.

Christine Adams
70 Glassbrook Road
Rushden, Northants, NN 10 9 TH
England

Debby Anderson
Post Office Box 497
North Haven, Maine 04853

Don Anderson
2218 East Colorado Boulevard
Pasadena, California 91107

Elizabeth Brandon
Brandon Porcelain Originals
5916 West 53rd Street
Mission, Kansas 66202

Patricia Ryan Brooks
3840 East Wynngate Drive
Martinez, Georgia 30907

Sonja Bryer
4108 Beechwood Drive
Bellbrook, Ohio 45305

Gillian Charlson
69 Babylon Lane
Anderton
Nr. Chorley, Lancashire PR6 9NS
England

Blythe Collins-Kretschmer
Blythelin Dolls
1635 Spruce Street
Chico, California 95926

Van Craig
417 West 46th Street
New York, New York 10036

Paul Crees
2 Angelo Terrace
Bath, Avon BA1 5NH
England

Edna Daly
5 Levi Eshkol Street
Rannana 4300
Israel

Ruth Ann Eckersley
6800 Ralston Road
Arvada, Colorado 80002

June Gale
49 Cromwell Road
Beckenham, Kent
England

Margaret Glover
42 Hartham Road
Isleworth,
Middlesex,
England

Jean Heighton
1669 South Norfolk Street
San Mateo, California 94403

Margaret Hickson
9 Durley Chine Court, West Cliff Road
Bournemouth BH 2 5 HJ
England

Julia Hills
c/o Crafts Council
12 Waterloo Place
London, England

Rebecca Iverson
Route 1, Box 60
Amery, Wisconsin 54001

Kezi
The Kezi Works
Post Office Box 17062
Portland, Oregon 97217

Helen Kish
10253 West Geddes Circle
Littleton, Colorado 80127

Michael Langton
RFD 1, Box 159
Alton, New Hampshire 03809

Lisa Lichtenfels
Doll Studio
1342 Berkshire Avenue
Indian Orchard,
Massachusetts 01151

Robert McKinley
31 Jane Street 17E
New York, New York 10014

Nerissa
Post Office Box 1045
Tallahassee, Florida 32302

Mary Ann Oldenburg
5515 South 12th Street
Sheboygan, Wisconsin 53081

Cathleen O'Rork
Route 8, Box 125AA
Clarksville, Tennessee 37043

Susanna Oroyan
1880 Parliament Street
Eugene, Oregon 97405

Ann Parker
67 Victoria Drive
Bognor Regis,
Sussex, England

Beverly Port
Post Office Box 711
Retsil, Washington 98378

Robert Raikes
Post Office Box 82
Mt. Shasta, California 96067

Cecilia Rothman
2240 27th Avenue
San Francisco, California 94116

Edna Shaw Dohl
675 Olive
Pensacola, Florida 32514

Marilyn Stauber
2263 University
Eugene, Oregon 97403

Tuck Dolls
Margy Tuck and Gary Henson
436 N. Ogden Drive
Los Angeles, California 90036

Ellen Turner
Route 1, Box 156
Horse Shoe, North Carolina 28742

Kenneth Van Essen
403 North Minnesota
Glendora, California 91740

Nancy Villaseñor
c/o Jesco
923 South Myrtle
Monrovia, California 91016

Susan Wakeen
Box 365
Brookline, Massachusetts 02146

Sheila Wallace
407 Garden Avenue
Grove City, Pennsylvania 16127

Carol-Lynn Rössel Waugh
5 Morrill Street
Winthrop, Maine 04364

William Wiley
310 Broadleaf Drive, Northeast
Vienna, Virginia 22180

Charlotte Zeepvat
1 Meadow Cottages
Elms Lane, Pett
Nr. Hastings TM 35 4 JF
England

about the authors

They said it could not be done.

And they had every reason to be right!

Who could believe that two people, 3000 miles apart who have only been nose to nose a total of, perhaps, 23 days in their whole ten-year acquaintance could successfully collaborate on the construction of a book?

Of course, they could and you are holding it in your hands this very minute because once upon a time...

certainly have been times when the respective spouses thought there was more cross-country conversation than cross-table). More than just thinking or talking with each other, an incredible rapport and understanding developed -- almost a mutual mind.

Who are these long distance ladies?...the literary long and short of it?

Oroyan, just managing five feet tall in her high heels is probably the world's shortest left-handed doll artist. (We know of

A long time ago, an Oregon doll maker ran a tiny ad in a obscure journal and it caught the eye of another doll maker on the other side of the country in Maine. The doll maker in Maine wrote to the Oregon doll maker to inquire about a purchase or trade. The Oregon doll maker was so excited to get a response, she replied with a few more lines than was probably necessary. This, in turn, prompted an eight-page reply from Maine.

What sparked off all this verbiage? Probably a whacky twist of phrasing along with some grounds for mutual mind meeting. Whatever, in the years that followed the post office paid off its debts for the first time in recorded history and actually made a profit on the cards, notes, letters, tapes, clippings and photos...probably amounting to nearly a thousand bits of communication...that criss-crossed the country between these two writing fools. It is not a correspondence in anything like the traditional sense. It is a never-ending conversation ranging over philosophical discussions, professional "rap" sessions, gossip, identity crises, highs, lows and hopes carried on in much the same way as you might talk to someone in the next room or across the kitchen table (and there

one other shorter but not left-handed.) In the dozen or so years she has been creating dolls, she has tried her hand at almost everything that does not require molds (because of under cut sculpture and potential plaster in the plumbing!) Through exaggeration, manipulation and elongation her knobby-kneed, nifty-nosed character figures have probed the "fringes" and "twilight zones" of interpreting the human form with tongue-in-cheek. In 1982 her work gained her election to membership in the prestigious National Institute of American Doll Artists.

Not just content to sit home and ply her needle, Oroyan has, among other things, applied her 11 years of academic study in linguistics to the stitching up of numerous in-depth and educational articles for the doll world press. Her off-the-wall and tell-it-like-it-is style has given her recognition as one of the foremost spokespersons and advocates of original doll art.

Believing anything is possible, she has written half this book, one of her own *(Dollmaker's Notebook: Working with Sculpey)*, arranged the opening night of the ballet and constructed a gaggle of larger-than-life figures for display. With her notable talent for

247

undertaking projects (including outrageous clothing of her own design), Susie has been artist-in-residence, guest lecturer, organizational office holder, program coordinator for the NIADA annual conference, and Chairlady of the 1985 UFDC Region I Conference. "Leisure time" is spent job sharing as an architectural office administrator, reading two or three novels a week and jotting down the occasional "rotten rhyme."

Waugh nears six feet in her socks. A multi-faceted woman: doll artist, Teddy Bear designer, author, editor, journalist, lecturer, photographer, painter and manufacturer's representative, she looks to have grown up to be her childhood heroine, Wonder Woman. She is without a doubt one of THE notables of the Teddy Bear world, writing columns, reviews, film scripts and articles for arctophile periodicals and the commercial world. She has lectured as a featured speaker on the Teddy Bear at rallies, jamborees, conventions, conferences and outings of the bear folk of America, Canada, and Great Britain, (appearing, on television in all three countries, bear in hand), and has been called upon to give interviews to the national media.

Carol-Lynn's credits also include, *Teddy Bear Artists: The Romance of Making and Collecting Bears, Petite Portraits* (a study of the small doll), *My Friend Bear*, a juvenile book based on the adventures of her young son and his ted, and a series of mystery anthologies co-edited with Martin Harry Greenberg and Isaac Asimov.

Carol-Lynn has applied her love of toys and two degrees in art history to the creation of subtle watercolors of children and well-loved bears, character bears of porcelain, composition and mohair, and the famous "Bearlock Holmes" and "Oop" paper dolls.

When not zapping around the country to promote bears and love, Carol-Lynn makes her home in Maine surrounded by hundreds of bears, books, a husband, two children and a lot of unironed laundry. She credits her prolific output to her word processor and the inspiration of her bear mentor, *Oop*.

Susanna Oroyan with *Aunt Sophia*.

Carol-Lynn Rössel Waugh with *My Friend Bear*. Photograph by Jenny-Lynn Waugh, March 1985.